THE CONCEPT OF STATE JURISDICTION IN INTERNATIONAL SPACE LAW

THE CONCEPT OF STATE JURISDICTION IN INTERNATIONAL SPACE LAW

A Study in the Progressive Development of Space law in the United Nations

by

IMRE ANTHONY CSABAFI

FOREWORD BY

DR. D. GOEDHUIS

Professor of Air and Space Law
Leyden University
Chairman, Space Law Committee
International Law Association
Advisor, The Royal Netherlands Embassy, London

MARTINUS NIJHOFF / THE HAGUE / 1971

ISBN 978-94-015-0358-7 ISBN 978-94-015-0921-3 (eBook)
DOI 10.1007/978-94-015-0921-3

To
The First Man
To Land on the Moon

TABLE OF CONTENTS

FOREWORD

Dr. Csabafi in his clearly and concisely written book sets out to confront the most pressing jurisdictional problems arising from the exploration and use of outer space, problems which the authors of the Outer Space Treaty of 27th January, 1967, have not attempted to solve.

He has recognized that in view of the lack of sufficient knowledge of technological capabilities present and anticipated of the utilization of outer space and its political, economic and social implications, the time is not yet ripe for the elaboration of specific rules to govern most of the highly complex issues in this context.

Apart from the lack of sufficient knowledge and experience, the achievement of a consensus on rules regarding jurisdiction in outer space is further hampered by the strongly divergent interpretations of the fundamental principles of the Outer Space Treaty namely the principle of freedom of outer space for exploration and use and the principle of non-appropriation of outer space. In various parts of his study Dr. Csabafi has, on the basis of a thorough study of the preparatory work of the Outer Space Treaty, expressed his views on the meaning of these principles. For instance on page 116 he writes that reference in Article I to the principle of sovereign equality and the framework of contemporary international law instantly sets the entire Treaty on the sobering basis of realism and he submits that it is this approach, rather than the lofty principles of the Preamble, that will shape State practice. On page 128 he observes that it would be fallacious to attempt to write law imposing obligations on individual nation states, which they are not willing to undertake in favour of a non-existing global community and he continues that until mankind *per se* assumes legal personality under transnational law, sovereign nation states and organizations created by them continue to be the carriers of international rights and obligations. He rightly considers that full credit must be paid to the lawful interests of States engaging in the exploration and exploitation of the natural resources of international spaces, because it is only they who are capable and willing to allocate financial and intellectual resources, develop technologies and employ manpower for its exploration and exploitation.

On the other hand the author in his reflections never loses sight of the fact that the common and real intention of the Parties at the time of the conclusion of the Treaty, was to acknowledge that apart from the specific national interests, there are wider interests which States in their utilization of outer space are obliged to take into account. He considers that international legal scholarship and the United Nations Outer Space Committee should tackle as a matter of priority the study of what would be an effective and acceptable legal regime for outer space affording an equitable sharing of the wealth and national resources to be found therein among States exploiting these resources and third States (see p. 128).

After giving in his Introduction various examples demonstrating the jurisdictional problems which arise in the application of both the Space Treaty of 27th January, 1967, and the Agreement on the Rescue of Astronauts, the Return of Astronauts and the Return of Objects Launched into Outer Space of 18th December, 1967, he gives a short exposé of the attitude regarding the jurisdictional problems in outer space of the "Institut de Droit International," "The International Law Association" and "The David Davies Memorial Institute of International Studies." In Chapter 2 he describes in general terms the concept of State jurisdiction in public-international law. In Chapter 3 he makes, on the basis of the available material, a thorough investigation of the definition of the concept of State jurisdiction by the United Nations Legal Sub-Committee on Outer Space and he considers in the following Chapter the law as it appears to be applicable today regarding the exercise of State jurisdiction over activities in outer space.

Detailed reference has been made to a number of issues such as the principle of non-appropriation, the definition of the term space object, the problem of nationality and registration of spacecraft etc.. Special attention is given to the legal value of the Declaration on Legal Principles accepted by the XVIII General Assembly of the United Nations in 1962. He expresses the opinion that the principles contained in this Declaration are binding upon the members of the United Nations. In view of the fact that a number of delegations, having reservations to make to *some* of these principles, was so large that the authors of the Declaration decided to make the record of the relevant proceedings an integral part of its report, it is possible to disagree with the author on the bindingness of all the principles of the Declaration. However, no doubt can exist as to the binding force of the two basic principles laid down in the Declaration, namely that of freedom of outer space for exploration and use and the non-appropriation of outer space, including the Moon and other celestial bodies. In this connection attention may be drawn to the Resolution on Space Law adopted by the Conference of the International Law Association held in Buenos Aires in 1968, which provides i.a. that the Outer Space Treaty supports the principle of freedom of outer space and that of non-appropriation of that space *as principles of general international law.*

The aspects in which the relevant proceedings of the Space Treaty differ from those of the Declaration have been clearly set out on page 104. He draws attention to the fact that as the Declaration contains no provision comparable to that laid down in Article XII of the Space Treaty concerning open access to all stations etc. on the Moon and other celestial bodies, under the Declaration the jurisdiction of the State of registration over its stations etc. on the Moon and other celestial bodies is unfettered. (see page 104).

In Chapter 5 the author has elaborated his ideas on State jurisdiction and outer space "de lege ferenda." He rightly stresses the fact that exploitation and uses of outer space are unimaginable without the extension of State authority or jurisdiction to the areas of spatial zones affected. He points out the difference between the concept of State jurisdiction in traditional international law and that in space law and he suggests for the jurisdiction in outer space the illustrative term of "functional" jurisdiction. This term is defined in the following words: " 'Functional jurisdiction' means the right of a State in international law to regulate rights of persons, to affect property, things, events and occurrences in designated zones in outer space or areas on celestial bodies, whether by legislative, executive or juridical measure to the extent and for the period of time that is necessary to safeguard and secure its right to explore and exploit outer space including celestial bodies." He states that the substance of this jurisdiction is determined by the safeguarding functions it is invoked to perform, and he considers that the right to exercise this jurisdiction is not only "functionally" defined, but is also limited in terms of time.

In assessing the legitimacy of the exercise of this "functional" jurisdiction it is of course clear that one of the crucial problems is that concerning the "designation" of the zones over which jurisdiction can be exercised. How can the difficulty be avoided between the principle of non-appropriation and the exercise of jurisdiction which might be claimed to amounting to a violation of this principle? The author considers this problem in the light of a practical issue which has already arisen.

He refers to the White Paper of the Canadian Government of 28th March, 1968, in which it was pointed out that space available for the location of synchronous communication satellites for Canadian domestic use was limited. It was calculated that the number of suitable parking locations for such satellites was limited to perhaps 6 or 7 at the most and it was stressed by the Canadian Government that a domestic satellite communication system was of vital importance for the growth, prosperity and unity of Canada and should be established as a matter of priority. In an article by the author published in the "Montreal Star" of January 3, 1970,[1] it was stated that the Canadian Government secured two parking locations for itself instead of the 6 claimed through negotiations with the United States Department, and that they will be occupied by satellites to be operated by Telesat, a Canadian Corporation for tele-communication by satellites, established by the Telesat Canada Act on June 27, 1969.

Though the agreement between Canada and the United States should certainly be welcomed, the question arises what happens when several States have an equally valid interest in a limited number of parking locations. Is the principle of "first comes first takes" applicable in this context? Dr. Csabafi expresses the opinion that if claims satisfy the requirement on functional jurisdiction, then it would be in conformity with the developing principles of international space law. (see p. 149). He suggests that the main principles enunciated by the Space Treaty and the emerging need for securing titles and avoiding of "first comes first serves" tactics and the ensueing conflicts could be fulfilled if regional intergovernmental organizations or mixed commissions could be established to carry out evidentiary and recording functions.

It should be borne in mind, however, that the recognition of the legitimacy of the right to jurisdiction over spatial zones on the basis of reasonably conceived requirements of exploration and use, does not solve the problem of the rights of "late-comers" whose requirements may be equally reasonable. Moreover the opinions as to the reasonableness in any context of conflicting views may differ and there is no provision in the Space Treaty as to the settlement of disputes. Without some internationally agreed upon arrangements a competition might occur which, apart from accentuating the present imbalance between the few users of outer space and the very great majority of non-users, would entail definite risks of conflict between the few countries which in the present phase are capable of utilizing that space.

Dr. Csabafi's expectations that "first comes first serves" tactics could be avoided by the establishment of regional organizations or mixed commissions to carry out evidentiary and recording functions, may be considered to be too sanguine. However, his postulation that no State could proceed

[1] "Canada needs to insure its right for 'parking sites' in outer space."

unilaterally with exploitation procedures based on unrestricted occupation of parking locations for synchronous satellites to the prejudice of all other States, should be strongly upheld.

Dr. Csabafi's book in which for the first time a comprehensive study has been made of the complex jurisdictional problems arising in outer space, effectively meets a need. He has made an important contribution to a clearer conception of these problems and his book will be of interest to all those who, in whatever capacity, are concerned with the question of how and when international arrangements, implementing the Space Treaty, could be achieved, which would ensure maximum benefits for mankind as a whole, with minimum impairment of the specific national interest in outer space.

D. Goedhuis

PREFACE

Space law has become a reality.[1] The Treaty on Outer Space of January 27, 1967, codified the basic legal principles which had developed into a consensus in the United Nations during the last decade.[2]

The function of State jurisdiction in outer space, as elsewhere, is to maintain legal order and stability. The growing importance of rules governing the exercise of State jurisdiction over space activities parallels the development of the exploitation of outer space including celestial bodies. Many delegates to the United Nations have urged in the UNCOPUOS that questions relative to the exploitation and uses of outer space should be studied without delay.[3] The Canadian delegate to the United Nations pointed out, for example, that "the landing of manned spacecraft on celestial bodies would give rise to a series of practical problems of jurisdiction".[4] In the light of the accelerating pace of space activities, the landing of men on the Moon, the construction of space platforms and the restricted number of parking locations for synchronous communications satellites the question arises: What is the law regarding the exercise of State jurisdiction in outer space?

We believe that with the conclusion of the Treaty on Outer Space and the acceptance by U.N. General Assembly Resolution 2345 (XXII) of December 18, 1967, of the Agreement on the Rescue of Astronauts, the Return of Astronauts and the Return of Objects Launched into Outer Space scholars in international space law are confronted with responsibilities of a new kind. Intellectual resources should now be channelled toward developing a systematic and comprehensive doctrine of international space law. This involves not only studious and elaborate work, but also requires the

1 Jenks, 25.

2 For the text of the Treaty on Outer Space, see *Appendix II*.

3 Cf. 4 *U.N. Monthly Chronicle* 40 (1967). See also, U.N. Doc. A/AC. 105/C. 2/SR. 62 at 4.

4 *Ibid.*

knowledge and mastery of source materials on which an inductive, positivist-realist approach to space law can scientifically be based.

Bearing in mind the reminder of M. Portalis – one of Napoleon's commissioners – as to "the dangerous ambition of wishing to regulate and foresee everything" [5], it was deemed necessary to narrow the scope of this study to one question only: the progressive development of the concept of State jurisdiction in international space law.

The contribution of the United Nations to the progressive development of space law, as evidenced in the documents of the UNCOPUOS, has not been studied. These documents have yet to be compiled, edited and published. Such a publication would be of inestimable practical and scientific value, since it would place for the first time at the disposal of governments, as well as scholars, practitioners and students the entire *corpus juris* of international space law. With such source material at hand a completely different approach is possible to international space law.

The present study is almost exclusively based on relevant U.N. documents. It is due to this approach that the doctrine of State jurisdiction is not treated in its entirety, which may be considered by the reader as a shortcoming.[6] But if consideration is given to our attempt at building up space law on what we consider to be the backbone of this branch of law, the "U.N. practice", then perhaps this calculated handicap will be appreciated. It is hoped that the present book will be followed shortly by another one to be entitled *International Space Law Reports 1958–1969,* also by the present writer, which is intended to fulfill the purpose described above.

Finally, the author wishes to acknowledge his great indebtedness to the many persons and institutions that have extended their generous assistance to him in the preparation of this work. Thanks are due to the Outer Space Affairs Group of the United Nations for providing the author with U.N. documents relative to the peaceful uses of outer space, to Dean Maxwell Cohen, Faculty of Law, McGill University, Sir Francis A. Vallat, K.C.M.G., Q.C., Legal Advisor, Foreign Office, and Director, Institute of Air and Space Law, McGill University, as he then was, without whose support, encouragement and criticism this research could not have been begun, much less finished. A special debt is owed to Dr. Edward McWhinney, Q.C., Professor of Law and Director, Institute of Air and Space Law at McGill University since 1966, through whom the author acquainted himself with the theory of "inter-bloc international law" and the research

[5] *In Re Piracy Jure Gentium* [1934] A.C. 600 in 3 B.I.L.C. 836–843.

[6] For example, we are familiar with the fact that *control* is exercised by States in several areas where sovereignty is not claimed, e.g. in the case of mandates, trust territories, military bases, enclaves, and Antarctic bases.

method of "comparative international law".[7] The author also wishes to avail of this opportunity of thanking Mr. J. E. Richardson, Dean, Faculty of Law, The Australian National University, Canberra, Visiting Professor, Institute of Air and Space Law, who supervised the research ultimately leading to this work in 1966–67, Mr. Bin Cheng, Lecturer in International Law and Air Law, University College, London, for his invariable courtesy in sending this writer his publications, Mr. G. I. Tunkin, Moscow State University, for letting the author have the benefit of his comments regarding space law while they were at The Hague Academy of International Law in 1966.

The author wishes to record his warm appreciation of the friendly and whole-hearted assistance which he has on numerous occasions received from Mr. Charles Schlacks, Jr., Assistant Professor in Russian History and Editor, *Canadian Slavic Studies,* Loyola College, Montreal, who has kindly read the typescript, René H. Mankiewicz, Faculty of Law, McGill University, M. Nicolas M. Matte, Professeur en Droit, Université de Montréal, M. Denis Szabo, Professeur et Directeur, Institut de Criminologie, Université de Montréal, Dr. John F. Kish, Instructor in International Law, St. John's College, Cambridge, England, and Dr. Gábor Both, Law Library, McGill University.

The following persons had a hand, at one time or another, in the preparation of the manuscript: Miss Jacqueline Benatar, Miss Elvira Bräuninger, Mrs. F. Dagenais, Miss May Polsky, and Mr. Laird D. Taylor who went through the proofs.

It only remains to record my thanks to Dr. D. Goedhuis, Professor of Air and Space Law at Leyden University, Chairman, Space Law Committee, International Law Association, Advisor to the Royal Netherlands Embassy in London, England, who on numerous occasions gave me the benefit of his experience and advice in the formative stages of this book.

Last but not least, the author's thanks go to the Publishers and Printers for their co-operation which has played no little part in the publication of this book.

It goes without saying that all errors and opinions in this work are entirely those of the author.

Imre Anthony Csabafi

Montreal, Quebec
January 23, 1969

[7] McWhinney, 122 *et seq.*

TABLE OF CASES

Abu Dhabi Oil Arbitration (1951) (Petroleum Development (Trucial Coast) Ltd. *v*. Sheikh of Abu Dhabi), 1 L.R., 1951 Case No. 37

Alabama Arbitration (1872) (G.B. – U.S.), B.F.S.P., Vol. Gl, p. 40

Alta, The, 136 Fed. 513 (9th Cir. 1905)

Ambrose Light, The, 25 Fed. 408 (S.D.N.Y. 1885)

Antelope, The, 23 U.S. (10 Wheat.) (1825)

Apollon, The, 22 U.S. (9 Wheat.) 362 (1824)

Att.-Gen., Hong Kong *v*. Kwok-a-Sing (1873) L.R. 5 P.C. 179

Behring Sea fur seal Arbitration (1893) (G.B. – U.S.) Moore, 1 I.A. p. 755

Chiquita, The, 19 F. 2d. 417 (5th Cir. 1927); Ann. Dig., 1927–28 Case No. 96

Chung Chi Cheung *v*. The King [1939] A.C. 160

Compania Mercantil Argentina *v*. U.S. Shipping Board, (1922) 93 L.K.I.B. 816; [1924] W.N. 129; 68 S.J. 666; 40 T.L.R. 601; 131 L.T. 388

Constitution of the Maritime Safety Committee of the Inter-Governmental Maritime Consultative Organisation, *I.C.J. Reports* 1960, p. 150

Cox *v*. Army Council [1962] 2 W.L.R. 950

Creole, The (1855) (G.B. – U.S.) Moore, 4 I.A. p. 4375

Cristina, The S. S. [1938] A.C. 485; [1938] W.N. 101; 107 L.I.P. 1; 54 T.L.R. 60 L.1.L. Rep. 147; 159 L.T. 394; [1938] 1 All E.R. 719; Amn. Dig., 1938–40, Case No. 86

Cushin and Lewis *v*. The King (1935), L.R. Ex. C.R. 103

Cutting Case, The, (Mexico) Bravos District Court of Chihuahua, 1886; Moore, Report on Extraterritorial Crime . . . , p. 9

Dickson Car Wheel Co. Claim (1931) (Mexico – U.S.) *U.N. Rep.*, Vol., IV, p. 669

Dujay Case (1929) (Mexico – U.S.) 4 R.I.A.A., p. 449

Palmas Island Case (Netherlands – U.S.) *V.N. Rep.*, Vol., II, p. 829 (1928)
Parlement Belge, The (1880) 5 P.D. 197; 42 L.T. 273; 38 W.R. 642
Pesaro, The, 255 U.S. 216 (1921). 277 Fed. 473 (S.D.N.Y. 1921)
Piracy *Jure Gentium, Re* [1934] A.C. 586
Porto Alexandre, The [1920] P. 30; 89 L.J.P. 27; 122 L.T. 661; [1919] W.N. 299; 36 T.L.R. 66

R. *v.* Anderson (1808) 1 L.R.C.C.R.
R. *v.* Carr and Wilson (1822) 10 A.B.D.
R. *v.* Godfrey [1923] 1 K.B. 24; [1922] W.N. 285; 128 L.T. 115; 92 L.J.K.B. 205
R. *v.* Gordon-Finlayson, *Ex parte* an Officer [1941] 1 K.B. 171; 57 T.L.R. 270; 110 L.J.K.B. 289
R. *v.* John Lewis (1851) 7 Cox C.C. 277; 26 L.J.M.C. 104; 5 W.R. 572
R. *v.* Joyce [1946] A.C. 347; 115 L.J.K.B. 146 174 L.T. 206; 62 T.L.R. 203; 31 Cr. App. R. 57; [1946] 1 All E.R. 186
R. *v.* Manoel Antonio de Mattos [1936] 7 Car. x P. 458; 3 B.I.L.C. 21–24
R. *v.* Martin *et al* [1956] 2 W.L.R. 975; [1956] 2 Q.B. 272; 120 J.P. 255; 100 S.J. 323; [1956] 2 All E.R. 86; 40 Cr. App. R. 68
R. *v.* Naylor [1961] 2 All E.R. 932
Rahimtoola *v.* Nizam of Hyderabad and Anor [1958] A.C. 379; I.L.R., 1957, p. 175
Republic of Bolivia *v.* Indemnity Mutual Marine Assurance Company Limited [1909] 1 K.B. 785; 78 L.J.K.B. 596; 100 L.T. 503; 25 T.L.R. 254
Right of Passage over Indian Territory (Portugal – India) *I.C.J. Reports*, 1960, p. 6
Rocha *v.* U.S., U.S., Cath. Cir. 1961) 288 F. 2d. 545

Schooner Exchange *v.* M'Faddon 11 U.S. (7 Cranch) 116 (1812)
Spanish Zone of Morocco Claims (G.B. – Spain), *U.N. Rep.*, Vol., II, p. 615 (1925)

Tempest, The, (1859) (France) D. 59. I. 88
The Newton and the Sally, The Bull. des Lois (1806) (France) No. 126

U.S. *v.* Chandler, 72 F. Supp. 230 (D. Mass. 1947), 171 F. 2d. 921 (1st Cir. 1948)
U.S. *v.* Cordova, 89 F. Supp. 298 (E.D.N.Y. 1950); I.L.R., 1950, p. 191
U.S. *v.* Eagle Indemnity Co., 18 F. 28. 135 (E.D. Va. 1926)

LIST OF ABBREVIATIONS

A & A	*Astronautics and Aeronautics*
A.J.I.L.	*American Journal of International Law*
Alberta L. Rev.	*Alberta Law Review*
Analysis and Background Data	Treaty on Principles Governing the Activities of States in the Exploration and Use of Outer Space, Including the Moon and Other Celestial Bodies. Staff Report. 90th Congress, 1st Session. 1967
AW & ST	*Aviation Week and Space Technology*
B.I.L.C.	British International Law Cases
Brierly,	The Law of Nations (1963)
B.F.S.P.	British and Foreign State Papers
B.Y.I.L.	British Yearbook of International Law
Cheng,	"Extra-Terrestrial Application of International Law", C.L.P. 133–152 (1965)
Christol,	The International Law of Outer Space (1966)
Colombos,	The International Law of the Sea (6th rev. ed., 1967)
Colum. L. Rev.	*Columbia Law Review*
Cranch,	Cranch's U.S. Supreme Court Reports. 1801–1815 (United States)
C.L.P.	*Current Legal Problems*
Current Problems	Current Problems in Space Law: A Symposium B.I.I.C.L. (1966)
C.Y.I.L.	Canadian Yearbook of International Law
Dep't State Bull.	*Department of State Bulletin* (U.S.A.)
Dods.	Dodson's *Reports of Cases Argued and Determined in the High Court of Admiralty,* etc. (1811–22) 2 vols., London, 1815, 1828. Reproduced in *The English Reports* (1220–1865) 176 vols., Edinburgh and London, 1900–30

D.L.R.	*Dominion Law Reports* 1912 – Canada
Draft Restatement	The American Law Institute's Official Draft of Foreign Relations Law of the United States, 1962
Edw.	Thomas Edwards: *Reports of Cases Argued and Determined in High Court of Admiralty,* etc. (1808–12) London, 1912. Reproduced in *The English Reports,* vol. 165
Exch. Div.	*Law Reports.* 2nd series Exchequer Division (1875–80) 5 vols., London, 1876–81
F.I.	*Flight International*
F.Rep.	Federal Reporter (United States)
F.Supp.	Federal Supplement (United States)
Hackworth	Digest of International Law (1943)
Harv. L. Rev.	*Harvard Law Review*
Harvard Research	Research in International Law. Under the Auspices of the Harvard Law School. Draft Conventions Prepared for the Codification of International Law
H.C.R.	James Brown Scott, *The Hague Court Reports,* 2 vols., New York, 1916, 1932
I.C.J.	International Court of Justice
I.C.J. Reports	Reports of Judgements, Advisory Opinions and Orders of the I.C.J.
I.C.L.Q.	*International and Comparative Law Quarterly*
I.J.I.L.	*Indian Journal of International Law*
I.L.C. Yearbook	Yearbook of the International Law Commission
I.L.R.	International Law Reports. 1950 (United Kingdom)
Jenks,	Space Law (1965)
Lachs,	"The International Law of Outer Space", 113 *Hague Recueil* (III, 1964) 7–115 (1966)
L.N.T.S.	League of Nations Treaty Series
Mann,	F. A. Mann, "The Doctrine of Jurisdiction in International Law", 111 *Hàgue Recueil* (I, 1964) 9–162 (1966)
McDougal, Lasswell and Vlasic	Myres S. McDougal, Harold D. Lasswell, and Ivan A. Vlasic, Law and Public Order in Space (1963)
McWhinney,	Edward McWhinney, "Peaceful Co-existence" and Soviet-Western International Law (1964)
Mich. L. R.	*Michigan Law Review*
Moore, D.,	Moore, D., A Digest of International Law, 8 vols., (1906)

Moore, I. A.,	Moore, B., History and Digest of the International Arbitrations to which the United States has been a Party, 5 vols. (1898)
O'Connell,	O'Connell, O. P., International Law, 2 vols. (1965)
Oppenheim,	International Law, Lauterpacht, 8th ed. (1955)
P.C.I.J.	Permanent Court of International Justice
P.I.L.J.	*Philippine International Law Journal*
Proceedings VI Colloquium	International Institute of Space Law (Washington, 1964)
Proceedings VIII Colloquium	International Institute of Space Law (Norman, Oklahoma, U.S.A. 1966)
Q.B.D.	*Law Reports,* 2nd series Queen's Bench Division (1875–90) 25 vols., London, 1876–91
R.I.A.A. (U.N.R.I.A.A.)	United Nations, *Reports of International Arbitral Awards,* 1948–
Schwarzenberger,	Schwarzenberger, G., The Inductive Approach to International Law (1965)
S.G. i P.	*Sovetskoe Gosudarstvo i Pravo*
Shawcross and Beaumont,	Air Law, 3rd ed. (1966)
Starke,	Starke, J. G., An Introduction to International Law, 6th ed. (1967)
S.Y.I.L.	Soviet Yearbook of International Law
T.L.R.	Times Law Reports (Eng. 1884)
UNCOPUOS	United Nations Committee on the Peaceful Uses of Outer Space
U.S.F.R.	Paper Relating to the Foreign Relations of the United States, Washington, 1862–
Yale L. J.	*Yale Law Journal*
U.N.T.S.	United Nations Treaty Series
Wheat.	Wheaton's United States Supreme Court Reports

CHAPTER I

INTRODUCTION

It has often been observed that progress in the field of science and technology is not necessarily followed by comparable progress in the field of ethics, or of international law or co-operation . . . What is needed is the elaboration of a "space code" forthwith to co-ordinate and discipline work in this field; it is vital that whatever new conquests science may soon make – and science is advancing very rapidly – shall find a legal framework and institutional arrangements already in existence to ensure that they serve the good of society and are not abused.

Message from Pope Paul VI
to the U. N. Conference on the
Exploration and Peaceful Uses
of Outer Space
14 August 1968

The Conference has already demonstrated that important and practical applications of space research for the direct benefit of mankind have already been developed and proven during this first decade of the space age. Discussions in the Conference have indicated that these practical applications could assist materially in alleviating some of the economic and social problems created by the explosive growth of population, the serious shortage of food, the spread of disease – problems of great concern to a vast majority of mankind. At the same time, the Conference has highlighted the fact that, because of their complex, expensive and specialized nature, these tools of outer space are known only to few nations. The developments in space science and technology have thus far benefited most those countries which are already far ahead in the eco-

> nomic and social time-table of the world. The space age is increasing the gap between the developed and developing areas of the world at an alarming rate.
>
> Note by U. N. Secretary-General U. Thant U. N. Conference on the Exploration and Peaceful Uses of Outer Space Vienna 14–27 August 1968

This work seeks to identify legal principles and rules governing the exercise of jurisdiction by States in outer space and on celestial bodies. We suggest that the legal basis of the concept of State jurisdiction in outer space differs from that of State jurisdiction in the traditional terrestrial environment. Further, it is the aim of this study to trace the process of changes and modifications – if any – in the concept of State jurisdiction and in the course of the progressive development of international space law.

This study intends to elaborate upon the contribution of the United Nations to the progressive development of international space law with respect to State jurisdiction. In view of the fact that the U.N. is the recognized *forum* for the "making" of space law, its "practice" has, as a matter of course, been placed in the centre of this inquiry.

The most important contribution of the United Nations to the progressive development of international space law to date is the *Treaty on Principles Governing the Activities of States in the Exploration and Use of Outer Space, Including the Moon and Other Celestial Bodies* of 27 January 1967, and the *Agreement on the Rescue of Astronauts, the Return of Astronauts and the Return of Objects Launched into Outer Space* of 18 December 1967.[1] Basic legal principles and rules have been agreed upon in a form "authenticated by one of the three generally recognised law-creating processes of international law."[2] The Space Treaty is not an attempt at codification *uno ictu* of each and every aspect of space law.[3] The framers of the

[1] Hereafter referred to as Space Treaty and Treaty on Outer Space. For a more detailed discussion, see Chapter IV. See U.N. Doc. A(6804) Add. 1 (16 December 1967). The latter Agreement will be referred to in this study as Agreement on Rescue and Return. For a detailed discussion of the Agreement, see Chapter IV(V) *infra*.

[2] The three law-creating processes in international law are: (1) consensual undertakings in the widest sense, (2) international customary law, and (3) the general principles of law recognised by civilised nations. Schwarzenberger, 5. See Article 38 of the Statute of the International Court of Justice.

[3] The applicability in this respect of the McWhinneyan theory of *comparative* international law is apparent. The adopted "U.N. practice" with respect to the limited codi-

Treaty neither intended nor were able to provide for principles governing the "uses" and forms of exploitation of outer space and celestial bodies. In view of the lack of experience and foreseeability of contingencies requiring specific regulation, too early or rapid a codification, it was thought, could have become an undesirable hindrance later. Consequently, no detailed rules can be found in the Treaty on Outer Space governing the exercise of State jurisdiction in outer space including celestial bodies. Article VIII of the Treaty provides a general rule only:

> A state Party to the Treaty on whose registry an object launched into outer space is carried shall retain jurisdiction and control over such object, and over any person thereof, while in outer space or on a celestial body ....

It is suggested that the clarification and systematization of legal rules governing the exercise of State jurisdiction over persons, things, occurrences and events in outer space is a task of primary importance. Of no less importance is the allocation by an international treaty of jurisdictional competencies with respect to events caused by space activities on earth, e.g. rescue and return of astronauts and space vehicles making emergency or distress landing on earth.[4]

The Agreement on Rescue and Return deals with the question of State jurisdiction in Articles 1 to 6 on the substantive rules. The provisions of this Agreement will be discussed together with Article VIII of the Treaty on Outer Space in greater detail in Chapter IV.

The Space Treaty marks the end of a stage in the progressive development of international space law. Now we are on the eve of the next stage. While the first stage may be characterized by successful attempts at creating a broad legal basis and framework for the law of outer space, the second stage appears to consist of attempts in the U.N. to draw up a number of international draft treaties some of the current problems associated with the increasing exploration and uses of outer space and celestial bodies. In addition to the two above-mentioned international agreements on outer space, a third one concerning liability for space vehicle accidents is still in the drafting stage.[5]

fication of space law by the Space Treaty is commensurate with both the "operational methodology for achieving an interbloc international law" in general, and the observations concerning "codification, *uno ictu* versus empirically-based, step-by-step methods" in particular. McWhinney, 86–87 *et seq.*

4 The French representative to the Legal Sub-Committee of the UNCOPUOS suggested that a distinction should be made between rules governing the terrestrial effects of space activities and the body of space law proper. See *infra.*

5 *Report of the Legal Sub-Committee on the Work of its Seventh Session* (4–28 June 1968) in Report of the Committee on the Peaceful Uses of Outer Space, A/7285 United Nations, New York, 128–134, 138–196. (1968)

The French representative to the UNCOPUOS made a similar observation in his commentary on the Space Treaty at the seventieth meeting of this committee. He said:

> However, consideration could also be given to the inclusion of a provision [in the *Space Treaty*] binding on all signatories to the effect that international commitments should be negotiated as soon as possible with a view to establishing rules which could be applied with the least possible difficulty and which covered the following points: reconciliation of the concept of freedom and the various criteria for restricting that freedom; negotiations on potentially harmful activities and on measures for preventing them; *the exercise of jurisdiction*; responsibility; taking into account the actual role of each participant where there was more than one; assistance to persons and the return of persons and objects, it being understood that commitments which were (sic) difficult to fulfill for technical or moral reasons should not be entered into; the registration of objects; the dissemination of information on the results of space activities; visits to installations or objects which were (sic) not longer on earth, taking particular account of the safety factor; the priority to be given to certain types of exploration and use; the direct broadcasting of programmes; and the consequences on earth of activities in space.[6] (Emphasis supplied)

This statement clearly shows it is not without reason that the importance of the issue of State jurisdiction in outer space is gaining momentum. Indeed, the regulation of any one of the enumerated questions would in essence amount to the allocation of specific jurisdictional competencies among the States involved in the exploitation of outer space and especially the Moon. Take for example the first question: reconciliation of the concept of freedom and the various criteria for restricting that freedom. These "various criteria" restricting the freedom of outer space bear directly upon the scope of jurisdiction that States may assume in a particular case. For instance, the freedom of access to outer space is restricted by the non-existence of a right to innocent passage of spacecraft through foreign national airspace under contemporary international space law. Thus the exclusive jurisdiction of the subjacent State in national airspace is unaffected. Under international law a trespassing spacecraft could be held responsible for violating the sovereignty of the subjacent State, except in cases of distress or emergency landing. The granting of the right to foreign spacecraft to fly across the national airspace constitutes a matter of absolute discretion of the territorial State. Such spacecraft would come under the jurisdiction of the subjacent State unless the terms of an agreement or an international treaty provide differently. Consequently, if the reconciliation of the freedom of outer space with the concept of absolute and ex-

[6] U.N. Doc. A/AC. 105/C. 2/SR. 70 at 15.

clusive sovereignty of the subjacent State in the national airspace were attempted with an aim to favour the less restricted exploitation of outer space, then it could be achieved only by excluding certain persons, things, events or occurrences from the exclusive jurisdiction of the subjacent State.

The openness of space stations on the Moon versus the non-openness of space vehicles and stations in outer space present jurisdictional problems too. The various questions relative to the exploitation of resources of outer space or the uses of certain areas on the Moon could also generate a number of unresolved potential jurisdictional conflicts. Take, for instance, State A which lawfully exploits and uses outer space of the Moon. The interests of State A associated with its space activities must be protected by law against all and sundry. In other words, it would follow from the principle of sovereign equality of States that the right of every State to enjoy the benefits of outer space through is activities is an *absolute* one and has an *erga omnes* effect. Legal titles could be adequately protected by specifying those contingencies which give jurisdiction to a State.

This example alone is sufficient to prove that the issue of State jurisdiction in space law occupies a key position. Reference to the U.N. "practice" would be incomplete without mentioning U.N. General Assembly Resolution 1962 (XVIII) of December 13, 1963, on the *Declaration of Legal Principles Governing the Activities of States in the Exploration and Use of Outer Space*.[7] Paragraph 7 of this Declaration provides that "the State on whose registry an object launched into space is carried shall retain jurisdiction and control over such object, and any personnel thereon, while in outer space."

Some of the "most highly qualified publicists in the field of international law"[8] commented on a few questions associated with State jurisdiction in outer space. Jenks argued that the concept of nationality should not be introduced in space law, because "Neither maritime law nor aviation law has yet accommodated itself to the need for an international flag and international registration for internationally-operated vessels and aircraft .... All that appears to be necessary is that every space object should be registered and on the basis of such registration responsibility for it should rest with a determined State or international organisation of States having jurisdiction and control over it."[9] Since the *Declaration of Legal Principles* did not consider the possibility that the State of registry and the launching State could be different from one another, Jenks called attention to the

[7] Hereafter referred to as *Declaration of Legal Principles*.
[8] Cf., Article 38 of the Statute of the International Court of Justice.
[9] Jenks, 236.

Resolution of the Institute of International Law on the Legal Régime of Outer Space[10] which provided that "the State under the authority of which the launching of a space object has taken place shall be liable . . . ."

Jenks' opinion is that there are no preliminary conditions, e.g. compliance with the applicable international rules, prompt registration with the U.N. and the use of marks and signals of identification, to be fulfilled before the State of registry could claim jurisdiction.[11] The term "jurisdiction and control" as used in the *Declaration of Legal Principles* was interpreted by Jenks as implying "that no other State is entitled to interfere, by electronic or other means", with the normal operation of the space object. The law of the State of registry applies to the space object and occurrences thereon "in the same manner in which occurrences on board a ship are governed by the law of the flag".[12] Disciplinary authority is vested in the master of the spacecraft. The jurisdiction of the State of registry of the spacecraft seems to be unlimited, except as Jenks said in the following two cases: while the spacecraft is in the territorial jurisdiction of another State and when third States may "for good cause" interfere with the activities in space of other States "for the purpose of self-protection against interference from space with matters within their territorial jurisdiction or for any other reason".[13]

The problems of State jurisdiction in outer space were again brought into the limelight by Jenks on the Conference held by The British Institute of International and Comparative Law on May 4, 1966. According to Jenks:

> The Declaration of Legal Principles provides that objects launched into space and any personnel thereon remain subject to the jurisdiction of the State of registry. How does this principle apply to manned orbital stations and manned space stations or settlements? The question may become an immediate one as soon as manned flights to the Moon become a regular occurrence. Presumably orbital stations and space stations or settlements remain subject to the jurisdiction of the State establishing them. Where, however, are we to draw the line between the exercise of jurisdiction and the principle that space and the celestial bodies are not subject to appropriation? And what relationship should we envisage between the law applicable to such stations or settlements and the personal law of persons in space? The problem is liable to become a matter of practical importance when it becomes possible to pass from one space station

[10] Institute of International Law, Resolution on the Legal Régime of Outer Space, adopted unanimously at Brussels on September 11, 1963. Reproduced in Jenks, 416–418, Appendix IX.

[11] Jenks, 237.

[12] Jenks, 238.

[13] *Ibid.*

or settlement to another, and at that stage the arrangements for the exercise of jurisdiction being evolved under the Antarctic Treaty, where there is a similar problem of intercommunication between isolated scientific settlements in an area not subject to national appropriation, may afford suggestive experience for consideration.[14]

The section of the Declaration of Legal Principles, 1962, dealing with jurisdiction and control over objects launched into outer space did not provide an altogether satisfactory answer. Paragraph 7, as Goedhuis pointed out in succinct terms, suffers from an inner contradiction. In the words of Goedhuis:

Paragraph 7 of Declaration 1962 provides that the State on whose registry an object launched into outer space is carried, shall retain jurisdiction *and control* over such object, and any personnel thereon, while in outer space. There is at present no agreed opinion as to which State should provide for the registration of a spacecraft. Let us suppose that State A registers the owner of a spacecraft and that State A, not disposing of launching facilities requests State B to launch this spacecraft. In such a case it might well be necessary that State A retains the control of the spacecraft once it has been launched. However, according to paragraph 7 State B would retain control over the said spacecraft. It seems doubtful whether those who drafted this provision realized all its implications.[15]

This observation has not lost its validity. In fact, neither the Space Treaty nor the Agreement on the Rescue of Astronauts, the Return of Astronauts, and the Return of Objects Launched into Outer Space contain uniform provisions regarding the designation of the State which may exercise jurisdiction. Article VIII of the Treaty on Outer Space is, for practical purposes, an exact replica of Paragraph 7 of the Declaration of Legal Principles. The Agreement on Rescue and Return of Astronauts and Space Objects consistently uses the term "launching authority" with whom States Parties to this Agreement are supposed to deal irrespective of whether or not "the State responsible for launching" is at the same time the State on whose registry the object launched into outer space is carried. It would seem that the "launching authority" retains control over objects launched into outer space under the Agreement on Rescue and Return of Astronauts

[14] C. Wilfred Jenks, "Space Law Becomes a Reality," *Current Problems,* 22, 23–24. But see the comment of J. E. S. Fawcett stating: "In regard to the jurisdiction over persons in space, this seems to me a question that has a low priority. Once the principle of State responsibility for spacecraft registered in it is accepted, it seems that for a long time ahead people inside such registered craft will be, in an ordinary meaning of the word, within the jurisdiction of that State . . . ." *Ibid.,* at 26–27.

[15] Dr. D. Goedhuis, "Reflections on the Evolution of Space Law," *Nederlands Tijdschrift voor Internationaal Recht,* 119–120 (1966, No. 2).

and Space Objects irrespective of the fact of registration. Thus, in the contingency Goedhuis referred to above, the spirit and letter of the Agreement on Rescue and Return, etc., creates an exception to Article VIII of the Treaty on Outer Space which links the right to exercise jurisdiction and control to the State of registration of the space object. In our opinion the resolution of the problem of jurisdiction and control in this fashion is attributable to deference to pragmatic considerations rather than a legal error. As a result, we have a flexible law at hand and the finger can be pointed at more than one State. Accordingly, it would seem quite permissible if the recovering State or the State on whose territory foreign spacecraft and astronauts landed communicated with either the "launching authority" or the State on whose registry the object is carried, or with both.

That the UNCOPUOS has an approach of its own toward the progressive development of international space law becomes apparent from the contrast between the "U.N. practice" and the resolutions of various learned societies. While the U.N. approach is characterized by the political nature of the Organization, the resolutions of the *Institut de Droit International,* the International Law Association, and the Draft Rules of the David Davies Memorial Institute of International Studies reflect to a certain degree the legalistic deliberations of detached academic bodies. It is for the sake of bringing out this contrast, rather than because of the supposed influence of the scientific argument contained in these documents on the work of the UNCOPUOS, that a brief reference is made here to them.

I. THE ATTITUDE OF THE *INSTITUT DE DROIT INTERNATIONAL*

The *Institut de Droit International* unanimously adopted a resolution entitled *Le Régime Juridique de l'Espace* on 11 September 1963. Paragraphs 2–6 contain provisions bearing on the question of jurisdiction. Accordingly:

2. Aucun objet spatial ne doit être lancé si ce n'est sous l'autorité d'un Etat. Chaque Etat est tenu de garantir que l'utilisation de tout objet spatial lancé sous son autorité sera conforme aux règles internationales applicables.
3. Tout lancement d'un objet spatial devra être enregistré sans délai, et avec les précisions à convenir, auprès des Nations-Unies ou d'un organisme spécial à créer, par l'Etat sous l'autorité duquel il a été effectué.
4. Tout objet spatial devra porter des signes d'identification de son origine et utiliser des signaux d'appel permettant de déterminer l'Etat sous l'autorité duquel le lancement a été effectué.
5. Tout objet spatial, lancé dans les conditions ci-dessus énumérées, reste soumis à la juridiction de l'Etat sous l'autorité duquel il a été lancé.

6. L'Etat établissant une installation spatiale est tenu d'y assurer l'ordre et la sécurité.

Sous réserve de tout accord international ultérieur, les personnes utilisant l'installation et les faits qui s'y produisent relèvent de la juridiction de l'Etat ayant établi l'installation.[16]

Thus according to this resolution, the right of a State to exercise jurisdiction over an object launched into outer space depends on three constitutive conditions. Namely, that the launching shall have taken place under the authority of a State, that the object is registered by this State, and finally the identification marks of this State are also displayed on the object. Astronauts are subject to the jurisdiction of the State which has the right to exercise jurisdiction over the space object. The solution provided by the resolution of the *Institut* has an indisputable logical appeal. It would seem doubtful, however, that it would be an acceptable formula for States because it does not afford any leeway for accomodation of divergent State interests. For example, it cannot be taken for granted, as the resolution of the *Institut* does, that the launching authority would be willing to exercise jurisdiction over a spacecraft launched on behalf of another State, nor, for that matter, that the latter State would relinquish its right to exercise jurisdiction over its object and perhaps personnel therein for the sake of adhering to a legally appealing construction.

II. THE ATTITUDE OF THE INTERNATIONAL LAW ASSOCIATION

The International Law Association has been considering questions relating to space law since its 49th Conference held in Hamburg in 1960. Its "Resolution on Air and Space Law" of 1962 set up a Space Law Committee within the Association which has been responsible since then for the circulation of questionnaires and preparation of reports. At its 51st Conference in Tokyo in September, 1964, the ILA passed five resolutions bearing on questions of space law. Resolution B on "The Upper Limit of National Space" recognised "the importance of the problems of the upper limit of national space and the right of innocent passage of foreign spacecraft through such space, and the many difficulties, at once theoretical and practical, which have to be resolved before satisfactory answers can be found to them." It expressed the ILA's desire "to contribute to the study concerning the possible demarcation of the upper limit of State sovereignty and the limitation of such sovereignty to any extent necessary for ensuring

[16] The text of the Resolution is reprinted in *Current Problems* at 134–135. Cf. Goedhuis, *loc. cit. supra* at 129-130.

that the benefits of the freedom of outer space shall be enjoyed by all States." For this purpose the Space Law Committee was requested "to give its attention to the study of this subject" and report to the next Conference of the Association.

Resolution C on "The Legal Status of Space Vehicles of International Organisations" noted that Paragraph 5 of the U.N. General Assembly Resolution 1962 (XVIII) "contemplates that international organizations as well as States may operate, and have responsibility for space vehicles," and requested the Space Law Committee to continue the study on the legal aspects of this subject and report to the next Conference of the Association.[17]

A Questionnaire was prepared by the Space Committee on the Legal Status of Spacecraft for the 52nd Conference held in Helsinki in 1966. Lack of time prevented the Conference from considering the issue and in its Resolution requested the Space Law Committee to continue the study and "present to the 53rd Conference recommendations for draft rules on the Legal Status of Spacecraft or a progress report on its study, as the case may be."[18]

Replies to and comments on the Questionnaire have been summarized in the Progress Report on the Question of the Legal Status of Spacecraft (hereafter referred to as Progress Report) prepared by the Rapporteur of the Space Law Committee.

The Space Law Committee held a preliminary meeting in Paris on 16 September 1967 to study the comments received, and considered a draft definition of the term "space objects." Decision regarding this question was postponed on account of the insufficiency of the draft and no final stand was taken by the ILA until now. However, the Committee adopted a resolution at this meeting which recommended that:

> All space objects to be launched should be registered by a State or inter-governmental organization in accordance with its own regulations. All launches by a State or inter-governmental organization should be notified to the United Nations in a way which allows the identification of the launched space objects.[19]

[17] International Law Association, *Report of the Fiftieth Conference, Brussels,* 1962, p. viii, (August 26, 1962). See also, Goedhuis, *op. cit.,* at 128–129.

[18] The present writer wishes to thank Professor René H. Mankiewicz, Faculty of Law, McGill University and Rapporteur of the Space Law Committee of the ILA for his helpful comments regarding the proceedings of the Buenos Aires Conference of the ILA and for providing him with a copy of the Progress Report which has not been published in the Proceedings of the ILA at the time of writing. See text of the Progress Report in *Appendix VI.*

[19] See *Appendix VI.*

A detailed examination of the substantive part of the Progress Report will follow. The comments reproduced in the Progress Report and the conclusions drawn therefrom reflect scholarly opinion which deserves attention, not only because of the extent they go into the details of the problem relative to the definition of spacecraft, classification, identification, nationality and registration thereof, but also because the Progress Report reflects the *opinio juris* of legal *honoratiores* in the period following the conclusion of the Treaty on Outer Space and the adoption of the Agreement on Return and Rescue. For this reason one may say that the Progress Report points beyond the "U.N. practice" and supposedly also foreward.

The Resolution adopted by the 53rd Conference in Buenos Aires in 1968 provided that the concept of nationality is not necessary for the determination of the launching authority. This complex question has, of course, not been settled and the ILA will have to concern itself with this question in the future.

1. Terminology

An acceptable definition of spacecraft would provide us with an accurate determination of the scope of State jurisdiction *ratione instrumenti.* The Progress Report pointed out the familiar fact that neither the Treaty on Outer Space nor the Agreement on Rescue and Return had solved the question of terminology, although several terms were used. The Treaty uses the term "objects" the most frequently. Occasionally the qualifying words "component parts" (Article VII) are added. Article XII mentions "stations," "installations," "equipment" and "space vehicles," but only regarding the moon and other celestial bodies. The term "Spacecraft" is not used at all and the term "space vehicle" is used only in two instances (Articles V and XII). On the other hand, the Agreement on Rescue and Return uses the expression "spacecraft" in Articles 1, 2, 3 and 4, and also the term "space object" in Articles 5 and 6. This seems to indicate that no consideration was given to the uniformity of terminology by the UN-COPUOS. For that matter, the variety of opinions and comments in the Progress Report does not present a different picture either.

To the Rapporteur there appears to be a general agreement that the term to be used should be all-embracing. It is felt that the word "object" cannot be used without additional qualifying descriptions, such as "space" and "its component parts." The Space Law Committee was also in favour of complementing an "all-embracing" definition with classification according to both technical and legal criteria.

The German Branch of the ILA proposed that the definition should include the launcher vehicle, debris and spent spacecraft from the beginning of the launching until landing on earth or disintegration of the spacecraft. The Soviet Branch felt that the chief criterion of definition should be the purpose of the space object: namely, that it is meant for the exploration and use of outer space including celestial bodies. It:

> should also embrace the spent space objects . . . [and] cover artificial satellites of the earth, the moon or other celestial bodies, spacecraft, orbiting space platforms, interplanetary stations and laboratories, stations, installations, equipment on the moon and other celestial bodies, separate stages of the carrier rocket, space probes as well as detached parties of space objects and separate debris of spacecraft that distintegrated. Land stations (rocket launching sites, tracking and control stations, transmitting and receiving stations) should not be covered by the definition of "space object," though they can be subject to appropriate legal arrangement.

In de La Pradelle's view,

> Il serait préférable d'adopter une définition à portée limitée qui pourrait être applicable aux fusées mais qui viserait essentiellement les capsules terminales et exclurait sans équivoque les installations terrestres fixes du tir spatial et de la poursuite du vol spatial.

The Progress Report drew attention to an important point of consideration, namely, whether the definition of "object" should apply to assembled spacecraft on earth prior to its launching. Under municipal law an assembled spacecraft on the surface of the earth is considered a movable object subject to the municipal law of the land. It was also suggested to be considered whether the analogy of municipal air law should be followed regarding the application of special rules during and/or after the assembling of the object.

The Space Law Committee soon was to run into the unresolved question of where the lower limit of outer space is. The definition of an "object" launched into outer space or capable of moving through space raises the question at what altitude would such an object enter space. The Report pointed out that in the final analysis "the criterion ought to be the 'capability' of spacecraft to move under said physical laws, [physical laws of astronautical flight] or any more appropriate definition of the forces or mechanics of its evolution". Attention is drawn in this context to an amendment by the Council of ICAO in 1967 of the traditional definition of aircraft ("any machine that can derive support in the atmosphere from the reactions of the air other than the reactions of the air against the earth's surface").

Turning to exact definitions, the Committee examined the following ones. The German Branch of the ILA proposed that:

"Spacecraft" means any objects designed to move in outer space, not needing support from the reactions of air.

Subsequently, it was suggested that the second part of the sentence, following the words "outer space" be deleted.

The Hungarian Branch suggested the following definition:

All artificial bodies (manufactured by man) shall be space objects which are launched from the earth, with or without crew, with the purpose of orbiting around the earth, moon or the sun by making use of the laws of Keppler (celestial mechanics) or of reaching from the earth another celestial body whether or not with the objective to stay at the place of destination.

This definition also covers objects which are assembled in space. In addition, it is based on the assumption that objects in orbit altitude around the earth are in outer space, which is a sensible approach toward the problem of demarcation. The definition, however, is not compact since it says more than is sufficient and necessary. For example, reference to Keppler's laws is redundant. The mention of the sole purpose of orbiting certain celestial bodies is too restrictive, and the closing part of the definition implying the possibility of installations on celestial bodies or direct launchings therefrom, is obscure.

The definition offered by the Soviet Branch reads as follows:

The definition of space object should [also] cover any object or its component part launched with the view of performing flight in outer space for exploration and use of space including the moon and other celestial bodies, till the moment of its scientific dismantling or demolition.

This "all-embracing" definition adequately covers foreseeable contingencies and also emphasizes the criterion of purpose. However, in order for it to become meaningful the term outer space still needs to be defined.

De La Pradelle offered the following definition:

On entend par engin spatial tout appareil susceptible de se déplacer dans l'espace extra-atmosphérique (et destiné soit à s'y désintégrer, soit à s'y maintenir conformément aux lois de la physique astronomique).

Cocca referred to the definition adopted at the First Colloquium on the Progress in Cosmic Exploration held in Buenos Aires in December, 1966:

Cosmic vehicles in the regime of the Treaty are all artifacts launched by man for the exploration or use of outer space including the moon and other celestial bodies, with peaceful purposes.

What makes this definition particular is that special mention is made of "peaceful purposes", a qualification that one might have expected to find in the Soviet definition which, however, preferred a terse technical language. This definition, like the Hungarian one, limited its scope to objects launched or manufactured by man. It is felt that this concern for precision is somewhat overdone. No mention of the qualification "manufactured by man" should have served the purpose better, because either the contingency of the appearance in our galactic space of objects manufactured by extra-terrestrial beings should have been considered remote, or if not it would be pretentious to withhold the status accorded man-made space objects from such presumably far more sophisticated devices.

Mankiewicz, the Rapporteur of the Space Law Committee, suggested a definition to the Committee for consideration which has the merit of being succinct:

> Space device means any object launched toward (in the direction of) space. *(Appareil spatial signifie tout objet lancé en direction de (vers) l'espace.)*

Or, alternatively:

> Space device means any object intended for launching into space. *(Appareil spatial signifie tout objet destiné à être lancé vers l'espace.)*

The first alternative would also cover misfired launching when the objects do not reach outer space. The Agreement on Rescue and Return uses the words "launched into space," which may be construed as referring only to those objects which reached outer space. The second alternative covers the object before the launching takes place.

2. *Classification of Spacecraft*

The Progress Report reflects a general consensus relative to the necessity of eventually classifying spacecraft according to technical and legal criteria. The Questionnaire prepared by the Rapporteur, which was considered by the Committee prior to the Progress Report, suggested the following criteria for classification:

A. 1. Should the definition of spacecraft be all-embracing (drafted in general terms) or proceed by distinguishing and enumerating classes or types of spacecraft?

   (a) If a unique definition is adopted, should it be followed up by a classification of spacecraft (regarding the possible need for providing exemptions or special rules for specific types of spacecraft), for instance:

      manned and unmanned spacecraft

active and passive spacecraft
"stationary" spacecraft
"space platforms"
classification by use such as:
(i) meteorological spacecraft
communications spacecraft
science research spacecraft
"navigational aids"
(ii) military and non-military spacecraft
(iii) spacecraft destined to return to earth,
and spacecraft destined to disintegrate
(iv) experimental and "permanent" spacecraft.

Cocca suggests that a distinction be made between manned and unmanned spacecraft, and also between rockets, satellites and space probes. de La Pradelle would prefer both a technical and a legal classification as follows:

Classification technique: Une distinction fondamentale pourrait être faite entre les fusées et les satellites, soit entre les engins ou véhicules d'exploration et d'exploitation spatiales satellisables.

Classification juridique: Elle pourrait prendre appui sur le rapport Cooper et les commentaires qui l'ont accompagné, et ferait apparaître des catégories d'appartenance et de contrôle ayant une incidence sur le status des activités spatiales.

Exemples: Engins spatiaux publiques (public spacecraft) Engins spatiaux ou de groupement d'Etats, engins spatiaux d'organisations internationales, satellites d'information, etc.

Engins spatiaux privés (private spacecraft) Engins d'entreprises privées (télécommunications) engins d'organisations non-gouvernementales.

The Soviet Branch submitted the most elaborate proposal regarding the criteria of classification. It would not suggest the inclusion of classification into a general definition of space object. The proposal points out, however, that in the future the elaboration of a definite system of the classification of space objects inevitably will become necessary. Three kinds of criteria are proposed: objects used for peaceful and military purposes, manned and unmanned spacecraft, and "classification of space objects depending on their purpose and use (communication satellites, meteorological satellites, navigational satellites)".

Great significance should be attached to the first criterion because it sheds some light on eventual Soviet practice regarding the Treaty on Outer Space and the Agreement on Rescue. The Soviet comments read as follows:

Important from the point of view of principles in this field is a strict distinguishing of space objects used only for peaceful purposes and space objects used for military purposes (for legal regulation of celestial bodies concerning the elaboration of the Convention on the rescuing of cosmonauts and a Convention on the liability for damage done by space objects). In connection with partial demilitarization of celestial bodies, certain importance is attached to the distinguishing of objects depending on their position in outer space or on a celestial body.

It would appear that the Soviet position at last reflects a realistic, matter-of-fact and legalistic attitude toward the military uses of outer space and its implications on law. In the face of the partial demilitarization of outer space (cf. Article IV of the Space Treaty), the Soviet intention now would seem to secure legal protection for objects to be launched, constructed and maintained for military purposes in outer space. It is not without significance that earlier propagandistic statements regarding the claimed illegality of military uses of outer space were not introduced into the above-cited comment. Thus, there is an indication on the part of the Soviet Branch of the ILA to accord appropriate legal status to military objects launched into outer space. However, no sufficient evidence is yet available as to what legal consequences the Soviet Government or scholars would be inclined to attach to the military nature of certain objects. Bearing in mind consistent Soviet condemnation of reconnaissance satellites, despite the well-known fact that the Soviet Government reciprocates in kind, and also the basic Soviet approach to the definition of spacecraft, i.e. the "purpose" should be the first criterion, it would seem prudent to conclude that the legal status, openness of and jurisdiction over certain kinds of space objects of military nature is open to negotiation. It may well be that unilateral action and municipal laws would precede an international settlement. The mention of military space objects specifically in the context of the Agreement on Rescue and Return and of liability for damage caused by space vehicle accident seems to bear out the basically pragmatic approach of Soviet scholars to what in fact concerns the exclusiveness of State jurisdiction over military space objects.

3. *Registration and Nationality of Spacecraft*

The Space Law Committee agreed that space objects need to be identified through registration by a State or international organization in accordance with its own regulations. It did not pass upon questions as to whether there should be an international agreement to prescribe which State or organization should be the "registration authority", or which State, international organization, or private entity should be obliged to apply for registration. It referred only to the fact that Article VIII of the Space Treaty, in line with the Declaration of Legal Principles, assumes that objects launched into outer space are registered within a State, but does not specify who the State of registration should be nor prescribe any rules relating to registration. The Progress Report considered the question of both national and international registration.

a. National Registration

The Draft Resolution of the Space Law Committee provided that space objects be registered in a State, but refrained from designating that State. Rather, it referred to Article VII of the Treaty on Outer Space under which the following States are accountable internationally: (i) the State that launches the object; (ii) the State that procures its launching; (iii) the State from whose territory the object is launched; and (iv) the State from whose facility it is launched. It should be recalled here that theoretically the following States may be involved in the launching and flight of a space object:

> (i) State of registration; (ii) State of manufacture of the booster (launch vehicle); (iii) State of manufacture of the space capsules; (iv) State or States of the manufacturers of the embarked equipment; (v) State from whose territory the spacecraft is launched; (vi) State whose nationals control and initiate the launching; (vii) State whose nationals programme and/or control the flight and activities of the spacecraft (space navigation); (viii) States that provide ground stations necessary for space navigation; (ix) State or States whose nationals man the stations mentioned under (viii); (x) States through whose airspace the spacecraft passes; (xi) State of landing (whether planned landing or emergency landing); (xii) State of nationality of the Astronauts.[20]

The Rapporteur preferred the registration to be effected in the State from whose territory the space object was launched, with the proviso that this State should be obliged to mention on its registry all other States that might be liable internationally – or otherwise – for damages caused by the object. Lissitzyn was favourably disposed toward multiple national registration, but the Soviet and German branches, as well as Cocca, were opposed.

b. International Registration

The Draft Resolution of the Space Law Committee which was adopted by the preparatory meeting in Paris provides for such registration without further elaboration. The question is left open whether international regis-

[20] See Progress Report in *Appendix VI*.

tration is to be effected with the launching organisation, a member of that organisation or a party to an *ad hoc* agreement, or with an international agency having jurisdiction in space matters, e.g. the United Nations, or a new specialized agency. Since this question would depend on the regulations of the organisation concerned, multiple registration could arise.

The Soviet Branch of the ILA "believes that the problem of international registration of space objects indisputably deserves attention and demands the most detailed study." It would appear that the Soviet position is not *ab ovo* hostile toward international registration – their main concern being the statutory powers of such an organization. Accordingly, they point out that "the solution of this question will largely depend on the general definition of the legal status of such an organization in international affairs." Moreover, the Soviet stand regarding joint space ventures is quite open-minded and realistic. The Soviet Branch suggests that "the parties to the agreement or members of the organization should themselves decide upon the question as to which State should carry the space object on its registry". This approach tallies with the resolution adopted on December 14, 1967 by the Council of ICAO with respect to the registration of aircraft operated by joint operating agencies. A statement made by academician Keldysh in January 1969, when commenting on the feasibility and great advantages of a joint Soviet-American space flight and the operation of joint space platforms, is in line with the above-mentioned position. A further indication of the flexibility of the Soviet Union toward a special international space agency can be found in the reference by the Soviet Branch to a statement made by the Representative of Canada during the sixth session of the Legal Sub-Committee of the UNCOPUOS, who "felt it was necessary to establish a special international agency for the registration of space objects." The Rapporteur advocated the establishment of a specialised agency of the United Nations with functions and responsibilities somewhat different from those of ICAO in the field of international civil aviation.

As to the conditions and particulars of registration, the Soviet Branch states that this is a matter of internal competence of States. However, it recognizes the necessity in the future to unify the registration procedure on an international level. The Hungarian Branch suggests a detailed system and obligations. Accordingly, States should be bound by international law to pass municipal laws requiring that domestic authorities "should list all launchings licensed or effected from national territory with information susceptible of making identification, the requirement for salvage, eventual liability for damages [sic] and the establishment of property rights." The registration should contain, as a minimum requirement, the following data: (i) place and date of launching; (ii) apogee and perigee; (iii) radio frequency; and (iv) identification marks and the name of the State of registry.[21]

With regard to the choice of identification marks and methods, the Soviet Branch points out that "identification markings make it possible to establish the State affiliation of a space object only after it has returned to Earth" and that "during the space flight such object can be identified with the help of special radio identification signals". Reference was also made to the voluntary identification of launchings to the U.N. Secretary-General in accordance with the U.N. General Assembly Resolution 1721. It was generally agreed that the designation of identification marks should be left to the State of registry.

The Space Law Committee in the face of German and Soviet opposition held that there was no need for nationality of space objects. But as the Soviet Branch pointed out, "one should not be in a hurry to dispose of the concept of nationality in determining the legal status of space objects". The Soviet Branch reckoned with the expansion of joint activities of States and also with the increase of the role of inter-governmental organisations; but in their opinion it "is not a sufficient argument in favour of rejecting the concept of 'nationality.'" It was decided at the 53rd Conference of the International Law Association that the questions discussed above should be studied further. With the opposition of Alex Meyer it was also decided that there was no need for nationality of space objects.

The comments of the present writer relative to the previous material may then be summarized as follows: although in the Progress Report of the Space Law Committee of the ILA, no *opinio juris communis* has chrystallized as yet into legal rules regarding who the launching authority is, what the registration procedures – national or international – are, and what the statutory responsibilities of an international space agency should be, the analyzed material has brought the consideration of the question to a higher level of sophistication. When in the future the Legal Sub-Committee of the UNCOPUOS addresses itself to questions of State jurisdiction, it could draw upon the suggestions contained in the Progress Report. The alternatives seem to have been charted, and now it is up to the States to bring into harmony their choices in the light of their needs and experience. These questions in due course will have to be regulated by new international treaties.

It is admitted that the definition of space objects is an important issue; and the more comprehensive and simple such a definition is, the better it

[21] For de La Pradelle's proposal, see *Appendix VI* Paragraph 19 c.

will be suited to serve its purpose, which in essence is to designate the State of jurisdiction *ratione instrumenti*. It should be recalled here that in the light of State and treaty practice, space objects in any event would be accorded a legal status under international space law. Consequently, a definition of space objects would not bring about a substantive change in the law. Basically it is an issue of terminology rather than one of law. The definition suggested by the Rapporteur of the Space Law Committee of the ILA succinctly sums up the gist of the matter. It would appear that classification prior to concrete experience serves only academic purposes. The Soviet position, based on the insights of a space power, is thus more realistic.

The International Law Association did not decide the most crucial question: who the State of registration should be and whether or not there should be either a national or international registration or both. Closely tied up with the search for the "launching authority" is the concept of nationality of spacecraft. It is this question that will be disposed of first. It was decided at the Buenos Aires Conference of the International Law Association in 1968 that there was no need for nationality of spacecraft.

It is submitted by the present writer that this resolution, if it correctly represents the position of the Space Law Committee of the International Law Association, is either imprecise or an *obiter dictum*. First, one cannot dispose of nationality by a stroke of the pen because the launching authority or State of registration, whoever it happens to be, will exercise authority over the space object. Thus it may be said in legal shorthand that the object possesses the nationality of the respective State. Nationality is neither more nor less than a link which, once established, will indicate both the State of jurisdiction and consequently the nationality of the spacecraft as well. What is expected of the concept of nationality of the space object is to show which State law applies to it, which State is responsible for it and liable for damage caused by it, and who should be dealt with in case of emergency. Nationality serves a very pragmatic evidentiary purpose.

The concept of nationality is, however, not an original one but a derived notion. We may not know what the nationality of a person or object is until the question is settled as to which State may exercise jurisdiction over them and on what grounds. In this sense we may truly say that we do not need nationality in order to pinpoint the source of authority because nationality is the effect and not the cause, although it affords of inference to the latter. In sum, first the State of jurisdiction is to be designated and in turn nationality will emerge as an indicator.

Mankiewicz, the Rapporteur of the Space Law Committee, summarized the discussion in that Committee at its Buenos Aires meeting in the following words:

L'engin spatial traverse les espaces aériens et extra-atmosphériques, le plus souvent sans personnel à bord. Il faut donc qu'on puisse l'identifier. Son identification n'est possible que s'il porte une marque d'immatriculation. Cette marque, permettant l'identification, lui sera attribuée par l'autorité, internationale ou nationale, auprès de laquelle il sera immatriculé. Il n'est pas nécessaire que cette marque – ou la désignation de l'autorité d'immatriculation – soit liée à la "nationalité" de l'engin. En fait, l'engin n'a pas besoin de nationalité.[22]

As to what should be substituted for the concept of nationality, Mankiewicz would suggest:

Du moment où l'on s'abstient de donner une nationalité à l'engin spatial, on n'a pas à se préoccuper de la question de savoir quels devraient être les critères constitutifs de nationalité . . .

Evidemment, il ne suffit pas que l'engin spatial puisse être identifié. Il faut encore qu'on puisse savoir quelle autorité nationale ou internationale – ou entité de droit privée – a jurisdiction sur l'engin spatial et les personnes à bord, indépendamment du lieu où ils se trouvent; à savoir quel est l'Etat, autorité publique ou entreprise privée, qui doit assurer le contrôle de la conduite de l'engin et sera tenu responsable de ses activités, ainsi que des dommages qu'il pourrait causer dans l'espace extra-atmosphérique, dans l'espace aérien et sur la terre. Quelles que soient les règles qu'on appliquera – ou qui s'appliquent déjà en vertu des résolutions des Nations-Unies et des traités – pour déterminer cette autorité ou entité, elle sera mentionnée sur le registre d'immatriculation. Or, du moment où le registre d'immatriculation comportera les mentions nécessaires à l'identification de l'engin et des autorités publiques, ou entreprises privées, ayant des droits et des responsabilités à l'égard de l'engin, son statut sera défini et connu sans qu'il soit nécessaire de lui attribuer une nationalité.

J'ajoute que je préfère l'immatriculation internationale à l'immatriculation nationale. Si l'immatriculation internationale ne peut pas remplacer l'inspection préalable de l'engin, qui me semble de plus en plus indispensable pour assurer que celui-ci ne se livre à une activité dangereuse ou dommageable, l'obligation faite aux intéressés de faire inscrire auprès d'une organisation internationale les détails concernant la composition, la programmation et les activités de l'engin constituerait un premier tri des lancements d'engin et retiendra peut-être les Etats d'entreprendre des activités dont l'innocuité n'est pas certaine. Par contre, si les engins sont immatriculés sur des registres nationaux, personne ne saurait d'avance à quelles fins ils seront lancés.

Finally, we should like to draw attention to an additional reason why the concept of nationality could not fulfill the function it does in general

22 Quoted from "Space Law Committee, Legal Status of Spacecraft, Résumé d'une Intervention Faite à Buenos Aires" (Unpublished, mimeo.). The present writer thanks Professor Mankiewicz for kindly providing him with this paper.

international law. When a State launches and registers its own space object, in this case the launching authority, the State of registration and nationality coincide. Obviously, this is not the case where more than one State is involved in the launching (cf. list of potentially interested States in the Progress Report). States may agree to divide up responsibilities relative to the space object among themselves. The notion of nationality could not adequately cope with such situations which would come to resemble a state of legal schizophrenia.

What is required now is to provide for the registration of space objects in a State. The present writer is of the opinion that no hard and fast rules as to who the State of registration should be, would suffice. In fact, the framework must be flexible so as to admit of optional arrangements for registration between the parties concerned *inter se*. In this way, the term State of registry would not always cover the same category of States. This is an important criterion which we propose is not only of the nature of a suggestion, but is imbedded in the paramount principle of sovereign equality of States. For the sake of peace, order and good government in outer space, a rebuttable presumption and legal obligation should be created to the effect that the State from whose territory the space object was intended to be launched toward outer space shall register the object and give adequate notification thereof internationally or notify an international agency. International space law need not be concerned with national registration; it is a matter of internal competence of States and should be left as such. It is international registration which is significant and indispensable for public order in outer space. The creation of a specialized international registration board performing exclusively evidentiary and notification functions would seem to be a feasible and sufficient objective. This International Space Registration Board would not require the creation of a complex international organization and could be established within or linked to the United Nations. It is not only for pragmatic purposes that we suggest international registration together with an international registration board, but also because we believe along with Sir Hersch Lauterpacht, that "an effective peaceful organization of the international community . . . is the legitimate business of international lawyers to promote."[23]

The legal presumption to the effect that the State from whose territory the space object was launched should be considered the State of registry, would provide sufficient incentive for the appropriate State to actually register the object. The registration would then be a matter of negotiation and agreement between the States concerned. Consequently, the terri-

[23] Lauterpacht, *The Function of Law in the International Community*, 437 (1933).

torial State would run the risk of having to carry the burdens of responsibility of the State of jurisdiction if it does not secure the contractual obligation to register the object from the State on whose behalf the launching was undertaken. In addition, it would enhance the efficiency and openness of international registration if the territorial State were granted a right to transmit the relevant information and documentation directly to the International Space Registration Board concurrently with the State of registration of the space object. The principle of openness of the national registry of space objects, if such is maintained, should be couched in the form of a legal obligation. But the rebuttable presumption, as has been mentioned above, is also a legal necessity. We submit that the mandatory designation of a single State of registration would be a contravention of Article I, paragraph 2 of the Treaty on Outer Space, which provides that space exploration and use shall proceed "without discrimination of any kind, on a basis of equality and in accordance with international law".

Thus, there is a legal obstacle in assuming that a system of registration without the freedom of optional choice would be acceptable, because it would require the designated State to assume jurisdiction over, as well as international responsibility for, the space object launched on behalf of another State and, vice versa, the relinquishing of authority and control by the latter State with respect to the space object. Such a system would penalize those States which do not have the capability to act for themselves regarding the exploration and use of outer space. In sum, it is proposed that space objects be registered by the State of registration with an International Space Registration Board (ISRB). The actual State of registration should be designated by the interested parties in a formal agreement, about which the ISRB should be duly notified by either of them with the proviso that failing notification the State from whose territory the object was launched shall be deemed the State of registration.

III. THE ATTITUDE OF THE DAVID DAVIES MEMORIAL INSTITUTE

The David Davies Memorial Institute of International Studies produced a "Draft Code of Rules on the Exploration and Uses of Outer Space" in 1962 and "Draft Rules Concerning Changes in the Environment of the Earth" in 1964.[24] Both these documents are notable for their detailed and well thought out provisions.

Paragraph 5.1 provides that every spacecraft shall be registered "in a

[24] The texts of the two documents are reprinted in *Current Problems,* at 123–131 and 159–164 respectively.

State" in accordance with municipal law regulations as well as with the UNCOPUOS. Spacecraft launched by international organisations are likewise to be registered with the UNCOPUOS. The proposal provides for a flexible system for determining the nationality of the spacecraft. According to Paragraph 5.3:

(a) every spacecraft to which Section 5.1 applies shall be deemed to have the nationality of the State in which it has been registered, and whose nationality and registration mark it bears, or in the absence of such registration, of the State responsible for its launching.

Paragraph 5.3(b) in effect provides that spacecraft or parts thereof, "so long as they are identifiable" are the property of the State of nationality and do not become *res derelicta* on account of launching.

As regards space stations, the State which establishes or permits its nationals to establish such stations may, according to Paragraph 3.5, exercise jurisdiction "over all persons in the station and in that area around it over which movement is necessary for the maintenance and use of the station." Section (xxii) of the Comments explains that "jurisdiction is to be understood as covering the internal administration of the station and its personnel and as including a right to exclude other persons, vehicles or craft from the area, upon a reasonable belief that their entry would be injurious to the station or its use." Further, the extension of U.N. supervision over installations on celestial bodies is advocated, initially through the UNCOPUOS and later a specially constituted international agency. If such stations are established by an international organisation, it is suggested that it "may exercise a similar jurisdiction by international agreement" (Paragraph 3.5(b)).

The drafting of Paragraph 4 dealing with the innocent passage of spacecraft through airspace reflects concern for the preservation of the legal régime of airspace. As a general rule, the right of innocent passage is not granted, but permission to this effect should not be withheld if prior notice (minimum 14 days in advance) has been given of the intended flight and the flight is solely for scientific and peaceful purposes. In any event, however, a spacecraft capable of operating also as an aircraft "shall for the purposes of its use of the airspace be deemed to be an aircraft." Manned spacecraft in emergency situations are not subject to this prohibition. Save in the case of emergency landings, the territorial State "may divert or destroy any spacecraft which enters its airspace without the consent prescribed in Section 4.1."

It is remarkable how close these proposals come to what actually may now be considered the applicable law. The Draft Code and the Draft Rules are also noteworthy for their appreciation of the role of international bodies with a measure of regulatory responsibilities.[25]

It has been extensively reported in scientific publications and government documents that the national space programs of the United States of America and the Soviet Union, as well as of some other States, are geared to the practical uses and commercial exploitation of outer space. The United States is preparing the launching of manned orbiting workshops and manned orbiting laboratories in the earth orbit. Likewise, the Soviet Union is known to be planning the launching of large space stations and orbital "greenhouses". Permanent bases will be established in outer space and on the Moon, providing living facilities and habitable environment for long-duration missions (up to one year and longer). Astronauts will be able to settle down and work under "shirt sleeve" conditions on the Moon. Astronomical observatories, scientific instruments and automatic data stations will be deployed and serviced by astronauts on the Moon. Space ferry service and lunar transportation vehicles will facilitate the rotation and exchange of space crews. The possibility of operating an ore processing plant on the Moon is already being studied.[26]

Thus, it should be obvious that space activities are becoming more sophisticated and habitation in outer space will assume the characteristics of a regular, planned and routine way of life. Consequently, administration and the exercise of State jurisdiction over such activities become a matter of efficiency and security. State control over space stations and crew personnel in outer space or on a celestial body will have to be exercised through the spatial extension of jurisdictional powers.

[25] See Goedhuis, *op. cit.* at 130.

[26] For technical literature on space projects, see *inter alia*: "The Space Program in the Post-Apollo Period" – A Report of the President's Science Advisory Committee, Prepared by the Joint Space Panels, the White House, February 1967, USGPO. For a survey of the report see, "PESAC Gives Post-Apollo Recommendations," 5 A&A 20–233 (March 1967), George S. Hunter, "NASA pushes Orbital Workshop Program," (March 6 1967) 86 AW & ST 70–71, 73, 75–76, 79, 81, "NASA Multi-Purpose Space Stations," 91 FI 420–421 (16 March 1967); "MOL Increases Opportunities in Military Space Activities," 86 AW & ST 117–119 (March 6, 1967); "Moon's Service Station Studied," 20 TW 14 (April 10, 1967); Charles D. La Fond, "Emplaced Data Station May Extend ALSER," 20 TW 32–34 (January 9, 1967); "Lunar Shelter, Taxi Work Getting Funds," 20 TW 3 (February 27, 1967); "Instant Moon Shelters From Ordinary Gelatin," 20 TW 23 (March 6, 1967); Arthur Hill, "Lunar 'Walking Staff' Design Under Way," 20 TW 24 (March 6, 1967). Regarding Soviet space projects see *The Montreal Star,* April 8, 1967; "Gagarin Predicts Shots," *N.Y. Times,* April 15, 1967. "Soviet Reported in Key Lunar Test, Cosmos Flights May Be Heat Shield Re-Entry Trials," *id.* "Russians Next To Fly In Space," *The Montreal Star,* March 28, 1967. See also, Report to the Congress from the President of the United States, United States Aeronautics and Space Activities (1966), 171 pp.

What law will apply to space vehicles, moon stations and the personnel there? Will astronauts be subject to the exclusive jurisdiction of their own national States during their residence in the space station of a third State? What is the extent of immunity from the law of the rescuing State when astronauts make emergency or distress landings? In what manner is a State entitled to protect the integrity of its scientific instruments and other devices? Can a State prescribe rules of conduct safeguarding its lawful interest in outer space and on celestial bodies, thereby in fact assuming a certain measure of control over a limited area of the Moon?

In order to give cogent answers to these and similar questions, it is necessary to clarify, elaborate and systematize the rules governing the exercise of jurisdiction by States in outer space including celestial bodies.

This study consists of three stages: (1) a survey of the applicable rules of public international law governing the exercise of State jurisdiction in outer space; (2) the Space Treaty and the Agreement on Rescue and Return, etc.; and (3) the U.N. General Assembly resolutions on outer space and the summary records and documents of the UNCOPUOS. The last two sources will frequently be referred to under the comprehensive terms of "U.N. practice". It would seem that these three sources constitute the most important legal means for determining the rules and principles of international space law. A consideration of the writings of publicists is – with a few exceptions – beyond the scope of the present work.[27]

The question of the upper limit of State sovereignty has puzzled the community of space lawyers since the inception of space law research. The delimination of airspace from outer space bears directly upon the upward extension of exclusive State jurisdiction. The existence, at least *in abstracto,* of such demarcation between airspace and outer space is, of course, undisputable. Airspace and outer space constitute two juridically different régimes and since they are contiguous a demarcation line is implicit. Now the question is, whether or not this demarcation line should be made *explicit* in international space law, and if so, by what means or criteria

[27] The substitution of the above-mentioned three "sources" of our inquiry for the reference to the jurisprudence of prize courts in Lord Sumner's statement in the Case *The Kronprinsessan Margareta* should illustrate the point. Lord Sumner said:

> Valuable as the opinions of learned and distinguished writers must always be, as aids to a full and exact comprehension of a systematic law of nations, Prize Courts must always attach chief importance to the current of decisions, and the more the field is covered by decided cases the less becomes the authority of commentators and jurists. [1921] 1 A.C. 486, at p. 495.

the demarcation of the two legal régimes should be made effective. No progress has been made in this respect within the U.N. nor in learned institutes, though numerous suggestions were proposed.[28] It was due only to these considerations, and not to the underestimation of the significance of the question, that we only *per tangentem* mention the question of delimitation.[29] Moreover, it will be well to point out here that the vertical extension of State jurisdiction beyond territorial space is also a matter of *demarcation,* and not exclusively that of delimitation or one of substance. Indeed, the demarcation of outer space and airspace is not primarily a legal, or for that matter, a technical question, but much more a political one in nature. And this being the case, no hard and fast rule would serve the international community or individual states equally well. However, the functional limitation of exclusive State jurisdiction in the terrestrial environment is a different matter and adequate reference will be made to it in subsequent pages.

Outer space is a new environment, the universal arena in and through which man communicates by a new medium electronic technology. Societies have always been shaped, says McLuhan, more by the nature of the media than by the content of the communication. "Electronic technology fosters and encourages unification and involvement. It is impossible to understand social and cultural changes without a knowledge of the workings of media."[30] Survival and accommodation of conflicting national interests involving space environment is equally impossible if one approaches "the social drama, with a fixed, unchangeable point of view the witless repetitive response to the unperceived."[31] Outer space is a collide-oscope of interfaced situations. We should be concerned with two problems. However, we are bogged down in the first, and consequently cannot even attempt to solve the second with a likely chance of success. First, the problem of war and peace in our "global village" bears heavily upon us. McLuhan conveys a message to international lawyers as well:

All the money that is being spent in NASA is exactly on a par with the budget for *Bonanza.* It is a Newtonian program, not a twentieth-century program. It is

[28] For a good survey see, Dr. D. Goedhuis, "Some Trends in the Political and Legal Thinking on the Conquest of Space," *Nederlands Tijdschrift voor Internationaal Recht,* 119 *et seq.* (1962, No. 2). See also by the same author, "An Evaluation of the Leading Principles of the Treaty on Outer Space of 27th January 1967," (1968, mimeo.), and *loc. cit. supra* at 129–130.

[29] For a discussion of questions relative to the definition of outer space, see Chapter 1 IV-A.

[30] Marshall McLuhan & Quentin Fiore, *The Medium is the Massage, An Inventory of Effects,* Bantam Books, 8 (1967).

[31] *Ibid.* at 10.

a misappropriation of funds. It has no relevance to our time anymore than *Bonanza* does. Projecting missiles into outer space is no different from the activities of Columbus and Magellan.

The new space, created by our electronic microscopes, points to the immediate possibilities of anti-gravitational transportation such as would eliminate the wheel and the miseries of our cities. The same rear-view pattern appears in connection with every innovation whatsoever. When anesthetics were discovered, they were naturally applied to surgery. Surgery was not new. The anesthetic was new. Moreover, the anesthetic made possible fiendish human torments that transferred all the human pain to convalescence. With anesthetics, what was really new was convalescence. Weeks and months of pains resulted from the new technology. Nobody has ever thought of applying anesthetics to convalescence.[32]

If our space research is "Newtonian" and could and should it be something other than "Newtonian?" then what are the characteristics of contemporary international law, our legal device which is destined to make order in our global village? In concepts and approach it is overwhelmingly concerned with individual state interests rather than the common interest of our global village. The unqualified extension of international law into space environment is the most striking example of juristic "rear-view mirrorism."[33] The silence of contemporary public international law regarding the questions posed by the uses and exploitation of sea resources is a case in point. The body of international legal rules and principles we have at our disposal now will not do better in space environment either, unless they are interpreted and developed in accordance with the message the space medium conveys to us.

In other words, as our second task we are faced with the thorny problem of how to preserve peace, order and good government, not only in our global village, but also in the universal space village. We have to use multiple models or the technique of suspended judgment for exploration; in other i.e., our approach to interpreting and developing international space law should be an approach that has in its focus the primary interests of our global village as a whole. It is only in this way that individual state and global interests can be aggregated and articulated in a realistic fashion. The space

[32] Marshall McLuhan & Quentin Fiore, *War and Peace in the Global Village*, Bantam Books, 127 (1968).

[33] *Id.* 18. See also, Marshall McLuhan & Quentin Fiore, *The Medium is the Massage, An Inventory of Effects*, Bantam Books, 74–75 (1967). "The past went that-a-way. When faced with a totally new situation, we tend always to attach ourselves to the objects, to the flavor of the most recent past. We look at the present through a rear-view mirror. We march backwards into the future. Suburbia lives imaginatively in Bonanza-land." *Id.*

environment should be appropriated by, or at least on behalf of, our global village. Should the exploitation of outer space be carried out and State jurisdiction be made to protect interests and titles therein exercised in the framework which our contemporary international law provides, then gross mismanagement may very well be the outcome. It will suffice here to refer to the distinct and real contingency of mismanagement of the resources of the sea. There too, the existing law has to be changed to assure some kind of an accommodation of community and individual state interests. Outer space is, however, a distinct environment due to its potentiality for becoming a powerful medium capable of reshaping our thoughts and perception of things in our global village. It is not difficult to read the message written in the sky, that one day the community of states will form a global village. This is, however, not a necessity, but only a contingency. It will be well to note that we do not suggest that the application of international law in space environment is an exercise in futility and contrary to the requirements of progress. Indeed, international law has a number of concepts, principles and rules that are good for almost all seasons and environments. Why not incorporate them into space law and why not develop new rules? We should, therefore, draw upon current methodology in approaches to international legal problems.

In order "to move beyond the impressionism of earlier approaches" to the study of international law, Falk suggested that "the body of practice" and the "set of attitudes associated with the interesting legal questions . . . need to be collected and organized in a systematic fashion to permit the formulation of well-evidenced generalizations".[34] Thus, method of inquiry becomes a question of primary importance because only the "right method secures the best results"[35] in ensuring that international studies acquire a scientific character. Some scholars have focused their attention on a "systematic framework of enquiry adopted to a number of relatively specialized subject matter[s]".[36] "Case" studies have become very popular.[37] This study also intends to conform to this practice. However, the point herein raised that the inquiry should be based on the U.N. practice, is believed to be novel.

The methodology of this work has many features in common with the

[34] Richard A. Falk, "New Approaches to the Study of International Law," 61 A.J.I.L. 487 (1967).

[35] L. Oppenheim, 2 A.J.I.L. 327 (1908) quoted from Schwarzenberger, 42.

[36] Falk, *op. cit. supra* at 487.

[37] The term "case study" has a double meaning. It may either mean the study of a judicial decision, or the study of an event, phenomenon or judicial concept, e.g. the scope of domestic jurisdiction. Cf. Falk, *op. cit. supra* at 495.

inductive approach[38] (as a technique of research) and with some of the current methodological orientations in the study of international law in the United States.[39] An attempt is made in this work to analyse and elaborate upon the rich legal raw material accumulated in the course of the progressive development of space law in the U.N. Frequent reference to U.N. General Assembly resolutions on outer space and random citation of passages from statements of delegates in the Legal Sub-Committee of the UNCOPUOS, the First (Political) Committee and the General Assembly of the U.N. a recurring practice of the past must finally be replaced by a systematic elaboration of the "U.N. practice" according to subject matter. The approach adopted in this study has many features in common with the methodologies of the *policy science, functionalism, systems theory and phenomenological* schools.[40]

When dealing with the problems of State jurisdiction in outer space, attention should be paid to the "factual events of community process" and to "all variables [past, present and future] that a fully rational decision-maker would want to take account of". (*Policy science*).[41] Evidently, a certain teleological approach is required in the study of space law, if the incorporation of new social goals representative of the changing international society in which contemporary international law must operate is a desired objective.[42]

Also, we must recognize that a more adequate theory should be developed regarding the basis of legal obligation in international law.[43] Article 38 of the Statute of the International Court of Justice does not necessarily give the best and only solution. Other criteria, such as a "com-

[38] Schwarzenberger, *op. cit. supra* at 8–42. See also, Mexican-United States General Claims Commission (1923): *Dujay Case* (1929), Opinions of Commíssioners, 1929, p. 180 at 185: "The existence or non-existence of a rule of law is established by a process of inductive reasoning." The Secretary-General of the U.N. in a Memorandum of March 7, 1949, observed that "there is a growing trend towards an inductive approach," (U.N. Doc. A/CN. 4/6, p. 114). Cited from Bin Cheng, *General Principles of Law as Applied by International Courts and Tribunals*, London, 1953, p. 1. This latter work is an example for the application of the inductive approach to the study of "the general principles of law recognised by civilised nations."

[39] See Falk, *op. cit. supra* at 488–495.

[40] For a detailed description of these methodologies see, Falk, *op. cit.* 487–496 (1967).

[41] *Ibid.* at 489–491. This approach is represented by Myres S. McDougal and Harold D. Lasswell as well as other associates.

[42] For a criticism of the doctrinal content of the so-called "inductive approach" see, Richard A. Falk, "Schwarzenberger, The Inductive Approach to International Law," (Book review) 61 A.J.I.L. 630 (1967).

[43] For the exposition of the traditional viewpoint see, James L. Brierly, *The Basis of Obligation in International Law* (1958).

munity-oriented notion of consensus",[44] and the law-creating effect of certain U.N. General Assembly resolutions[45] must also be considered. They seem to be well-suited to the dynamics of law-creation, supplementing those criteria listed in Article 38 of the Statute of the International Court of Justice. If this is so, the Declaration of Legal Principles (U.N. General Assembly Resolution 1962 (XVIII) can provide a legal basis on which claims against States, not signatories or parties to the Space Treaty after its entry into force, can adequately be founded.

The distinction between interests perceived by States as *vital* or as *non-vital* is very useful when dealing with problems of allocation of jurisdictional competencies. It is the proposition of the *functionalist methodology* that the development and study of international law must be correlated with "the satisfaction of certain social functions in the international system".[46] Indeed, so far as interests are perceived as vital in relation to space activities and their effects on earth, it should not be expected that States would consent to a curtailment of their exclusive jurisdiction over persons, things, acts and occurrences. The examples for the allocation of exclusive jurisdiction of the State of registry over its space objects and personnel thereof (cf. Article VIII of the Space Treaty) and the non-existence of the right of innocent passage for spacecraft through the national airspace of third States illustrate the point. On the other hand, when the satisfaction of common needs is required, concurrent or complementary jurisdiction is willingly substituted for exclusive jurisdiction. These "non-

[44] Jenks, *Law, Welfare and Freedom,* 83–100 (1963).

[45] See Falk, *op. cit.* at 486. In the course of the litigation in the *South-West Africa* cases the Applicants argued that the practice of *apartheid* is "illegal" because of the law-creating effect of the formal acts of the General Assembly. For the text of the judgment and a digest of dissenting opinions see, 61 A.J.I.L. 116–210 (1967). The present author has suggested elsewhere that Resolution 1962 (XVIII) of the General Assembly on the *Declaration of Legal Principles* is a *"formal declarative source of international space law."* Cf. also, Csabafi, "The U.N. General Assembly Resolutions on Outer Space as Sources of Space Law," 337–361 *Proceedings VIIIth Colloquium* (1966). This proposition received some favourable comments in the literature, cf., Marko G. Markoff, "Problèmes juridiques de l'exploration Planétaire," *Revue Générale de l'Air* 225 (1966); and John Michael Kemp, "Evolution Toward a Space Treaty: An Historical Analysis," 93 NASA, HHN-64, 1966. Note also the use of the term "declaratory" in the *Shimoda* decision where *"declaratory"* rules of warfare were mentioned in order to support inferences about obligatory standards of behaviour. Cf. Falk, "The Shimoda Case: A Legal Appraisal of the Atomic Attacks upon Hiroshima and Nagasaki," 59 A.J.I.L. 759–793 (1965). For the text of the decision see, Richard A. Falk and Saul H. Mendlovitz (eds.), *The Strategy of World Order: Toward a Theory of War Prevention,* 314–353 (1966).

[46] Falk, *op. cit.* at 491, 492–493. The functionalist approach is represented by Percy Corbett, C. Wilfred Jenks, Wolfgang Friedman, Julius Stone and David Mitrany.

vital" interests may include: rescue and return of astronauts and space vehicles making emergency or distress landings, as well as safety and open access to moon stations. The problem of the so-called *"functional jurisdiction"* over areas surrounding moon stations or lawfully utilized territory on the moon belongs in this context. It is believed to be a novel proposition, and it is argued that such a claim would be tenable under international space law.

The approach adopted by the *systems theory*[47] is also helpful in specifying analytical models describing the way in which jurisdictional competencies are distributed only between those space powers which are in a position to possess space stations on the moon, and not among every State irrespective of the fact whether they are able to "reciprocate" or not. Thus, Article XII does not provide for international control over moon stations. One may wish to put this model-building technique to a greater use in searching for further generalisations, should the objectives of research so require.

Space law is a novel phenomenon on the scene of contemporary international society. It displays the general attributes of the international legal system, as well as the unique evolution of law. The technique of depth analyses of "cases" had been elaborated and practiced by the *phenomenological school*[48] drawing heavily on the philosophical tradition created by phenomonology.

It is only a short distance from the phenomenological perspectives to the theory of *inter-bloc international law*.[49] Space law, as a new legal phenomenon, is the vintage of inter-bloc international law. The study of space law can be fitted conveniently into the framework of inquiry developed by the McWhinneyan theory of *inter-bloc or comparative international law*.[50] In the words of McWhinney:

[47] Cf. Falk, *op. cit. supra* at 493–494. This approach was used by Nicholas de Katzenbach, Kaplan, Stanley Hoffman, Saul Mendlovitz and Richard A. Falk.

[48] Cf. Falk, *op. cit.* at 494–495. This technique has been used by B. Currie and Falk.

[49] The inter-bloc international law or comparative international law theory has been developed by Edward McWhinney. See, Edward McWhinney, 115–116, 122–125; *Federal Constitution-Making for a Multi-National World* 123, 126–127 (1966).

[50] It is submitted that an effective system of State jurisdictions in outer space and on celestial bodies can be created only on the basis of a balanced adjustment of competing claims of competency. Jurisdiction is a process by which the limits of legal competence are specified and the authority to regulate is identified. Such allocation of jurisdiction must be suited to the requirements of contemporary international society in general and to the needs of the bloc-leader space powers in particular. Katzenbach has aptly pointed out that the allocation of jurisdictions concerning the uses of resources

There seems good reason to believe that the apparent genesis of an empirically-based, inter-bloc law represents not just a temporary truce between two great military antagonists, but that it is something in the way of a continuing, evolving process with the number and range of the "rules of the game" continuing to expand all the time, and with their degree of explicitness and concreteness also improving constantly.[51]

The growth of international space law is living evidence of the viability of the theory of inter-bloc international law. The scope of inter-bloc international law has been expanding rapidly. The Cuban Missile Confrontation of October, 1962, which as a "moment of truth" demonstrated "to both sides that they had a good deal of mutuality of interest in the solution of certain problems, apart from the more obvious and glaring points of discord between them,"[52] paved the way for the Moscow Partial Test Ban Treaty of August 5 1963. The example of the Test Ban Treaty was followed in 1967 by the Treaty on Outer Space. It demonstrates that despite the long-lasting confrontation in Vietnam between the two blocleader space powers, it was possible for them to select "the highest common denominator of agreement among the principles of the two systems"[53] regarding outer space. These two examples eloquently argue in favour of the theory of inter-bloc international law. The scope of agreement is greater by far with respect to the Space Treaty than it is to the Moscow Test Ban Treaty. The Treaty on Outer Space governs a great variety of activities, and its geographical scope is infinite; moreover, it complements the former.[54] In addition, it provides a framework around which the body of international space law is supposed to grow. Outer space is one of the arenas where the McWhinneyan theory faces a challenge; and it is the field of international space law where this theory can be tested in order for it to make significant contributions to legal science.

In the light of current developments in the field of space law, the pertinence of the following passage is obvious:

has been and increasingly is a function of political power. He proved that the technological developments which facilitate the exploitation and uses of outer space and celestial bodies demonstrated that earlier propositions of nineteenth-century doctrine of State sovereignty had become rapidly dated and outmoded. Nicholas de Katzenbach, "Sharable and Strategic Resources Outer Space, Polar Areas and the Ocean," *Proceedings of the American Society of International Law* 206–212 (1959).

[51] See McWhinney, 115. See also Myres S. McDougal, "The Comparative Study of Law for Policy Purposes: Value Clarification as an Instrument of Democratic World Order", 61 *Yale L. J.* 915 (1952); "Law and Power", 40 A.J.I.L. 109–111 (1952).

[52] McWhinney, 115.

[53] *Ibid.* at 87.

[54] Article 1 (1a) of the Moscow Test Ban Treaty and Article IV of the Space Treaty.

And insofar as they [the minimum rules of the game] may reflect, far more nearly than traditional international law doctrine frequently does, in the areas of cold war conflict, the working facts of present-day East-West international relations with their actual record of accomodations and adjustments of conflicting interests of the rival power blocs, they may, as we have said, meet the ultimate pragmatist test of the usefulness of any theory, whether of international law or otherwise, that they seem to work.[55]

It was the inquisitive approach and methodology of the McWhinneyan theory that influenced this elaboration of the "U.N. practice" regarding the progressive development of the concept of State jurisdiction in outer space.

We can now conclude with a brief clarification of terminology:

The *concept (doctrine) of State jurisdiction* means the right of a State to regulate the rights of persons, to affect property, things, events and occurrences whether by legislative, executive or judicial measure.

Prescriptive (legislative) jurisdiction or "jurisfaction" means the jurisdiction to prescribe what is mainly personal in nature.

Prerogative (enforcement) jurisdiction or "jurisaction" means jurisdiction to enforce what is mainly territorial in nature.

The term *exclusive jurisdiction* means a State has an exclusive right to exercise jurisdiction.

Concurrent jurisdiction means more than one State may simultaneously assume jurisdiction over persons, things or occurrences.

Complementary jurisdiction means a State may under international space law assume jurisdiction supplementing the jurisdiction of a third State.

International space law is interchangeably used with the term space law, especially when public international legal aspects are emphasized in opposition to those aspects related to municipal law.

U.N. practice means the totality of U.N. contribution to the progressive development of international space law. The term, as it is used in this work, should be understood to mean both the proceedings of the various U.N. organs and the specialized agencies bearing upon the progressive development of space law, as well as the resolutions of the U.N. General Assembly, the summary records of the meetings of the UNCOPUOS and its two sub-committees and other documents.

In the subsequent pages, we shall discuss the subject of State jurisdiction in outer space and on celestial bodies under the following headings:

[55] *Ibid.* at 116.

(a) The Legal Basis of the Progressive Development in the United Nations of the Concept of State Jurisdiction in International Law.
(b) The Progressive Development of Certain Legal Principles Governing the Exercise of State Jurisdiction in Outer Space and on Celestial Bodies.
(c) The *Lex Lata* Regarding the Exercise of State Jurisdiction in Outer Space.
(d) Observations *De Lege Ferenda.*

CHAPTER II

THE LEGAL BASIS OF THE PROGRESSIVE DEVELOPMENT IN THE UNITED NATIONS OF THE CONCEPT OF STATE JURISDICTION IN INTERNATIONAL SPACE LAW

I. THE PRINCIPLE OF APPLICABILITY OF INTERNATIONAL LAW TO SPACE ACTIVITIES

As early as 1959 the Ad hoc Committee on the Peaceful Uses of Outer Space observed in its report (A/4141) that the provisions of the U.N. Charter and the Statute of the International Court of Justice "as a matter of principle . . . were not limited in their operation to the confines of the earth."[1] In General Assembly Resolution 1721 (XVI) of December 20, 1961, the principle was stated explicitly for the first time that "international law, including the Charter of the United Nations, applies to outer space and celestial bodies."[2] The Declaration of Legal Principles (General Assembly Resolution 1962 (XVIII) of December 13, 1963) provided that "outer space and celestial bodies are free for exploration and use by all States on a basis of equality *in accordance with international law*"[3] and further that "the activities of States in the exploration and use of outer space shall be carried on *in accordance with international law,* including the Charter of the United Nations, in the interest of maintaining international peace and security and promoting international cooperation and understanding."[4]

[1] United Nations *Ad Hoc* Committee on the Peaceful Uses of Outer Space, Report to the United Nations General Assembly, Fourteenth Session, New York, 1959 U.N. Doc. A/4141, July 14, 1959. The Resolution is reproduced in *Legal Problems of Space Exploration – A Symposium,* Washington, March 22, 1961, pp. 1268, 1247–1275. For a discussion of the Resolution see, *Official Records of the General Assembly, Fourteenth Session, First Committee,* 1079th to 1081st meetings; and *ibid. Plenary Meetings,* 856th meeting. For the statement of U.S. Ambassador Stevenson, see U.N. Doc. A/C. 1/SR. 1210 (December 4, 1961).

[2] The wording of the principle was criticised, because international law cannot be regarded as applicable to outer space and celestial bodies as such. "What it applies to is activities undertaken there by the subjects of international law." See Jenks, 203.

[3] *Ibid.* Paragraph 2.

[4] *Id.* Para. 4. (Emphasis added). Concerning the change of wording see Jenks, 203.

Article III of the Treaty on Outer Space brought forth this principle in the same manner:

> States Parties to the Treaty shall carry on activities in the exploration and use of outer space, including the Moon and other celestial bodies, in accordance with international law, including the Charter of the United Nations, in the interest of maintaining international peace and security and promoting international cooperation and understanding.

It may be stated, then, that the U.N. practice has always been consistent and clear regarding the above-mentioned legal principles. The question now arises as to which rules and principles of international law governing the exercise of State jurisdiction are applicable and in what manner. The rule providing that international law is applicable to activities in space should be understood to include, when appropriate, the applicable rules of general international law regarding jurisdiction. To insure greater precision, the meaning of the principle of applicability of international law to outer space needs some clarification.

The summary records of the Legal Sub-Committee of the UNCOPUOS show that there was no unanimity of opinion regarding the meaning of the principle that international law is applicable to outer space activities. The French delegate commented that reference to international law was ambiguous, and he said that if the well-established principles of traditional international law relating to land, sea and air were meant, then that law "could not be applied as it stands in regard to outer space."[5] He argued that national appropriation of outer space and celestial bodies has been specifically banned, while this principle is established in general international law. If the reference to international law was to be regarded as relating "to the law of outer space", then the provisions of such a law were still in the process of formation. France maintained her position on this point and the French representative suggested in the course of the fifth session of the Legal Sub-Committee of the UNCOPUOS on 21 July 1966 that it was necessary "to determine which principles of international law were meant when international law in general was mentioned."[6] The

See also, U.N. Doc. A/C. 1/L. 301, A/C. 1/SR. 1210; A/C. 1/857; A/C. 1/L. 301: Rev. 1 and Rev. 1/Corr. 1; A/C. 1/SR. 1214; A/5100, 6–7; U.N. Doc. A/AC. 105/C. 2/Sr. 20; U.N. Doc. A/C. 1/PV. 1289; A/AC. 105/C. 2/SR. 28.

[5] U.N. Doc. A/5549/Add. 1 of November 27, 1963, p. 16–17. For the statement of the Brazilian delegate, see *id.* at 27.

[6] U.N. Doc. A/AC. 105/C. 2/SR. 64 at 6. The statement of Mr. Deleau, representative of France in the Legal Sub-Committee is cited in full for the illustration of the point. He said:

French delegate could not accept the occasional references in the drafts of the Space Treaty to the U.N. Charter as "entirely convincing."[7] He said that "the Charter did not rule out the existence of arms so long as general disarmament had not been achieved, and it provided for and even codified the right of self-defence."[8]

The French representative had a point in suggesting that a distinction should be made between "the earthly consequences of space activities" and "their effects in space and on celestial bodies."[9] "In the first case", said Mr. Seydoux, "it was largely a matter of transposing legal rules which already existed; it was the second case that brought into play the law of space proper, which would give rise to new legal rules to meet new situations."[10] In this light, it is not at all surprising that the French representative attempted to challenge the "advisability of referring in the draft treaty to international law and the United Nations Charter, which might not be applicable to space activities for long."[11] While it is difficult to agree entirely with this latter proposition, it must be conceded that the French position pointed out two significant aspects of space law. First, that as emphasis is shifted from the exploration to the "uses" of outer space,[12]

> ... the reference to conformity with international law in both the Soviet and the United States texts [of the Space Treaty] was perhaps not as clear as it seemed *a priori*, for if international law was based on sovereignty, how could one act within that law if the principle was proclaimed that there was no sovereignty in space and on celestial bodies?

[7] *Id.*

[8] *Id.* The French representative suggested, for instance, that the principle of sovereign equality of States should be made more specific by the stipulations of "conditions on which non-space Powers would have access to the results of the exploration of outer space and celestial bodies".

[9] U.N. Doc. A/AC.105/C.2/SR.57 at 15. For an illustration of the significance of the suggested distinction see: "The *open access* provided for in article 6 of the United States draft concerned installations in space and on celestial bodies and did not apply to installations on earth, i.e. launching or observations. There again, there was a difference of concept between the terrestrial part and the purely space part of space law". SR.64 at 6. The French delegate suggested consistency in referring in the Space Treaty to the terrestrial effects of space exploration as well. SR.66 at 11.

[10] *Ibid.*

[11] U.N. Doc. A/AC.105/C.2/SR.70 at 14 (3 August 1966).

[12] The French representative in the Legal Sub-Committee of the UNCOPUOS claimed that "There was little existing material on which to base the development of space law: a number of resolutions by the General Assembly, and the draft Treaties put forward by the United States of America and the USSR respectively". He went on stating that: "Traditional international law was based on the concepts of sovereignty and continental approach. No State had yet attempted to apply those concepts in space, and the draft treaties submitted on the subject rightly established the rule of non-appropriation. *Thus, it was not so much general international law that was applicable to space as the law of the high seas and it, too could hardly be applied without modifi-*

more specific rules governing such activities will have to be elaborated. In other words, broad principles of general international law will not be able to cope with the need for special rules. The exercise of State jurisdiction in outer space is a function of exploitation and uses of outer space. Analogous developments with respect to the high seas show that the more intensified the uses and exploitation of the resources of the oceans become, the more diversified the forms of State jurisdiction over such activities are (e.g., jurisdiction in the territorial sea, contiguous zone, continental shelf, seabed, fishing zones, adjacent airspace and in the air defense identification zones).

Further, it seems convenient and useful to distinguish between the "terrestrial" and the "spatial" effects of space activities when the applicable rules of general international law governing State jurisdiction in outer space are to be identified. The following two presumptions are suggested as working hypotheses:

(1) Established principles and rules of general international law governing the exercise of State jurisdiction should be deemed to govern the jurisdictional aspects of the *terrestrial* effects of space activities, unless they are modified by a subsequent rule of international space law.

(2) International space law should be deemed to govern the exercise of State jurisdiction over persons, things, acts and occurrences in outer space, the Moon and other celestial bodies. Should there exist no such special rule, general international law should be regarded as *mutatis mutandis* applicable but only if there is sufficient evidence to the effect that such rules are not in conflict with the established rules and principles of international space law and also are applicable to the unique conditions prevailing in outer space.

The French representative's suggestion was supported by other representatives to the United Nations who also shared the view that internation-

cation. Similarly, the United Nations Charter could not be extended to space without mature reflection. Moreover, the Sub-Committee would have to decide *how far the principle of non-appropriation was compatible with effective exploration and exploitation,* for the same resolutions that forbade the appropriation of celestial bodies encouraged their use". U.N. Doc. A/AC.105/C.2/SR.57, 15–16. (Emphasis added.) N.B. the parallel between the unregulated relationship of the principle of non-appropriation and the freedom of exploitation and uses of outer space and celestial bodies on the one hand, and that of the former principle and the right to exercise jurisdiction over activities in the exploitation and uses of outer space and celestial bodies.

[13] See the statement of the U.S. Representative to the U.N. Arthur J. Goldberg in Committee I (Political and Security) of the General Assembly, *Dep't State Bull.* January 9, 1967, pp. 78–83. See also the USSR Representative's statement in the Legal Sub-Committee U.N. Doc. A/AC.105/C.2/SR.57, 8–14. For the general debate on the Space Treaty, see SR. 57–64.

al law and the Charter of the U.N. are not applicable to space activities *in toto*. Mechanical application of established rules of general international law to outer space is also beyond question.[13] The doctrine of international space law unanimously supports this proposition.[14]

We must still define the precise ambit of the rule of applicability of international law to space activities. At the outset, we have suggested that the applicability of international law may be conceived both in terms of extension of law to a new environment and the regulation of new human activities and juridical relations. With this distinction a more accurate definition can be put forth. We propose that the rule of applicability of international law and the U.N. Charter to outer space has two aspects (i) formal and (ii) substantive.

(i) The *formal aspect* means the geographical extension of the scope of international law into outer space including celestial bodies. The novelty of the matter is illustrated by the Roman maxim *ubi societas ibi jus*. Law must follow man regardless of the environment where human activities are carried on. "Thus no legal system," argues Professor Lachs now Judge of the International Court of Justice "and no rule within it can dispense with the dimensional element of space concerning the phenomena which it is intended to embrace."[15] From the aspect of the operation of international law our entire universe may be divided into two legal "spaces": national "space" (territory, water and airspace subject to national sovereignty) and international "spaces" (the high seas, polar regions and outer space including celestial bodies). The so-called international "spaces" have one basic thing in common: they are governed primarily by international law.[16] It is international law as such that is applicable to space activities. International law *ipso facto* applies to inter-State relations in every environ-

[14] See *inter alia* Jenks, who said: "In a limited sense this observation appears to be valid. There are certain matters in respect of which the law of space is clearly tending to diverge from accepted international law," *op. cit.* at 204. Lachs, 41 *et seq.* Christol, 190–192, 201, 212–230, 290–291. G. P. Zhukov, "Problems of Space Law at the Present Time", *Proceedings V. Colloquium* (1962). For recent literature in the East European "socialist" countries, see Kopal, Csabafi, Bakotic, "Space Law in the Socialist Countries of Eastern Europe: Czechoslovakia, Hungary and Yugoslavia," 1 *Canadian Slavic Studies* 60–78 (1967). See also, Domas Krivickas and Armins Rusis, "Soviet Attitude Toward Space Law," in *Soviet Space Programs,* 1962–65. 493–528 (1966). Ian Brownlie, "The Maintenance of International Peace and Security in Outer Space," 40 B.Y.I.L. 1–31 (1964).

[15] Lachs, 40.

[16] For details regarding the so-called "theory of international spaces" proposed by J. F. Kish, St. John's College, Cambridge, England, see *A Nemzetközi Térségek Jogállása* (Legal Status of International Spaces) Közdok, Budapest, 1964, p. 104. (With summary in English). For the review of the book by the *present writer* see, 33 J.A.L.C. 506–507 (Summer 1967).

ment. Consequently, the rule in question is not of a constitutive (i.e., law-making) but of a declarative nature.

(ii) The *substantive aspect* of the rule of applicability of international law to space activities concerns the status of outer space within the framework of international law.[17] This proposition admits of an approximation of the problem.

It is implied in the proposition that international law as such is applicable, that "law" and not arbitrariness, political discretion or comity is supposed to govern activities in outer space. It also follows that only "principles which are in force between all independent nations,"[18] are applicable. The rules of international law which can be derived from international conventions, customary international law and the "general principles of law recognized by civilized nations" are also *mutatis mutandis* applicable to space activities. This conclusion *a fortiori* applies to principles and rules governing the exercise of state jurisdiction. The question now is, which established rules of general international law regarding State jurisdiction are applicable? Unfortunately, this question cannot be answered immediately and completely. It should be understood that the answer requires a process of applying the relevant rules of general international law and developing special rules of international space law. These rules do not spring forth suddenly like Athena fully-armed from the head of Zeus.[19] Instead, we have at our disposal certain tests which can be used to apply international law. They follow from the integrity of the system of international law as an independent body of law. The legal principles declared by General Assembly Resolution 1962 (XVIII) and the Space Treaty provide the second legal test. In addition, the unique physical conditions in outer space and on celestial bodies provide objective criteria against which the applicability of an extended rule must be tested.[20]

[17] Lachs, 40.

[18] The *Lotus Case,* P.C.I.J. A/10 p. 17, Lachs, 41.

[19] Regarding the pertinence of the operational methodology of the McWhinneyan theory of inter-bloc or comparative international law, see *op. cit.* at 86 *et seq.* See also, Richard A. Falk, "New Approaches to the Study of International Law," 61 A.J.I.L. 477–495 (1967).

[20] Jenks mentioned the examples of acquisition of sovereignty and demilitarisation of space where space law deviates from general international law. He concluded: "There must therefore be an implied exception to the principle that international law is applicable to the activities of States in space in respect of matters for which a new rule has been or is in process of being evolved for space on grounds of international public policy as well as for matters in respect of which the facts of space are so different from the facts of Earth as to make some familiar principle or rule inapplicable; this exception clearly includes matters in respect of which the Declaration of Legal Principles states

In our opinion, the meaning of the rule that international law applies to activities in space can be satisfactorily described by the following propositions:

(1) *Certain rules and principles of general international law directly (ipso jure) govern activities in space including celestial bodies.*

Thus Jenks stated:

> The law governing recourse to force, providing for the peaceful settlement of international disputes and defining the limits of the right of self-defence has an immediate and direct application to space activities. It includes, in addition to the Charter of the United Nations and the Statute of the International Court of Justice... the General Treaty for the Renunciation of War, the Hague Conventions on the Peaceful Settlement of International Disputes, and the customary law on the subject.[21]

We draw attention to the significance of that part of law which preserves the integrity of a particular legal system, that is, which governs the development of international law itself. Quite clearly, the principle of good faith, *res judicata,* that what is not forbidden is allowed, the principle proscribing the abuse of right, the principle *lex specialis generalibus derogat,*[22] the binding force of custom, the scope for the application of general principles of law and the "general concept of law as a living growth rather than as a body of hard and fast rules,"[23] are to be considered applicable to activities in outer space.

The principle of the absolute and exclusive jurisdiction of a sovereign State within its national territory is unimpeachable.[24] The rules governing the exemption of vessels in distress from the jurisdiction of the coastal State, and in this context the notion of necessity and the principle of self-preservation, may also be regarded as valid law for spacecraft and astronauts making emergency or distress landings in the territory of third States.[25] Further, the principle, *par in parem non habet imperium* also remains applicable in space law.

In addition, certain rules of procedure,[26] as well as the law relating to

or foreshadows a rule differing from or supplementing existing international law". *op. cit.* at 204.

[21] Jenks, 205.

[22] Cf. Bin Cheng, *General Principles of Law as Applied by International Courts and Tribunals,* 24–26 (1953).

[23] Jenks, 205.

[24] See e.g. *Palmas Case* (1928), U.S./The Netherlands in Scott, *The Hague Court Reports,* vol. 2, 92 (1916, 1932). *The Lotus Case* (1927), P.C.I.J. A.10 pp. 44, 69, 94.

[25] Bin Cheng, *op. cit.* at 75–78, 158. *The Alabama Arbitration* (1972), U.S.A./G.B., 1 *Pièces relatives aux délibérations du Tribunal d'arbitrage à Genève,* p. 178.

[26] *Ibid.* at 257–394.

the conclusion of treaties, validity, effect, interpretation and discharge of treaties, are applicable to international space law.

It may very well be argued that the "rules of the game" as expounded by the McWhinneyan theory of inter-bloc international law have indisputable competence in governing inter-State relations in outer space. The principles of bipolarity, bloc territorial integrity, and of non-intervention of each bloc (*inter se*), renunciation of total (nuclear) war as an instrument of political change, the limitation of the membership of the "nuclear club" and the three nuclear age "due processes": (the duty to avoid "surprise" or sudden change in the inter-bloc balance of power relationship, the principle of economy in the use of power, and the principle of mutual self-restraint) are reinforced by the "factual" (political, strategic, legal and physical) realities of outer space. These "principles" govern space activities through the transmission of established legal processes which they condition.[27]

The applicability in space law of a general rule of international law having the character of *jus cogens* presents an interesting and delicate problem. It should be recalled here that the mechanical extension of international law to outer space is unacceptable. Is this conclusion valid with or without reservation also in respect of rules having the nature of *jus cogens*? The practice of States, the jurisprudence of the International Court of Justice[28] and municipal courts,[29] the theory of international law and the writings of distinguished publicists,[30] all confirm that certain rules of general international law have the character of *jus cogens*. Article 50 of the Draft Articles on the Law of Treaties prepared by the International Law Commission provides that:

> A treaty is void if it conflicts with a peremptory norm of general international law from which no derogation is permitted and which can be modified only by a subsequent norm of general international law having the same character.[31]

Article 61 of the Draft Articles complements this provision by stipulating that "if a new peremptory norm of general international law of the

[27] McWhinney, 92–100, 115–116.

[28] See Advisory Opinion of the International Court of Justice concerning *Reservations to the Convention on the Prevention and Punishment of the Crime of Genocide* (1951) I.C.J. Reports, 23.

[29] Stefan A. Riesenfeld, "Jus Dispositivum and Jus Cogens in International Law: In the Light of a Recent Decision of the German Supreme Constitutional Court," 60 A.J.I.L. 511–515 (1966).

[30] For details and reference to literature see Alfred Verdross, "Jus Dispositivum and Jus Cogens in International Law," 60 A.J.I.L. 55–63 (1966).

[31] For text see, 61 A.J.I.L. 409–437, 263–463 (1967).

kind referred to in Article 50 is established, any existing treaty which is in conflict with that norm becomes void and terminates."[32]

The concept of *jus cogens* in international law provides a fundamental criterion for the distinction between applicable or inapplicable rules of general international law to activities in space. It also can tell us whether a new norm of international space law has developed which would modify a previous peremptory norm of general international law. Consequently, States may not derogate from a peremptory norm of general international law regarding outer space and celestial bodies. In this respect the applicability of *jus cogens* to outer space is absolute. Yet one could not say that, when a peremptory norm of general international law is applied to activities in outer space, States are free to disregard the special circumstances which were responsible for the emergence of a rule having the nature of *jus cogens*. Consequently, even a peremptory norm of general international law may not be applied mechanically to outer space.

If the applicability of a peremptory norm to space activities is absolute, then it would seem to be a logical proposition to find out which rules, if any, of general international law regarding State jurisdiction have the character of *jus cogens*. Unfortunately, however, no authoritative or complete list of rules having the character of *jus cogens* is available. The International Law Commission refrained from either mentioning some cases of treaties void for conflict with a rule of *jus cogens*, or from drawing up, even on a selective basis, a list of peremptory norms of general international law.[33] The ILC decided "to leave the full content of this rule (Article 50) to be worked out in state practice and in the jurisprudence of international tribunals."[34]

Some members of the Commission, however, suggested a few examples. They included (1) a treaty providing for the unlawful use of force contrary to the principles of the U.N. Charter; (2) a treaty contemplating the performance of any other *criminal act under international law;* (3) a treaty contemplating or conniving at the commission of *acts, such as trade in slaves, piracy or genocide;* (4) treaties *violating human rights;* (5) treaties

[32] *Id.* at 437 *et seq.*

[33] The reasons for not listing rules having the character of *jus cogens* were to avoid "misunderstanding as to the position concerning other cases not mentioned in the article" and, "a prolonged study of matters which fall outside the scope" of the article in question. See *ibid.*, at 411. Indeed, the problems associated with the enumeration of subject-matters or cases which is for one reason or another not complete are many. Note, for instance, the prolonged debate and contradictory jurisprudence regarding Sections 91 and 92 of the British North America Act, 1867. See Dawson, *The Government of Canada* (4th ed., revised by Ward) 80–104 (1967).

[34] See 61 A.J.I.L. 410 (1967).

violating the equality of States; and (6) treaties *violating the principle of self-determination.*[35]

Verdross defined the term *jus cogens* in the following words:

> The criterion for those rules consists in the fact that they do not exist to satisfy the needs of the individual states but the higher interests of the whole international community. Hence these rules are absolute. The others are relative, because the rights and obligations created by them concern only individual states *inter se.*[36]

Bartos, Lachs, de Luna, Pal, Rosenne and Tunkin stated in the International Law Commission that rules of *jus cogens* as such exist in the interest of the whole international community. For Yasseen, a rule of *jus cogens* must be "necessary to international life and deeply rooted in the international conscience."[37] Lachs said that such rules exist in the "interest of the international community as a whole."[38] Tunkin argued in favour of the existence of *jus cogens* by pointing out that certain international relations "had become an interest to all."[39]

Verdross pointed out that "all treaties encroaching upon the rights of third states seem to be contrary to *jus cogens.*" He also said that "all rules of general international law created for a humanitarian purpose" are rules of *jus cogens.*"[40]

Another group of rules having the character of *jus cogens* may be found in Articles 2(4), 51, 2(3), and 2(5) of the U.N. Charter.[41] Accordingly, States are bound to refrain from the threat or use of force against the territorial integrity or political independence of any State, except in the case of individual or collective self-defense. Secondly, States are bound to settle international disputes by peaceful means. Finally, States are legally bound to give the United Nations every assistance in any action taken in accordance with the Charter, and to refrain from giving assistance to any State against which the United Nations is taking preventive or enforcement action. Article 2(4) of the Charter gives a good example illustrating how a rule of *jus cogens* is supposed to be applied in outer space. The reference to territorial integrity of any State bears the connotation of the traditional terrestrial application of international law, where sovereignty and territoriality are concepts of primary importance. In outer space the concept of

[35] *Id.* at 410–411.
[36] Verdross, *op. cit. supra* at 58.
[37] 1 *I.L.C. Yearbook* (1963) at 64, see also, at 62, 65, 66, 67, 68, 69, 72, 76–77.
[38] *Id.* at 68.
[39] *Ibid.* at 69.
[40] Verdross, *op. cit. supra* at 58–60.
[41] *Id.* at 60.

territoriality cannot be accommodated because Article II of the Space Treaty proscribes "national appropriation by claim of sovereignty, by means of use or occupation, or by any other means." The rule provided by Article 2(4) of the Charter has the character of *jus cogens* and is nonetheless applicable to both the terrestrial effects of space activities and to space activities with no such effects.

The idea we wish to stress here is that a rule of general international law having the character of *jus cogens,* when applied to activities in outer space including celestial bodies which do not primarily affect inter-State relations on Earth, must be adopted to the conditions and facts of outer space. In case of doubt the presumption is in favour of the applicability of rules of *jus cogens.*

One final question must still be settled in this context. Namely, are the legal principles declared in the Declaration of Legal Principles and the Space Treaty of the nature of a peremptory norm of international space law? There are many arguments favouring this proposition. The legal principles in question have already become part of general international law. General Assembly Resolution 1962 (XVIII) recognised the "common interest of all mankind" in the exploration and use of outer space and declared that space research and exploration "should be carried on for the betterment of mankind and for the benefit of States irrespective of their degree of economic or scientific development."

Article I of the Treaty on Outer Space provided that "the exploration and use of outer space, including the Moon and other celestial bodies, shall be carried out for the *benefit and in the interest of all countries,* irrespective of their degree of economic or scientific development, *and shall be the province of mankind.*" (Emphasis added). Thus, it can clearly be seen that the language of the two above-mentioned documents is very similar to that used in the definitions of the term *jus cogens.*[42] The U.N. practice indicates that it was the intention of the framers of the Space Treaty to lay down fundamental legal principles which would determine the future development of space law. The fact that the Space Treaty mentions principles and not rules should not be considered an insuperable obstacle, because the principle of non-appropriation, for example, can be precisely concretized. Moreover, some of the examples relating to rules of *jus cogens* likewise have wide ambit. There are, nonetheless, two obstacles to certitude in the matter: the absence of relevant State practice, and jurisprudence of international tribunals. Moreover, the *jus cogens* or *non-jus cogens* character of a rule of international space law would not make a

[42] See *supra* at 45.

great deal of difference in practice now. In our opinion, most of the legal principles declared by the Space Treaty are well on their way toward acquiring the character of *jus cogens*. There is evidence in the U.N. practice that States regard these legal principles as part of international law. States assumed legal obligations to respect these principles, and demonstrated the effectiveness of these legal principles in the course of the elaboration of further special rules of space law in the field of liability, return and assistance.[43] Any consideration of State jurisdiction in outer space must not lose sight of the fact that these rules must satisfy not only the needs of States, but also serve the benefit and interest of all countries. This follows from the legal obligations assumed by States under the Declaration of Legal Principles and the Space Treaty.

Besides the provisions of the Charter referred to above, the following chapters are also applicable: Chapters VI and VII relating to the peaceful settlement of disputes; Chapters IX and X relating to the coordination of the policies and activities of the specialised agencies; Chapter XIV relating to the International Court of Justice; Articles 102 and 103 relating to the registration of international treaties and the effects of no-registration; and Articles 104 and 105 relating to the legal capacity, privileges and immunities of the United Nations Organisation.[44]

What we said above may be summarized in the following words: There is now sufficient evidence that the principle of non-appropriation of outer space including celestial bodies has become *jus cogens*. The maxim, *par in parem non habet imperium* applies in space law in equal force as it does in general international law. As a rule of *jus cogens,* derived from the principle of sovereign equality, every State has exclusive jurisdiction over its spacecraft, installations and personnel therein. Consequently, States other than the flag State may not exercise jurisdiction over spacecraft in outer space. In accordance with Article II of the Treaty on Outer Space, States may not exercise exclusive jurisdiction over outer space as such either. As far as personal jurisdiction is concerned, the rules of general international law seem to be applicable.

(2) *Certain concepts of general international law are applicable to and indispensable for international space law.* Such concepts include that of State jurisdiction as such, State responsibility, personality in international law and objects in international law. These concepts are constitutive ele-

[43] The statement of the Soviet representative to the Legal Sub-Committee of the UNCOPUOS is, we think, also a good example, cf. U.N. Doc. A/AC.105/C.2/SR.48, 10–11.

[44] Jenks, 208–209; Lachs, 42–43.

ments of an independent branch of law. They may be used as "prefabricated elements" for the edifice of space law. The rules shall have to be adopted or created according to specific requirements. Some of the established rules of State jurisdiction in international law cannot be applied to outer space at all because they may have been destined for different environments or are unsuitable *ex definitione*. We propose here that even the acceptability in space law of the legal basis of State jurisdiction in general international law should be questioned. Summarily, it is that the principle of non-appropriation (Article II of the Space Treaty) calls for a re-adjustment of the doctrine of State jurisdiction which, as far as the author is aware, has never been suggested before.[45]

(3) *Certain principles of general international law are applicable or analogous.* Thus, the Principles of Peaceful Coexistence taken as a whole apply to outer space. The real difficulty arises only when an attempt is made to elaborate *secondary* principles which are "immediately utilisable in terms of current problem-solving."[46] It is also obvious that principles governing the freedom of the seas, the exploitation of the oceans and exercise of State jurisdiction over parts thereof and activities thereon provide useful patterns.

(4) *The following rules of international law are not applicable to activities in outer space and on celestial bodies:* (i) Those which as *lex specialis* govern one or some of the other environments only and (ii) those which have been replaced or modified by a rule of international space law.[47] Some of the bilateral or multilateral agreements which are not *expressis verbis* applicable to outer space may be reviewed and amended accordingly. In some cases their replacement may become necessary in order to extend their scope to outer space including celestial bodies.[48] Thus, the modification of the *Chicago Convention on International Civil Aviation*, 1944, to govern some of the aspects of aerospace flights may become necessary, should outer space be utilized for transportation of passengers, cargo and mail. Also the *Tokyo Convention on Offenses and Certain Other*

[45] For details, see *infra* at 124 *et seq.*

[46] For details see, McWhinney, 36–27, 45–51, 30–34. See also, Ian Brownlie, *loc. cit. supra* at 6–7.

[47] See Lachs, 46. Examples on non-applicability by Jenks include: the principle of national appropriation, Article 2(7) of the Charter regarding space activities, the membership provisions of the Charter in respect of extra-terrestrial communities, and Chapters XI and XII. *loc. cit.* at 209.

[48] Lachs illustrates the point with treaties of non-aggression, *op. cit.* 42. Brownlie mentions the Kellog-Briand Pact (L.N.T.S. [1929] No. 29.), the Hague Convention V of 1907, the NATO and Warsaw pacts, *loc. cit.* at 6–11.

Acts Occurring on Board Aircraft, 1963, may be amended in order to apply its provisions to aero-spacecraft used in civil aerospace transport.[49]

In order to determine the international legal basis of the progressive development in the U.N. of the concept of State jurisdiction we shall proceed with a summary description of the concept of State jurisdiction in general international law. The aim of the following survey is to provide a basis of reference necessary for the purpose of progressive development of rules governing the exercise of State jurisdiction over activities, persons, objects and events in outer space and on celestial bodies.

II. THE CONCEPT OF STATE JURISDICTION IN PUBLIC INTERNATIONAL LAW

The concept of State jurisdiction may be defined as follows: State jurisdiction in public international law means the right of a State to regulate or affect by legislative, executive or judicial measures the rights of persons, property, acts or events with respect to matters not exclusively of domestic concern.[50] The notion of jurisdiction finds its origin in the concept of territory, the principle of sovereign equality and non-interference with the domestic affairs of States.

The doctrine of jurisdiction emerged in the seventeenth century from the concepts of sovereignty and territoriality. Its development led through the *statue theory*[51] to the *Huber-Storyan maxim*[52] and it became es-

[49] See Bin Cheng, *The Law of International Air Transport* (The Library of World Affairs, No. 47) 75, 111–112. (1962). Shawcross & Beaumont, 701–715. Cf. also, Resolutions A15–1 adopted by the 15th Session of the Assembly, ICAO; reproduced in Andrew G. Haley, "ICAO Space Resolutions," *Proceedings of the XIIIth Colloquium,* 116–118 (1966).

[50] For further definitions of the notion of State jurisdiction, see Mann, 9 *et seq.;* Schwarzenberger, *International Law as Applied by International Courts and Tribunals,* vol. I, 184 *et seq.* (1957); Oppenheim, 325 *et seq.;* Brierly, 222 *et seq.;* Starke, 199 *et seq.* Christol, 416; Bin Cheng, "The Extra-Terrestrial Application of International Law," 18 C.L.P. 134 *et seq.* (1965). O'Connell, 655–957. Beale defined the concept of jurisdiction in the following words: "the power of a sovereign to affect the rights of persons, whether by legislation, by executive decree, or by the judgment of a court." "The Jurisdiction of a Sovereign State," 36 *Harv. L. Rev.,* 241 (1923); In *Mc Donald v. Mabee* (243 U.S. 90 [1916]) Mr. Justice Holmes said that the ultimate basis of jurisdiction is "physical power," and in *Wedding v. Meyler* he equated jurisdiction with "authority" (192 U.S. 573, 584 (1904)). The American Law Institute's Official Draft of Foreign Relations Law of the United States, 1962 (hereinafter referred to as *Draft Restatement,* (1962)) uses the term "capacity of State." Mann speaks of "States' *right* to exercise certain powers" (Emphasis added). *loc. cit.* at 9 *et seq.*

[51] For details on the development of the doctrine of jurisdiction, see Mann, 9–30. The term formulated by Paulus: *"Extra territorium jus dicenti impune non paretur. Idem est et si supra jurisdictionem suam velit jus dicere"* has for a long time influenced the doctrine. In Italy the concept *"statutum non ligat nisi subditos"* became accepted

tablished in the nineteenth century.[53] The doctrine of international law distinguishes four categories of principles which provide a legal basis for national jurisdiction: (1) territory as a basis for jurisdiction; (2) nationality as a basis for jurisdiction; (3) the protective principle and (4) the universality principle.[54]

Further, the concept of State jurisdiction may be divided into three *types:* territorial, quasi-territorial and personal.[55] Jurisdiction as a whole may also be separated into two complementary *elements:* (a) *jurisdiction to prescribe,*[56] (prescriptive, legislative jurisdiction[57] or "jurisfaction"),[58] and (b) *jurisdiction to enforce*[59] (enforcement, prerogative jurisdiction[60] or "jurisaction").[61] The classification of the concept of State jurisdiction according to types and elements serves the purpose of convenience. When using this classification, the selection of applicable rules governing State jurisdiction becomes easier.

around 1200 A.D. In effect it denied the absolute power of *lex fori: "statutum non ligat forensem"*. In the fourteenth and fifteenth centuries the intra- and extra-territorial effects of legislative jurisdiction were pointed out by Meijers and Bartolus respectively. In the sixteenth century Bodin developed the concept of sovereignty in terms of internal strength and external limitation of power. At the same time Bertrand d'Argentre distinguished between *potestas* and jurisdiction (*"omnis enim potestas extra fines potestatis attributae aut propriae private est persona, et finitae potestatis finita jurisdictio et cognitio; ideo et statuta extra territoria sua sine usu sunt"*.) spelling out the essence of the statute theory.

[52] Ulricus Huber, *De Conflictu legum diversarum in diversis imperiis,* (1948). For his "trois illustres axiomes" see Gutzwiller, *Le Développement Historique du Droit International Privé,* Rec. 29 (1929 IV) 327; Mann, 26; See also *The Apollon,* 9 Wheat, 362, 370 (1824).

[53] *The Apollon, ibid.; S.S. Cristina* [1938] A.C. 485, 496, 497.

[54] McDougal, Lasswell and Vlasic listed in the following principles: active personality, 699; act of state, 644–648; nationality, 647, 691, 695–696, 699–703; passive personality, 647, 693, 699–700, 700n; territoriality, 647, 692, 694, 698–699, 703, 717; protective principle, 647, 700; universality, 647, 701; impact territoriality, 647. See also, *Draft Restatement,* (1962) p. 25. For its criticism, see Mann, 40–43. See also Johnson, "Bases of International Jurisdiction", *Report of International Law Conference,* David Davies Memorial Institute of International Studies 32–33 (1962).

[55] See generally, Ch. Rousseau, "Principes de droit international public", 93 *Hague Recueil* (1958), p. 369, at pp. 394–395. Bin Cheng, "Crimes on Board Aircraft", 12 C.L.P. 177 (1959); *op. cit.* 134 *et seq.;* "Inter Astra Silent Leges? – A Prolegomenon to Jural Cartography", 18 Glim (Michaelmas, 1961).

[56] See *Draft Restatement,* (1962). O'Connell, 655 *et seq.*

[57] Mann, 9 *et seq.*

[58] Cheng, *op. cit.* 134 *et seq.*

[59] *Draft Restatement,* (1962). O'Connell, *op. cit.*

[60] Mann, *op. cit.* at 9.

[61] Cheng, *op. cit.* at 134.

1. *Territorial Jurisdiction*

In terms of the *Storyan maxim* territorial jurisdiction means that each State has exclusive jurisdiction within its own territorial domain over persons, property, things and legal transactions done within it, including the extraterritorial activities of such persons.[62] The territorial domain includes *terra firma,* the adjacent territorial sea, and the superjacent airspace. Accordingly, third States may not exercise territorial jurisaction within the territory of another State. However, every State has the right to regulate the conduct of its subjects wherever they may be (jurisfaction). Territorial jurisdiction is not absolute because it is subject to certain limitations imposed upon States by international law. Foreign States and heads of Foreign States, diplomatic representatives, and consuls of foreign States, as well as international institutions, are wholly or partially withdrawn from the state's jurisdiction by a rule of international law. It is commonly described by the term "exterritoriality".

The term, itself a metaphor, is a good example showing that the relationship between jurisdiction and territoriality was considered to be so close that it was taken for granted in many cases without discrimination. Indeed, the concept of territoriality is a constitutive element of a large part of rules governing the exercise of State jurisdiction. The evolution of the concept of State jurisdiction clearly shows that the notions of national territory and sovereignty are the authors of rules governing the exercise of territorial jurisdiction. Thus, the concept of State jurisdiction is, at least partly, firmly anchored through the element of territoriality in the notion of sovereignty and the principle of national appropriation. It follows, therefore, that rules of territorial jurisaction are not applicable to space activities proper, since Article II of the Space Treaty, as well as the Declaration of Legal Principles, proscribed the principle of national appropriation from outer space and celestial bodies. Nevertheless, the rules of international law governing the exercise of territorial jurisaction are applicable with respect to the terrestrial effects of space activities. In other words, these rules must be considered applicable when they are supposed to operate in their traditional environment, unless a subsequent norm of international space law overrides them. Also, a State may exercise territorial jurisfaction affecting outer space from its national territory on earth.

The point intended to be made here is that the concept of State jurisdiction in space law is not similar to the concept of State jurisdiction as it

[62] Starke, 207–238, Brierly, 222–243, Oppenheim, 325–334, Christol, 418–420. Schwarzenberger, *op. cit.* 186, 292–253. Jenks, 236 *et seq.*

is established in general international law. The exercise of State jurisdiction in outer space cannot be linked to the appropriation of any part of outer space or of the territory of a celestial body. This fact makes necessary the development of special rules governing the exercise of jurisdiction in outer space.

Yet one cannot say that the concept of territorial jurisdiction is of no use for space law. The basis of territory has the merit of affording jurisdiction to a State which is in possession of persons, things and evidence required for legal judgment.

Under the so-called principle of "transient jurisdiction" a British Court may exercise jurisdiction over persons during a mere fleeting visit to British territory. Astronauts do not seem to be exempt from such jurisdiction merely on account of their status under contemporary international law. Where a spacecraft causes damage as a result of its landing in the territory of a foreign State, this State could assume jurisdiction to adjudicate claims. Such case would undoubtedly raise the questions of enforceability of foreign judgments,[63] conflicts of law and characterization problems. Similarly, where astronauts prior to their entry to the territory of a third State violate the criminal laws of such a State while outside its territory, they would be subject to the criminal jurisdiction of that State if their acts constitute a threat to its security, peace and good order.

For the purposes of territorial jurisdiction, it is customary to include as belonging to State territory the territorial sea, the national airspace, ports, vessels and aircraft flying under the flag of the State wishing to exercise jurisdiction.

The coastal State exercises exclusive jurisdiction in the *territorial sea*. Vessels of third States have the right of innocent passage through the waters of the maritime belt, but there is no right of innocent overflight for foreign aircraft. Thus, foreign spacecraft and crew thereof would be in the same position in or over territorial waters as on land territory.

Articles 19–22 of the Convention on the Territorial Sea and Contiguous Zone, signed at Geneva on April 28, 1958, impose some limitations on the jurisdictional rights of the coastal State. Accordingly, the coastal State may not arrest any person or conduct any investigation except in the following cases: (1) if the consequences of the crime extend to the coastal State; (2) if the crime is of a kind to disturb the peace of the country or the

[63] "It follows from the principle of territorial supremacy that States must not perform acts of sovereignty within the territory of other States. For the same reason ... the courts of many countries ... decline to give effect to public law ... of foreign States. To enforce them would mean, in effect, to assist States in the performance of acts of sovereignty in foreign countries in derogation of their territorial supremacy." Oppenheim, 327–330.

good order of the territorial sea; (3) if the assistance of the local authorities has been requested by the captain of the ship or by the consul of the country whose flag the ship flies; or (4) if it is necessary for the suppression of illicit traffic in narcotic drugs. These rules may provide a useful analogy should innocent passage be granted to foreign spacecraft.

Every State has complete and exclusive sovereignty over the *airspace* above its territory. (Article 1 of the Chicago Convention, 1944). Spacecraft do not enjoy the right of innocent passage through foreign airspace. Thus, until *lex specialis* develops the subjacent State may exercise exclusive jurisdiction over foreign spacecraft and personnel thereof in its national airspace. The principle stated in the *Hoff Case (The Rebecca)* (1929) would also apply to spacecraft in distress exempting it to a certain extent from the operation of local laws. It may be an arguable point that the rigidity of exclusive jurisdiction enjoyed by a subjacent State in national airspace is somewhat softened by the universal community interests attached to the principle of the freedom of outer space. Nevertheless, it is not known how far this proposition can be stretched in practical terms, as of now. The difference between the legal status of outer space and airspace accentuates the importance of a clear-cut frontier between territorial space and outer space. The legal basis and validity of acts of jurisdiction is basically determined by their *locus*.

The principles of international *river law* also provide an analogy for regulating the joint enjoyment of the benefits of outer space. Attention ought to be drawn in this context to the arbitration between France and Spain concerning the waters of Lake Lanoux, where the following broad principles were laid down:

> (1) Where a river system drains the territories of two or more states, each state has the right to have that river system considered as a whole and to have its own interests taken into account together with those of other states; (2) each state has in principle an equal right to make the maximum use of the water within its territory, but in exercising this right must respect the corresponding rights of other states; (3) where one state's exercise of its rights conflicts with the water interests of another, the principle to be applied is that each is entitled to the equitable apportionment of the benefits of the river system in proportion to their needs and in the light of all the circumstances of the particular river system; (4) a state is in principle precluded from making any change in the river system which would cause substantial damage to another state's right of enjoyment without that other state's consent; (5) it is relieved from obtaining that consent, however, if it offers the other state a proportionate share of the benefits to be derived from the change or other adequate compensation for the damage to the other state's enjoyment of the water; (6) a state whose enjoyment of the water is not substantially damaged by a development in the

use of a river beneficial to another state is not entitled to oppose that development.[64]

There is no uniform legal regime for international rivers. In the light of current research and developments it is doubtful that the principles stated above are actually effective today.

Maritime *ports*[65] are fully part of State territory; nevertheless, merchant and public vessels are subject to a special regime. Every vessel in distress has a right to seek shelter in a foreign port. In such cases it is considered immune from local jurisdiction. This immunity is only a qualified immunity. Similarly, the immunity that spacecraft and astronauts entering national territory in distress may enjoy is also limited. Public vessels are subject to special rules of jurisdiction and their status will be discussed in the context of quasi-territorial jurisdiction.

Where offences are committed on board vessels berthed in foreign ports, two sets of practice have crystallized regarding the *criminal jurisdiction* of the State of the port. The British view is that foreign merchant vessels in British ports and British merchant vessels in foreign ports are subject to the local criminal jurisdiction, but as a matter of comity concurrent criminal jurisdiction is claimed and granted to the flag State of the vessel. Usually British authorities intervene and enforce local jurisdiction where their assistance is requested, either by the consul of the flag State of the vessel or by those in control of the vessel.

According to the French and the U.S. practice the authorities of the flag State have jurisdiction in matters of internal discipline or economy of the vessel and the local authorities of the territorial State intervene only where the offence affects the peace and good order of the port.[66]

[64] Brierly, 231–232. For literature on the subject, see *inter alia:* Garretson, Hayton, Olmstead (eds.), *The Law of International Drainage Basin* (1967); Berber, *Rivers in International Law* (1959); Baxter, *The Law of International Waterways* (1964); For East European literature, see, Herczegh, Géza, "A nemzetközi folyóvizek hasznositásának néhány jogi kérdése," 11 *Állam- és Jogtudomanyi Közlöny* 12–30 (1968); See also *On the Uses of Waters of International Rivers,* The International Law Association 2–4 (1967).

[65] Starke, 211–212. Cf. in this context the Convention and Statute of December 9, 1923 on the International Régime of Maritime Ports.

[66] See Brierly, 223 regarding the Opinion of the French Council of State in 1806 referring to the case of the two American ships in French port, *Sally and Newton*. The decision of the French Courts in *The Tempest case* (1859) proves that, in fact, everything but disciplinary and minor offences committed on board vessels among the crew will fall under local jurisdiction. See Fauchille, *Traité de droit international public* (8th ed.), and Bonfils' *Manuel de droit international public,* vol. I, part ii, p. 1034. *The Wildenhus' Case* (1887), 120 U.S. 1 confirms this conclusion too.

Thus, it is clearly shown that absolute territorial competence is not exercised in every case "for reasons of general policy and expediency."[67] This principle is sound enough so that it may be applied to spacecraft entering the territory of a foreign State under emergency conditions or otherwise.

To what extent may the local authorities inquire into the regularity of the custody of a person on board a foreign spacecraft? In the *El Kantara* case (1922) the Australian court refused an application for a *habeas corpus* on the ground that there was no *prima facie* evidence regarding the irregularity of custody under the law of the flag (French) State. The decision implies that the local State may inquire into the regularity of custody and may also release persons whose custody appears to be irregular under the law of the flag State of the vessel.[68]

It is also pertinent to consider here the applicability of the *subjective territorial principle*[69] and the *objective territorial principle,*[70] which are commonly known as the technical extensions of the principle of territorial jurisdiction. These two principles are meant to justify the criminal jurisdiction of States over acts or offences which were committed outside their territory. According to the first principle, the *State in whose territory the commission of the crime commenced* (but was completed or consummated in the territory of another State) assumes criminal jurisdiction. Starke holds that this principle is not a general rule of international law.[71]

The application of this principle to spacecraft would suggest that the State of registry of such craft may exercise jurisdiction. States which adopt the principle of objective territorial jurisdiction assume jurisdiction over offences which were consummated or completed within their territory or produced harmful effect therein, but which had commenced in the territory of another State. Classical illustrations of this theory are: (a) a man firing a gun across a frontier and killing another man in a neighbouring country; and (b) a man obtaining money by false pretences by means of a letter posted in country A to a recipient in country B.[72] Great Britain and the United States base their jurisdiction on the principle of territoriality in criminal matters, but adopt the fiction that a crime may be committed

[67] Brierly, 225.

[68] *Journal of Comparative Legislation* 246 (1926), Brierly, 225–226. *The Creole Case* (1855), Moore, 1 *International Arbitrations*, p. 4375, at pp. 4377, 4378.

[69] Starke, 213.

[70] *Ibid.*

[71] *Id.*

[72] Report of the Sub-Committee of The League of Nations Committee of Experts for the Progressive Codification of International Law (1926), on Criminal Competence of States in respect of Offences committed outside their Territory.

within the territory of a State even though the actor may be outside the territory.[73] The Soviet Union, the East European countries, Germany, France and a majority of States admit certain exceptions to the principle of territoriality, if the act is directed against the security of the State or its financial interest. Thus, under this principle the U.S.S.R. could prosecute foreign astronauts for intelligence gathering activities carried out in outer space, prior to their entry into her territorial domain, even though such activities in our opinion do not constitute a violation of international law.[74] A third group of States, including Turkey and Italy, according to Brierly, reject the principle of territorial criminal jurisdiction.[75]

The question of criminal jurisdiction over an act causing collision on the high seas between a French mail steamer, the *Lotus*, and a Turkish collier *Boz-Kourt* was decided by the Permanent Court of International Justice in 1927 in the *Lotus Case*.[76] The Turkish authorities instituted proceedings also against the French officer upon the *Lotus*' arrival in Constantinople, claiming that the sinking of the Turkish ship and the loss of life of eight Turkish nationals was allegedly due to the gross negligence of the French officer of the watch on board the *Lotus*. By a majority decision the Court held that the action of the Turkish authorities was not inconsistent with international law and also stated that:

> It does not . . . follow that international law prohibits a State from exercising jurisdiction in its own territory, in respect of any case which relates to acts which have taken place abroad, and in which it cannot rely on some permissive rule of international law.[77]

The *Lotus* case was cited as an example both for the "objective territorial jurisdiction"[78] and also as a decision representing a further inroad

[73] *Rex v. Godfrey*, [1932] 1 K.B. 24. *Ford v. United States* (1927), 273 U.S. 593. The case of "Lord Haw-Haw" illustrates the jurisdictional difficulties of the principle of the territoriality of criminal jurisdiction. *Joyce v. Director of Public Prosecutions*, [1946] A.C. 347. But see, *The Cutting Case* (1887), *Moore's Digest of International Law* (1906), vol. II, p. 228.

[74] See Christol, 422.

[75] Brierly, 300.

[76] P.C.I.J., Series A. No. 10 (1927).

[77] P.C.I.J., Series A. No. 10 (1927) p. 19. Restricting itself to the domain of criminal law the Court of International Justice stated: "The territoriality of criminal law, therefore, is not an absolute principle of international law and by no means coincides with territorial sovereignty". *Id.*, at 20. The Court based its decision in favour of Turkey on the assumption that a ship is a "place assimilated to the national territory". The decision has in effect been overruled by the Brussels Convention of May 10, 1952, and the Geneva Convention on the High Seas of April 29, 1958 (Art. II.) The Court could equally have based Turkey's jurisdiction on the principle of nationality.

[78] See Brierly, 303.

into the domain of the territoriality principle.[79] The applicability of the rule to spacecraft as laid down in *The Lotus* case is questionable, because special rules are being developed to govern liability for collision of spacecraft.[80]

The *Lotus* case also illustrates that no presumption of immunity arises from the fact that a person who is subjected to the criminal jurisdiction of a State is an alien. Consequently, an *alien astronaut* could claim no exemption from the criminal jurisdiction of the local authorities unless he can prove that he is, by reason of some special immunity, not subject to such jurisdiction, or that the exercise of such jurisdiction would violate the minimum standards of international law.

2. *Quasi-territorial jurisdiction*

Cheng defines the term as

> The sum total of the powers of a State in respect of ships, aircraft and spacecraft (to the extent to which they are also granted legal personality) having its nationality . . . . Quasiterritorial jurisdiction differs from personal jurisdiction in that it extends not only to the craft in question but also to all persons and things on board, including the activities of such persons, whether on board the craft or elsewhere.[81]

In this context we are concerned with the operation of rules of jurisdiction *ratione instrumenti.*

Vessels bearing the flag of a State are subject to the jurisdiction of the flag State.[82] The Geneva Convention on the High Seas confirmed the rule that the flag State has exclusive jurisdiction over its ships. It negates the ruling of the Permanent Court of International Justice in *The Lotus* case (1927). Criminal proceedings may be instituted only before the appropriate authorities either of the flag State or of the State of nationality. (Cf. Article 11 of the High Seas Convention). Jurisdiction on the ocean is mainly connected with the maritime flag with two *provisos.* First, jurisdiction is not jurisdiction over the high seas as such, but only over persons and things. Secondly, men-of-war of all nations have the right under

79 See Mann, 38.

80 See *Report of the Legal Sub-Committee on the Work of its Seventh Session (4–28 June 1968) to the Committee on the Peaceful Uses of Outer Space.* U.N. Doc. A/AC. 105/45 (July 11, 1968) at 3–91.

81 Cheng, 135.

82 *Le Louis* (1817), 2 Dods. 210, *The Antelope* (1825), 10 Wheaton 66. See also the dissenting opinion of Judge Moreno Quintana in *Constitution of the Maritime Safety Committee of the Inter-Governmental Maritime Consultative Organisation,* I.C.J. Reports (1960) p. 178. *The Lotus Case* (1927), P.C.I.J. Series A. No. 10 p. 25.

customary international law: (1) to visit, search and seize neutral vessels for carriage of contraband; (2) to require suspicious private vessels on the open sea to show their flag; (3) to seize and punish foreign vessels sailing under the flag of a State without authority. (Article 22 of the High Seas Convention). Men-of-war or specially designated public vessels may exercise the right of "hot pursuit" of a foreign vessel. (Cf. Article 23 of the Geneva Convention on the High Seas, 1958).[83]

International law does not contain rules regarding the claim of vessels to sail under a certain maritime flag. The conditions of granting the flag and registration of vessels are regulated by municipal law. But no State may allow a vessel to sail under the flag of more than one State. The High Seas convention also provides that a "genuine link" must exist between the flag State and the ship. The State must be able to effectively exercise its jurisdiction and control over ships of its flag. Changes of flag during voyage or the sailing of a vessel under two or more flags are also prohibited.

Status changes (birth,[84] marriage and death), wills, contracts and the commission of crime[85] on board ships are governed by the law of the flag State.[86]

As a general rule aircraft are also subject to the jurisdiction of the "flag State". Aircraft have the nationality of the State of registration and cannot be validly registered in more than one State. Registration may, however, be changed from one State to another subject to the conditions established by municipal law.[87]

Under Article 12 of the Chicago Convention, 1944, aircraft are subject to the following three forms of State jurisdiction: (1) the territorial jurisdiction of the Contracting States when the aircraft is within the territories of such States; (2) the quasi-territorial jurisdiction of the national State of

[83] See Starke, 243; Brierly, 314 *et seq.*

[84] Cf. *Marshall v. Murgatroyd* (1870), L.R. 6 Q.B. 31. Oppenheim, 597.

[85] Cf. *The United States of America v. Santos Flores,* 289, L.S. 137; 27 A.J.I.L. 569–579 (1933). Oppenheim, *op. cit.*

[86] Since every State has the right to exercise territorial jurisfaction over its nationals abroad, such nationals remain under the personal supremacy of their home State even when on board a foreign vessel. Regarding jurisdiction over aircraft, attention ought to be drawn to an interesting suggestion made by Giannini in 1932 to the effect that ultimate control be vested with the League of Nations. (Saggi di diritto aeronautico). Oppenheim, note 5 at p. 597. For detailed study on the nationality of ships, see H. Meyers, *The Nationality of Ships,* The Hague, 1967. But, see *R. v. Gordan-Finlayson* [1941] 57 T.L.H. 270 where it was held that a British ship on the high seas was not part of the U.K. within Article 41 of the Army Act, 1881. Oppenheim, *op. cit.*

[87] Articles 18–19 of the Chicago Convention, 1944. Cheng, *op. cit.* 128–129, 191, 192, 491. See, also Art. 77 of the Convention and the proceedings of the 1966 Conference of the International Law Association in Helsinki, regarding the nationality of aircraft operated by International operating agencies.

the aircraft when the aircraft is on or over the high seas and *terra nullius;* and (3) personal jurisdiction over their own aircraft on or over foreign territory.[88] Shawcross and Beaumont pointed out that the rules and principles of international law are inadequate to settle the complex jurisdictional problems which may arise in connection with aircraft. Aircraft may, in principle, be subjected to the jurisdiction of several States (e.g., State of registry, the State of nationals possessing substantial ownership in the aircraft and the State of departure, overflight or arrival).[89]

The *Tokyo Convention on Offences and Certain Other Acts Occurring on Board Aircraft,* 1963,[90] to some extent[91] resolves jurisdictional difficulties insofar as crimes are concerned. The Convention applies with respect to offences against penal law and acts which may jeopardize the safety of the aircraft, persons or property on board, or which jeopardize good order or discipline on board, if such offences or acts have been committed on an aircraft registered in a Contracting State while the aircraft is in flight. [Articles 1(2), 4(d), 9(1), 1(3), (52)]. The Convention also applies when (a) the aircraft is either over the high seas or (b) on or over any other area outside the jurisdiction of any State at the time of the commission of the crime. [Article 1(2)]. It could easily be argued that aerospacecraft which may be used in the future in commercial aerospace transport could also be brought under the scope of the Convention, since Article 1(4) excludes aircraft used in "military, customs or public services" only.

Under Article 3(1), (2) the *State of registration* is competent to exercise

[88] Cheng, *The Law of International Air Transport,* London, 1962, p. 110.

[89] Shawcross and Beaumont, 28–29.

[90] *Ibid.* 701–715. See also, M. Fauchille, "Proposals" in 19 *Annuaire de l'Institut de Droit International* 51 (1902); *Harvard Research,* "Jurisdiction with Respect to Crime," 29 A.J.I.L. Special Supplement (1935). Honig, *The Legal Status of Aircraft* (1956). Meyer, "Le Statut Juridique de l'Aéronef par Rapport aux infractions à bord," (1958) *I.L.A. Conference.* De Visscher, "Les Conflits de Lois en Matière de Droit Aérien," 48 *Hague Recueil 285 (1934).* Royal Aeronautical Society, Study on Crime and Offences on Board Aircraft: Final Report by Bin Cheng (Duplicated) (1962). Wilberforce, "Crime in Aircraft," 67 *J. Royal Aeronautical Soc.* 175 (1963). Fitzgerald, "The Development of International Rules Concerning Offences and Certain other Acts Committed on Board Aircraft," 1 C.Y.I.L. 230 *et seq.* (1963); "Offences and Certain Acts Committed on Board Aircraft: The Tokyo Convention of 1963," 2 C.Y.I.L. 191–204 (1964). Boyle and Pulsifer, "The Tokyo Convention . . . ," 30 J.A.L.C. 305–354 (1964); Gutierrez, "Should the Tokyo Convention of 1963 be Ratified?," 31 J.A.L.C. 1–21 (1965). For the text of the Convention, see Shawcross & Beaumont, vol 2, Appendix B.

[91] See the Statement of the U.S. representative to the Rome Conference, 1962: ICAO Doc. 8302–LC/150–1, p. 56. See also Gutierrez, *loc. cit. supra.*

jurisdiction over offences.[92] The primary interest as to the exercise of jurisdiction of the State of registry is expressly recognised by the Convention [Articles 5(2), 16(1)]. Should Contracting States establish joint air transport operating agencies or international operating agencies, they have to designate a State of registration for the purposes of the Convention. (Article 18).

This principle is believed to be a good analogy for spacecraft. Indeed, the draft agreements on liability and on the assistance and return of spacecraft and astronauts in distress also accepted the concept of State of registration of spacecraft.[93]

The Convention can rightly be criticised for not having closed serious gaps.[94] [Article 3(3)] of the Convention does not exclude any criminal jurisdiction in accordance with national law. It does not eliminate the possibility of conflicting jurisdictions.[95] Thus, where aircraft are chartered to another State, the State of registration remains under the legal obligation to establish its jurisdiction over such aircraft. Further, any Contracting State which is not the State of registration may interfere with an aircraft in flight in specified cases.[96] The Convention does not exclude the possibility that several States may exercise jurisdiction in relation to the same offence or act.[97] The alleged offender may be tried successively in several States for the same offence. Unlike in the Rome Draft Convention the *non bis in idem*

92 As to nationality and registration of aircraft under the Chicago Convention, 1944, see, Shawcross & Beaumont, 22–223, Cheng, *op. cit.* 108, 128–132, 166, 194, 491, 275 (1962).

93 Article VIII of the Space Treaty.

94 Gutierrez, *loc. cit. supra.*

95 The following cases may illustrate the nature of jurisdictional problems: *U.S. v. Cordova* (1950), U.S. Av. R. 1; *R. v. Martin* [1956] 2. Q. B. 272; [1956] 2 All E. R. 86; But see, *R. v. Naylor* [1962] 2 Q. B. 527; [1961] 2 All E. R. 932; *Cox v. Army Council* (1963), A. C. 48; [1962] 1 All E. R. 880.

96 These cases include: (1) where the offence has effect on the territory of that State (cf. Article 19 of the Geneva Convention on the Territorial Sea and the Continuous Zone, 1958); (2) where the offence has been committed by or against its nationals; (3) where the offence consists of a breach of any of the State's rules relating to the flights or manoeuvre of the aircraft, or (4) where the exercise of jurisdiction is necessary to ensure the observance of the State's obligations under a multilateral international agreement.

97 The following examples given by Shawcross & Beaumont illustrate the point:

When a crime occurs on an aircraft registered in	State A;
while flying over	State B;
committed by a national of	State C;
against a national of	State D;
after which the aircraft lands in	State E;

all five States, A, B, C, D, and E may claim jurisdiction. In addition, the aircraft operator, captain, crew, passengers and ground authorities all have particular interests requiring consideration. Cf., Shawcross & Beaumont, 701.

principle has not been included in the Convention. Such discrepancies and flaws should not be repeated in space law.

Finally, attention should be drawn to another important aspect. The nature of rules governing jurisdiction varies also according to the kinds of vessels and aircraft. The following categories of vessels and aircraft are known in international law: private and public vessels, civil, State and private aircraft. The term public vessel means vessels used in military, customs or police services. A distinction among comparable types of spacecraft may become necessary in the future.

3. *Jurisdiction Over the High Seas and The Antarctic*

In this context we are concerned with a category of rules which determines the spheres of their validity *ratione loci.*

a. *The High Seas*

The high seas or open sea [98] are not, and can never be, under the sovereignty of any State. This principle is commonly called "freedom of the high seas." [99] The term means (a) prohibition of national appropriation of the high seas; [100] (b) freedom of navigation for vessels of any kind and of all nations; [101] (c) jurisdiction over vessels as identified with the maritime flag; [102] (d) freedom of fishing; [103] (e) freedom to lay submarine cables and oil pipelines ("freedom of immersion"); (f) freedom of flight over the high seas. It will be well to recall here Article 2 of the High Seas Convention, which provides that the principle of freedom of the seas includes other freedoms in addition to those *expressis verbis* enumerated therein.

The freedom of the open sea has never meant unregulated lawlessness.

98 The high seas are all parts of the sea that are not included in the territorial sea or in the internal waters of a State. Cf. Article 1 of the High Seas Convention. See also, Oppenheim, 588 *et seq.*

99 The historical development of the principle includes the following stages: freedom of the oceans, claims to exercise sovereignty over the open sea, and the freedom of the high seas. The Papal Bull called *Inter Caetera* issued by Pope Alexander VI of 4 May 1493 is a landmark in the historical development of the principle despite its subsequent withdrawal. Grotius' *Mare Liberum* (1609) arguing in favour of the freedom of the Seas and John Selden's *Mare Clausum* (1635) maintaining the English claims over large areas of the seas are the classical expositions of the two then opposing theories. Article 2 of the Geneva High Seas Convention only declared the principle of freedom of seas which had become part of international customary law.

100 Article II of the *Space Treaty.*

101 *Ibid.* Article I. But note the difference concerning the prohibition to orbit satellites carrying nuclear weapons or weapons of mass destructive effect, and to install such weapons in outer space and on celestial bodies.

102 *Id.* Article VIII.

103 *Id.* Article I wherein "the exploration and *use* of outer space" are mentioned.

The exercise of jurisdiction became necessary as a matter of course. Jurisdiction with respect to the high seas *is not jurisdiction over the high seas as such.* This we think is a primary analogy that is applicable as a concept to State jurisdiction in outer space. The point is well illustrated by Brierly. He said:

> So far as concerns jurisdiction, the freeing of the high seas from the exclusive sovereignty of individual states did not leave them subject to no jurisdiction. The right of jurisdiction, like the rights of navigation and exploitation, became vested in each and every state. It was not, however, a condominium with all the states exercising concurrent jurisdiction over all vessels and persons on the high seas; the jurisdiction of each state was limited to its own vessels and nationals.[104]

The principles of freedom of the seas and exclusive jurisdiction over national vessels became inseparable "twin principles". Consequently, aspects of the exercise of jurisdiction on the high seas came to be regulated by separate treaties.[105] Similarly specific problems bearing upon the exercise of State jurisdiction in outer space shall have to be dealt with in new international agreements. Such questions include the uses and exploitation of outer space, jurisdiction over and around installations in outer space and on celestial bodies, jurisdiction over "space" resources and space personnel.

Under the High Seas Convention the coastal State may exercise jurisdiction over foreign vessels outside the maritime belt where there is grave suspicion that such vessels threaten the sovereignty or security of that State. On the analogy of this rule States likewise can claim jurisdiction over and around space stations or installations where their sovereignty, security or vested interests are jeopardized.[106]

It has become an established practice that specific "warning areas" on the

[104] Brierly, 306–307. Cf., the practice of the U.S. concerning international cooperative projects in space research shows that outer space cannot be regarded a condominium. See generally, Arnold W. Frutkin, *International Cooperation in Space,* 186 (1965).

[105] Convention for Regulating the Police of the North Sea Fisheries, 1882; Convention for the Protection of Submarine Telegraph Cables, 1884; Convention Respecting the Liquor Traffic in the North Sea, 1887; the General Act of Brussels of 1890 for the Repression of African Slave Trade, the Brussels Convention of 1910 for the Unification of Certain Rules of Law Respecting Assistance and Salvage at Sea; Convention of June 10, 1948, on the Safety of Life at Sea; Convention for the Unification of Certain Rules Relating to Penal Jurisdiction in Matters of Collision and Other Incidents of Navigation, 1952; Interim Convention of February 9, 1957, for the Conservation of North Pacific Fur Seal Herds; Convention on Fishing and Conservation of the Living Resources of the High Seas, Geneva, April 29, 1958.

[106] The legal basis of this jurisdiction is the principle of self-preservation. Cf., Cheng, *General Principles of Law,* 29–102 (1953).

high seas are closed from vessels and aircraft of third States for the purpose of conducting rocket experiments. Under Article 2 of the High Seas Convention the various freedoms of the high seas must be exercised "with reasonable regard to the interests of other States in their exercise of the freedom of the high seas". It may be argued that on the basis of this analogy "control areas" may also be designated by a State on the Moon and other celestial bodies, if the establishment of such zones is reasonable and instrumental to the lawful exercise of one of the "freedoms of outer space".

If the regulation of the free exploitation of the resources of outer space including those of celestial bodies becomes possible and economical, it should be achieved only by special agreements between the interested States. The *Behring Sea Fur Seal Arbitrations* of 1893 and 1902 showed that under customary international law States could apply conservation measures only to their own vessels.[108] Clearly there is very little in international law in terms of applicable rules or principles upon which one could draw. The Fisheries Conservation Convention and bilateral agreements provide a measure of analogy. They show that States are willing to compromise for the sake of achieving a reasonable system of conservation. There are no universal criteria, however, upon which States can agree regarding how to divide the profits of common resources. So far, case by case negotiation and agreement between interested States provided patterns for profit sharing. The Interim Convention on Conservation of North Pacific Fur Seals of February 9, 1957 is based on the "abstention" principle which may provide a useful analogy for space law.[109]

(i) Fishing Zones.[110] Canada and the United States along with 48 other

[107] *Fur Seal Arbitration* (1893), G. B./U. S. 1 Moore, I. A.; *Whaling and Sealing Claims* (1902), Russia/U.S. U.S.F.R. Appendix I, p. 467 at p. 471.

[108] Brierly, 308, 315–316; Starke, 237–239.

[109] The Convention came into force on October 14, 1957 (314 U.N.T.S. 105). The Convention was amended and its duration extended by a Protocol signed on October 8, 1963, which entered into force in 1964 (494 U.N.T.S. 303). For further reference, see Carroz and Roche, "The Proposed International Commission for the Conservation of Atlantic Tunas", 61 A.J.I.L. 673–678 (1967); Chapman, "Fishery Resources in Offshore Waters", in Alexander (ed.) *The Law of the Sea,* (1967) 87–105.

[110] The Act Respecting the Territorial Sea and Fishing Zones of Canada of July 23, 1964 (Statutes of Canada, 1964, 13 Eliz. c. 22.) defined the breadth of Canadian territorial waters as three miles, adopted the straight baseline system, and established a fishing zone of 12-mile breadth from the baseline (i.e. 9 miles from the outer limits of the territorial sea). The purpose of this act was to give greater protection to Canadian interests in its adjacent shores. Foreign fishermen may not come into the fishing zone except if fishing is permitted under treaty provisions. See, A. E. Gottlieb, "The Canadian Contribution to the Concept of a Fishing Zone in International Law," 2 C.Y.I.L.

States including the U.S.S.R. claim fishery jurisdiction extending 12 miles from the baseline from which the breadth of the territorial sea is measured. The coastal State has exclusive fishing rights in the "fishing zone". Foreign States may not fish in such zones unless they enjoy traditional fishing rights or have obtained fishing rights from the coastal State. In view of the recent developments in international practice, the U.S. Department of State claimed,

> action by the United States at this time to establish an exclusive fisheries zone extending 9 miles beyond the territorial sea would not be contrary to international law. It should be emphasized that such action would not extend the territorial sea beyond [the] traditional 3-mile limit and would not affect such traditional freedoms of the sea as freedom of navigation or of overflight.[111]

The net "legal" result of the establishment of fisheries zones is that the exclusive jurisdiction of the coastal State over fishing moves forward into the high seas, and the jurisdiction of third States proportionately shrinks. The jurisdiction of the coastal State in the "fisheries zones" is limited according to its purpose. We propose that this type of jurisdiction should be called "functional jurisdiction." [112]

One might contend that exclusive fisheries jurisdiction beyond the territorial sea is an encroachment upon the freedom of fishing. From a static point of view this may well be so. On the other hand, it should be borne in mind that the needs of the international community of States may change in the course of time and such developments call for a readjustment of conventional or treaty law. Surely the exercise of the so-called "functional jurisdiction" meets this very need. As long as it is reasonably exercised and does not interfere with the freedom of navigation or of overflight, the concept of "functional jurisdiction" is compatible with the established principles and rules of international law. Contemporary State practice regarding the establishment of "fisheries zones" is conclusive evidence to this effect.[113]

55–76 (1964); Jacques-Yvan Morin, "La zone de pêche exclusive du Canada," *op. cit.* 77–106.

[111] 60 A.J.I.L. 831 *et seq.* See also Edward W. Allen, "Freedom of the Sea," 60 A.J.I.L. 814–816 (1966), where it is claimed that the relationship between the problems of "freedom of the seas for navigation and the handling of the current ocean fishery situation" is "wholly antiquated and illogical." The author urged that "a new international conference on conservation of fisheries" should be convened. Alexander (ed.) *The Law of the Sea* (1967) 321.

[112] It is recalled here that the nature of jurisdiction exercised by Canada and the United States in their air defence identification zones may also be regarded "functional jurisdiction."

[113] The following classes of coastal States claiming fishery jurisdiction can be dis-

We believe that the analogy of fisheries zones could eventually be applied on celestial bodies as well, if the exploitation of the resources or certain uses of outer space and the Moon required the extension of State jurisdiction beyond the confines of space stations and installations. While on earth the interest of the coastal States is emphasized, in outer space including celestial bodies the interests of the State of registration of space stations will require special attention.

(ii) The Contiguous Zone. The contiguous zone is another geographical location where the coastal State may exercise functionally restricted jurisdiction under international law. Article 24 of the Convention on the Territorial Sea and Contiguous Zone provides that the littoral State may not exercise sovereignty, but it may exercise control for the purpose (1) to prevent infringement of its customs, fiscal, immigration, or sanitary regulations within its territory or territorial sea, and (2) to punish infringements of such regulations committed within its territory or territorial sea.[115]

(iii) The Continental Shelf. Article 1 of the Convention on the Continental Shelf defined the term continental shelf as "the seabed and subsoil area of the territorial sea, to a depth of 200 metres or, beyond that limit, to where the depth of the superjacent waters admits of the exploitation of the natural resources of the said areas".[116] Article 2 grants the coastal State "sovereign rights" for the purpose of exploring and exploiting the natural resources of the shelf. For this reason the concept itself and the body of relevant rules of international law governing the continental shelf could not be accommodated in space law. Nevertheless, the example of the continental shelf is a useful illustration of contemporary developments whereby the exclusive jurisdiction of States is extended for specific purposes into areas having an international legal status.[117] It is a process, we

tinguished according to the breadth of such jurisdiction: (1) 3 miles: 15 States; (2) 3 to 12 miles: 10 States; (3) 12 miles: 50 States; and (4) beyond 12 miles: 17 States. This information was provided to the U.S. Senate Committee on Commerce by the Department of State and is up-to-date as of June 1, 1966. Cf., 60 A.J.I.L. 832 (1966).

114 A parallel may be drawn between the legal construction of the concept of the contiguous zone and the prohibition of national appropriation of outer space (Article II of the Space Treaty) and Article VIII of the Space Treaty. For details see *infra* at 152 *et seq.*

115 For details see Starke, 192–193.

116 This elastic definition of the continental shelf is the cause of divergent interpretations affecting the legal régime of the deep-sea floor. For an analysis of this question see Young, "The Legal Regime of the Deep-Sea Floor," 62 A.J.I.L. 641–653 (1968).

117 For details, see Starke, 196 *et seq.* Schwarzenberger, 2 *International Law* 309, 349–352. See also *Petroleum Development (Trucial Coast) Ltd. and the Sheikh of Abu Dhabi* (1951), 18 *International Law Reports* 144 *et seq.*

think, to which future developments regarding the uses and exploitation of the Moon and outer space – the latter especially for satellite communications may well be analogous.

(iv) Air Defence Identification Zones. For security purposes the United States, Canada and the Philippines have established so-called "air defence identification zones" above the maritime approaches to their coasts.[118] Foreign aircraft flying in such zones are supposed to provide identification data subject to enforcement measures and penalties. This interesting post-war development gives further support to the conclusion that State jurisdiction is not based solely on the concept of territoriality, and also that the exercise of jurisdiction by States may be extended under international law to specified types of activities beyond territorial domains. The legality of such unilateral action ultimately depends on whether the exercise of jurisdiction is within reasonable limits. In other words, State jurisdiction in such zones may not interfere with the freedom to fly over the high seas. An analogous situation would arise if a State intended to establish control zones around and above stations on the Moon for reasons of safety. In our view the exercise of State jurisdiction in such zones on the Moon could no longer be regarded as unparallelled legal phenomenon lacking status in international law.

b. The Antarctic

The legal regime of Antarctica has been the most frequently cited analogy regarding outer space. It is now obvious in the light of the negotiations leading to the Space Treaty that the analogy is but apparent and only certain similarities exist between the legal status of outer space and Antarctica. In fact, each of them has a status of its own in international law. Article IV of the Antarctic treaty did not abolish, but only froze, existing claims to territorial sovereignty in Antarctica. Quite clearly, no such claims have ever been submitted in respect of outer space or celestial bodies. It follows therefore that the legal basis of State jurisdiction in the Antarctic does not exclude the concept of territoriality with respect to States that made such claims while State jurisdiction, as it is understood in space law, excludes the concept of territoriality.

118 See generally, Robert D. Hayton, "Jurisdiction of the Littoral State in the 'Air Frontier'," 3 P.I.L.J. 369–398 (1964). Ivan L. Head, "ADIZ, International Law, and Contiguous Airspace," 3 *Alberta L. Rev.* 182–196 (1964). Murchison, *The Continuous Airspace Zone in International Law,* 97–100 (Rev. ed. 1955). Martial, "State Control of the Airspace over the Territorial Sea and the Contiguous Zone," 30 *Canadian Bar Review* 245 (1952). Debbasch, "La Zone Contiguée en Droit Aérien," 14 *Revue Générale de l'Air* 249, 256 (1961).

Article VIII of the Antarctic Treaty[119] provides that observers and scientific exchange personnel "and members of the staffs accompanying such persons, shall be subject only to the jurisdiction of the Contracting Party of which they are nationals." The treaty did not affect the territorial claims previously made with respect to areas of Antarctica. Therefore, the immunity of the said categories of persons from the jurisdiction of the territorial authorities is "without the prejudice to the respective positions of the Contracting Parties relating to jurisdiction over all other persons in Antarctica." The extent of the immunity corresponds to the requirement that such persons can freely exercise their functions. The subjection of the officially designated observers to the jurisdiction of the State of their nationality constitutes the treaty's major infringement upon the sovereignty of those States which made territorial claims. The law of nationality penetrates into the geographical area where, in principle, another State may exercise territorial jurisdiction. Hayton pointed out that it may become desirable to establish consular courts in the Antarctic when the bases become larger and the research programs more elaborate.[120]

The system of State jurisdiction on Antarctica is rather complex. Article VIII(1) does not affect "the respective positions of the Contracting Parties relating to the *jurisdiction over all other persons in Antarctica*." The category of "all other persons in Antarctica" includes every person except observers [Article VII(1)] and scientific exchange personnel [Article III(1b)]. In practical terms this rule means the following:

(i) State A, having no territorial claims over Antarctica, does not recognize the right of State B (e.g., Argentina) to exercise territorial jurisdiction over nationals of State A while they are within the sector claimed by State B. The same applies in the relationship of States which do not recognize each other's claims (e.g. Chile and Great Britain).

(ii) The Contracting States may exercise exclusive national jurisdiction over their own nationals wherever they may be in Antarctica and refrain from exercising jurisdiction over foreign nationals.

[119] For the text of The Antarctic Treaty see, *Legal Problems of Space Exploration* ... 1297–1303 (1961). 54 A.J.I.L. 476 (1960). See generally, *Soviet space Programs* ... 203–205 (1962). Lissitzyn, "The American Position on Outer Space and Antarctica", 53 A.J.I.L. 131 (1959). Philip G. Jessup and Howard J. Taubenfeld, *Controls for Outer Space and the Antarctic Analogy* (1959). Hayton, "The Antarctic Settlement of 1959", 54 A.J.I.L. 349–371 (1960). See also, *The Antarctic Treaty*, Hearings before the Committee on Foreign Relations United States Senate, Eighty-sixth Congress, Second Session, on Ex. B. 86th Congress, 2d Session, June 14, 1960 (U.S.G.P.O., Washington, 1960) pp. 42–71; concerning the application of The Antarctic Treaty to Outer Space, see *ibid.* at 70.

[120] Hayton, *loc. cit. supra* at 361 *et seq.*

(iii) The Antarctic Treaty acknowledges the difficulties which may arise from conflicting jurisdictions and therefore it provides for immediate consultation between the parties concerned "with a view to reaching a mutually acceptable solution." [Article VIII(2)]. Such jurisdictional conflicts may include an incident between members of a scientific group from two different countries in an area claimed by a third State; the application of an exchange scientist for refuge or political asylum; problems of criminal jurisdiction over non-nationals; and the exercise of control and administrative powers within sectors claimed by a third State.[121]

The importance of these provisions may be summed up in the following two points. Firstly, The Antarctic Treaty illustrates how rules governing the exercise of State jurisdiction operate in an area whose legal status is frequently compared with the regime of outer space and celestial bodies. Secondly, the nature of State jurisdiction varies according to the categories of persons. On this analogy it seems safe to conclude that different rules will govern the exercise of State jurisdiction on celestial bodies according to whether the persons involved are astronauts, exchange scientists and space personnel or designated observers.

4. Personal Jurisdiction

Personal jurisdiction is the totality of powers of a State with respect to natural and legal persons bearing its nationality, enjoying its protection or owing it allegiance wherever they may be. The concept of nationality is the

[121] The following passage taken from the Hearings before the U.S. Senate Foreign Relations Committee on the Antarctic Treaty illustrates some of the jurisdictional problems which may arise in Antarctica:

> *Senator Aiken:* Suppose that there became a sudden tremendous demand for emperor penguins and the people start killing off all the emperor penguins down there. Who could prevent that?
>
> *Mr. Phleger:* The people in each of the geographical areas covered by the seven claimant nations would claim they had a right to protect those penguins.
>
> *Senator Aiken:* But how about our penguins where we don't claim them?
>
> *Mr. Phleger:* If it was an American society that was going down there to get penguins, they would claim they had a right to go into the Chilean area and take the penguins. That is not covered by this treaty. Those relationships are left as they are.
>
> *Senator Aiken:* So long as the Soviet and the United States don't make any geographical claims down there, what is to hinder Denmark and Norway from laying claim to the territory that we have seen – I won't say occupied, but that we have seen?
>
> *Mr. Phleger:* There is nothing to prevent them from doing it, but their claims would not have any validity under international law because they have never discovered or explored or occupied the territory.

Hearings ... *op. cit. supra* at 62.

legal basis of personal jurisdiction.[122] In its decision in the *Nottebohm Case* (1955),[123] the Court of International Justice stated that nationality was within the domestic jurisdiction of every State which settled through its own legislation the rules relating to the acquisition of its nationality. But to exercise its protection, the Court stated, "is to place oneself on the plane of international law which determined whether a State is entitled to exercise protection . . . ,"[124] thus there must exist a "genuine link" between the State and persons over whom it wishes to exercise personal jurisdiction under international law. This principle is fully applicable to astronauts and spacecraft. The applicability of municipal laws shall have to be extended by a special legislative act in many countries.[125]

The concept of nationality is the basic connecting factor which enables States to exercise jurisdiction over their astronauts and space vehicles under international space law. By accepting nationality as the basis of State jurisdiction in space law the concept of territoriality becomes irrelevant.[126] The jurisdiction of the State of nationality follows every person to outer space. Thus, under present international law, the active nationality principle, the passive nationality principle and the protective principle are also applicable in outer space. According to the first principle jurisdiction would be assumed by the State of which the astronaut, against whom proceedings are instituted, is a national. According to the second principle the State of which the victim is a national would assume jurisdiction. The protective principle is meant to afford jurisdiction to a State over crimes endangering its security or its vital interests.[127] The protective principle is sound, but it may lead to "extravagant extensions of State power".[128]

[122] Starke, 238 *et seq.* Christol, 420 *et seq.* Cheng, 135. Cf. *inter alia* the following British cases: *Rex. v. Manoel Antonio de Mattos* ([1936] 7 Car. & P. 458) in 3 B.I.L.C. pp. 21–24. *Regina v. John Lewis* ([1857] Dears. & Bell 182) in 3 B.I.L.C. pp. 27–29. *Regina v. Adolf Bjornsen* ([1865] Leigh and C. 545) in 3 B.I.L.C. pp. 29–40. *The Queen v. Anderson* ([1868] L.R. 1. C.C.R. 161) in 3 B.I.L.C. pp. 40–45. *R. v. Joyce* ([1945] 2 A11 E.R. 673) in 3 B.I.L.C pp 45–51. *Joyce v. Director of Public Prosecutors* ([1946] A.C. 347) in 3 B.I.L.C. pp. 51–72.

[123] *Nottebohm Case* (Second Phase), I.C.J. Reports 1955, 4–65.

[124] *Ibid.* at 20–21. See also *Restatement* at 80–81.

[125] See Christol, 420.

[126] The *Restatement* does not refer to the concept of territoriality in connection with jurisdiction over ships and aircraft either. *Ibid.*, 421.

[127] See *U.S. v. Chandler* (1947), 72 F. Supp. 230. *U.S. v. Rodriguez* (1960), 182 F. Supp. 479. *Rocha v. U.S.* (1961), 288 F. (2d) 545. See also, McDougal, Lasswell and Vlasic, 647, 693, 699–700 and 700 n. McDougal, Burke, and Vlasic, "The Maintenance of Public Order at Sea and the Nationality of Ships," 54 A.J.I.L. 25 (1960).

[128] Jessup, *Transnational Law*, 50 (1951). See also, *Harvard Research, Jurisdiction*, Articles 7 & 8 at 543–563. Values protected by this principle include: security, terri-

Because of this reason the applicability of the latter principle to space activities should be circumscribed by treaty provisions.

5. *Jurisdiction According to the Universal Principle*

Under the principle of universality all States may assume jurisdiction over offences and acts wherever committed, if they are subject to such jurisdiction. The basis for universal jurisdiction is that certain offences are contrary to the interests of the international community, and, thus, may not go unpunished. Obviously, the applicability of this principle to space law cannot be disputed. According to Starke, the crime of piracy *jure gentium* and war crimes are two clear-cut cases of universal jurisdiction.[129] Genocide, narcotics, trafficking in women and children and the counterfeiting of currency are additional instances of the application of the principle of universal jurisdiction.

The principle of universal jurisdiction may have several useful functions. As regards piracy *jure gentium* in particular, it may well be questioned whether or not its reception into space law is desirable. Under international law private vessels or aircraft can only commit piracy. Since under space law the State of registry is internationally responsible for national space activities, the lack of distinction, as regards the launching State's international responsibility, between private and public spacecraft becomes irrelevant in the context of piracy. If a ship in the employ of her government commits acts that would pass for piracy were they committed by private ships, and that if she commits unjustified acts of violence redress must be asked from her flag State, which has to punish the commander, and to pay damages where required.[130]

The *raison d'être* of piracy in international space law could, of course, be that the commission of certain acts in outer space *ipso facto* constitutes such a grave encroachment upon the interests of the international com-

torial integrity, political independence, fiscal and monetary stability. See Christol, p. 225 at 423.

[129] Starke, 248, 249–252, 441–444. Cf. *The Ambrose Light* (1885), 25 Federal 408. See also, *In Re Jure Piracy Gentium* ([1934] A.C. 586) in 3 B.I.L.C. pp. 836–843. *The Attorney-General of Our Lady the Queen for the Colony of Hong Kong and Kwock-A-Sing* ([1873] L.R. 5 P.C. 179) 3 B.I.L.C. 812–825. *Republic of Bolivia v. Indemnity Mutual Marine Assurance Company, Limited* ([1909] 1 K.B. 785) 3 B.I.L.C. 325–336.

[130] Oppenheim, 610–611. According to Article 15 of the Geneva High Seas Convention, 1958 piracy consists of any illegal acts of violence, detention, or any act of depredation, committed for private ends by those aboard a *private ship* or *private aircraft,* and directed, either on the *high seas,* against a ship or aircraft, or persons or property thereon, or, in *territory or waters of the nature of terra nullius.*

munity that every State must be entitled to assume jurisdiction to apprehend and punish offenders "as if for an act of piracy".[131]

The case of the Huascar[132] shows that there is precedence where a public ship was treated as piratical. Bearing in mind the global interest in the peace and good order of outer space the following acts could be regarded as piratical under international space law: Orbiting or stationing nuclear weapons or other weapons of mass destructive effect in outer space or on celestial bodies respectively; pirate broadcasting from a space orbit which may cause radio interference and thus endanger the safety of space communications and thereby violating the freedoms of outer space or international radio regulations. It is clear that the concept of piracy would need revision if and when this institution will be incorporated into space law, in other words, the concept of *"piracy in international space law"* would have to be established. It follows that the common features between piracy *jure gentium* and piracy in international space law are only formal. It remains for international space law to determine what acts constitute piracy, i.e., under what conditions, if any, should the "pirate" lose the protection of the State of registration of the spacecraft or the State of his nationality.

It would be difficult to introduce the concept of piracy into space law as it is now established in international law. Since the launching State is directly responsible for acts perpetrated through the means of objects launched into outer space, irrespective of whether or not such instruments would qualify as private or public craft, three options are at hand regarding the application of piracy in space law. First, a clear-cut distinction be made between "private" and "public" space vehicles and the consequences of piratical acts should then attach to the former category. It would expose private vehicles engaged in acts defined as piratical to the jurisdiction of all States. The State exercising jurisdiction over such craft could, under Article VI of the Space Treaty, directly address its claim for redress, if relevant, to the State bearing "international responsibility for national activities". Under this construction, then, public spacecraft would be exempt from the jurisdiction of third States without prejudice to Article VI of the Space Treaty. This solution requires the definition of public and private spacecraft and acts that may be considered piratical. (E.g., "pirate" communications satellites, satellites equipped with nuclear weapons or other weapons of mass destructive nature).

Secondly, no distinction is necessary between public or private spacecraft

[131] Treaty of Washington, 1922, Article 3. 16 A.J.I.L. (1922) Supplement p. 67. Oppenheim, 613.

[132] Oppenheim, 611–612.

because every Sate could exercise jurisdiction and prosecute any spacecraft committing piratical acts, and the launching State would bear direct responsibility for such acts. This construction involves two difficulties. It would entail the modification of the concept of piracy, since it would extend its scope to government operated spacecraft. Consequently, States probably would be reluctant to give up the immunity they enjoy, though not the responsibility they bear regarding their spacecraft.

The third solution would be to reserve exclusive jurisdiction over piratical acts to the State which bears international responsibility for the national activity in question. This construction would negate the concept of piracy for space law. Useful as the concept of piracy might be, it is highly doubtful that its scope and contents could be determined without difficulty. The acceptability of the concept seems, therefore, to be low. The major powers would certainly not be in agreement with respect to the use of or stationing of weapons in outer space.

National jurisdiction is also based on the universality principle with respect to collision and salvage. Collision between spacecraft is no impossibility, but liability for collision between spacecraft, as well as ancillary legal issues, will be regulated in a separate international agreement.[133]

6. *Immunities from and Restrictions upon State Jurisdiction*

Foreign States, Heads of foreign States, diplomatic representatives and consuls, public ships and other property of foreign States, armed forces of foreign States and international institutions enjoy immunity from the territorial jurisdiction of States under international law.[134] International law also imposes certain limitations upon a State's treatment of aliens and its own nationals.[135] For the purpose of this study only two aspects of immunity from State jurisdiction in international law are deemed relevant. First, it should be considered to what extent astronauts and space vehicles can be regarded as immune from the territorial jurisdiction of a third State. It may be well to recall here that it is necessary to distinguish between two scopes of application of rules governing State jurisdiction: (a) application in respect of the terrestrial effects of space activities, and (b) application to activities in outer space and on celestial bodies proper.

[133] See *inter alia,* Houston Lay and Howard J. Taubenfeld, "Liability and Space Activities: Causes, Objectives and Parties," 6 *Virginia Journal of International Law* 250–288 (1966). See also, McNair, *The Law of the Air,* 3d ed., 288–289 (1964).

[134] See generally Starke, 216–238, Brierly, 243–276. Oppenheim, 264–267, 271–275, 800–801. Schwarzenberger, 192–194, 83–85, 185–186, 189, 257. Cheng, *The Law of International Air Transport,* 37, 40–42. (1962).

[135] See *inter alia* Brierly, 276–299.

Secondly, it is a rule of customary international law that foreign Heads of State are not subject to the jurisdiction of any other State.[136] The applicability of this rule is not restricted to the earth; it applies to outer space as well. The concept of immunity of diplomatic representatives from the jurisdiction of the receiving State[137] is also applicable to space law, should the need arise to establish such representations on celestial bodies. We hold, however, that special rules will have to be created to govern such contingencies. It is clear that astronauts do not enjoy any privileged position on account of their status in the territory of foreign States, despite the fact that the Declaration of Legal Principles and the Space Treaty refer to them as "envoys" of mankind. The Vienna Convention on Diplomatic Intercourse and Immunities of April 18, 1961,[138] deals with diplomatic agents as such, and for this reason astronauts cannot be regarded as diplomatic agents of their national State or the State of registration of the spacecraft. Their characterization as "envoys" of mankind is only a figure of speech.

Public ships of foreign States are in great measure exempt from the territorial jurisdiction.[139] State-owned commercial ships are not exempt from civil process *in rem* if they are within territorial waters or are passing through the territorial sea after leaving internal waters.[140] These rules are closely linked with the specific national and community interests regarding sea navigation. We think that the extension of these rules to outer space is not possible. For the present time there appears to be no difference between public or private spacecraft with respect to the obligation of third States to return such craft to the State of registration in case of distress landing in their territories. Nevertheless, it may become necessary to create special rules governing the question of immunity of various types of spacecraft from the territorial jurisdiction of States. In this context the abovementioned rules regarding public and private vessels may provide a useful analogy. Accordingly, the principle adopted in *Chung Chi Cheung v. R.* that the immunity of public ships is based not on the theory of "floating territory," but on the implication that immunity is granted by the local

[136] *Schooner Exchange v. McMadden* (1812), 7 Cranch 116.

[137] For a thorough study of the subject see, Yoram Dinstein, "Diplomatic Immunity from jurisdiction *Ratione Materiae*," 15 I.C.L.Q. 76–89 (1966).

[138] United Nations Conference on Diplomatic Intercourse and Immunities, 1961 Official Records ("/CONF. 20/14 & Add. 1.). See also, 10 I.C.L.Q. 600 (1961). The Convention entered into force on April 24, 1964.

[139] *Parlement Belge* (1880), 5 P.D. 197. *Porto Alexandre* (1920), P. 30. *Compania Mercantil Argentina v. U.S. Shipping Board* (1924), T.L.R. 601.

[140] *S.S. Cristina* [1938] A.C. 485. *Rahimtoola v. Nizam of Hyderabad* [1958] A.C. 377. But cf. *Pesaro* (1926), 271 U.S. 562 where the Supreme Court granted immunity to an Italian Government vessel wholly engaged in trade.

municipal law, is of relevance. If the public character of the vessel is proved,[141] "no legal proceedings will lie against it, either *in rem* for recovery of possession, or for damages for collision or in respect of members of its crew."[142] The purpose of jurisdictional immunity is to ensure the efficient functioning of the public vessel.[143] Thus the vessel is bound to observe the ordinary rules of the port. In case of extreme danger asylum may be granted to said vessel. It should not be forgotten that the possibility of legal proceedings against space vehicles is rather remote. The previous material indicates that there are certain principles and analogies in general international law on which the international lawyer may rely.

[141] In *Juan Ysmael & Co. v. The Republic of Indonesia,* [1955] A.C. 72, the Privy Council held that a bare assertion of interest by a foreign State is not enough to claim immunity. For exceptions as to the general rule of immunity, see *Larivière v. Morgan* (1875), L.R. 7 H.L. 423, and Brierly, 254.

[142] Starke, 230.

[143] See *Chung Chi Cheung v. The King* at 176.

CHAPTER III

THE PROGRESSIVE DEVELOPMENT OF CERTAIN LEGAL PRINCIPLES GOVERNING THE EXERCISE OF STATE JURISDICTION IN OUTER SPACE AND ON CELESTIAL BODIES

In this chapter we shall examine how the Legal Sub-Committee of the UNCOPUOS developed the concept of State jurisdiction with respect to (1) liability for damage caused by space vehicle accidents; (2) rescue, and (3) return of astronauts and space vehicles making an emergency landing. The summary records of the Legal Sub-Committee indicate the positions of States regarding their preference as to legal goals and practice. The summary records constitute the *sedes materiae* where some of the principles included in the *Space Treaty* find their origin. The summary records of the meetings of the UNCOPUOS serve as *travaux préparatoires* in the interpretation of the rules and principles of international space law.

First, we shall clarify the competence of the United Nations and of the UNCOPUOS in relation to the progressive development of international space law.

I. THE COMPETENCE OF THE UNITED NATIONS

The competence of the United Nations regarding the progressive development of space law is based on the relevant provisions of the U.N. Charter and on the common consent of Member States as expressed in the General Assembly resolutions on international cooperation in the peaceful uses of outer space.

Article 1 of the Charter determining the purposes, and Article 2 stipulating the principles according to which the Organization and its members shall act, subsume the responsibilities and legal competence of the United Nations regarding outer space.[1] In pursuance of the provision contained in

[1] See generally, Brownlie, *op. cit. supra* at 1 *et seq.* Jenks, 207. Christol, 332–340. Cheng, "The United Nations and Outer Space," 14 C.L.P. 247–279 (1961). – "United Nations Resolutions on Outer Space: "Instant" International Customary Law," 5 I.J.I.L. 23–28 (1965).

Article 1 (4) that the United Nations shall be "a center for harmonizing the actions of nations" in the attainment of its purposes, Paragraph 1 (a) of Article 13 provides:

> The General Assembly shall initiate studies and make recommendations for the purpose of:
>
> (a) promoting international cooperation in the political field and encouraging the *progressive development of international law* and its *codification*. (Emphasis added)

The meaning of these two terms was defined in Article 15 of the Statute of the International Law Commission: [2]

> In the following articles the expression "progressive development of international law" is used for convenience as meaning the preparation of draft conventions on subjects which have not yet been regulated by international law or in regard to which the law has not yet been sufficiently developed in the practice of States. Similarly, the expression "codification of international law" is used for convenience as meaning the more precise formulation and systematization of rules of international law in fields where there already has been extensive State practice, precedent and doctrine.

The General Assembly has treated the progressive development and codification of international law as a single process of development wherein the latter is the consequence of the former. However, Article 18 and Article 24 of the Statute of the International Law Commission established different procedures for the progressive development and codification of international law respectively. Consequently, where no codification proper is possible because of the absence of customary rules of international law, the progressive development of international law is an independent and unitary activity. Therefore, due to its inherent doctrinal and technical implications, the codification of international law was, as a whole, assigned to the International Law Commission. The General Assembly, Member States, the principal organs of the U.N., the specialized agencies and special bodies established by the General Assembly and international organizations equally have competence with respect to the progressive development of international law.[3]

This is the reason why the task of progressive development of international space law has been assigned to the Legal Sub-Committee of the UNCOPUOS. The interrelationship between legal, political, strategic, mili-

[2] See also Articles 10–14, 24–26 and 51. The International Law Commission was set up in pursuance of General Assembly Resolution 174 (II) to give effect to Article 13 (1a) of the U.N. Charter.

[3] See generally, Ustor, "Progressive Development of International Law and the United Nations," 6 I.J.I.L. 315–334 (1964).

tary and economic interests, as well as the metajuridical considerations as to priority treatment of certain legal issues, required that space law should be treated at a different – although not necessarily superior – level.[4] The evidential value of materials relating to the proceedings of the Legal Sub-Committee and other organs of the U.N., as well as the General Assembly resolutions on outer space range from their role as *fons cognoscendi* to a formal declarative source which evidences the fact and scope of *opinio juris communis*.

Up to June, 1968, the Legal Sub-Committee had held seven sessions.[5] The terms of reference of the UNCOPUOS were determined in General Assembly resolutions. The Legal Sub-Committee is expected to continue its work on preparing a draft agreement on liability for damage caused by space vehicles. It will also have to study questions relative to the definition of outer space, and the utilization of outer space and celestial bodies including the various implications of space communications.[6]

The doctrine of State jurisdiction, unlike the question of sovereignty, was discussed in a rather summary fashion in the Legal Sub-Committee. The reason may probably be found in the assumption that if an agreement is reached regarding the principle of non-appropriation of outer space, States do not have to worry too much at this stage about more detailed rules clarifying the exercise of State jurisdiction in outer space. Indeed, States were content with a general principle in regard to which there was no difference of opinion among them to the effect that space vehicles and personnel therein should remain under the jurisdiction and control of the State of registration.

[4] *Ibid.*

[5] The following table indicates the session of the Legal Sub-Committee of the

UNCOPUOS:	28 May–29 June	1962	Geneva	A/AC/105/C.2/SR. 1– 15
First Session	16 April–3 May	1963	New York	SR.16– 28
Second Session	9–26 March	1964	Geneva	SR.29– 37
Third Session	5–23 October	1964	New York	SR.38– 40
Fourth Session	20 Sept.–1 Oct.	1965	New York	SR.41– 56
Fifth Session	12 July–4 August	1966	Geneva	SR.57– 70
	12–16 September	1966	New York	SR.71– 73
Special Meeting	19 April	1967	New York	
Sixth Session	19 June–14 July	1967	Geneva	SR.74– 85
Special Session	14–15 December	1967	New York	SR.86– 89
Seventh Session	4–28 June	1968	Geneva	SR.90–110

[6] U.N. General Assembly Resolution 2222(XXI) December 19, 1966. See also U.N. Doc. A/AC.105/45 (11 July 1968).

II. THE REPORT OF THE AD HOC COMMITTEE OF THE UNCOPUOS

The Report of the Ad Hoc Committee on the Peaceful Uses of Outer Space of June 25, 1959, identified legal problems in two categories.[7] Among the problems which were regarded as requiring priority treatment the re-entry, landing and identification of space vehicles bear upon the problem of exercise of jurisdiction in outer space.

ad 1. *Inter alia,* the Ad Hoc Committee's Report stated relative to the first problem:

> Where space vehicles are designed for re-entry and return, it will be appropriate for the *launching State* to enter into suitable arrangements with the State on whose territory the space vehicle is intended to land and other States whose air space may be entered during descent. Recognizing, moreover, that such landing may occur through accident, mistake or distress, members of the Committee called attention to the desirability of the conclusion of multilateral agreements concerning re-entry and landing, such agreements to contain suitable undertakings on cooperation and appropriate provisions on procedures. Among the subjects that might be covered by such agreements would be the return to the launching State of the vehicle itself and–in the case of a manned vehicle–provision for the speedy return of personnel.[8]

Thus, the Ad Hoc Committee made three important presumptions. First, it regarded that the launching State may enter into suitable arrangements with other States, on the basis that the launching State has jurisdiction over manned and unmanned space vehicles. Secondly, the Committee presumed that the principle of freedom of outer space[9] does not *ipso facto* modify the rules governing the exercise of State jurisdiction in national territory. For example, the right of "innocent passage" through foreign airspace could not be inferred from the principle of the freedom of outer space. Thirdly, it appears, that the Ad Hoc Committee was inclined to regard the landing of space vehicles on foreign territory "through accident, mistake or distress" as a distinct problem. It also recommended the conclusion of multilateral agreements. However, the language used and the indication of the subject

[7] U.N. Doc. 4/4141 (July 14, 1959). For the text see, *Legal Problems of Space Exploration, A Symposium,* 1246–1272. The two categories included questions susceptible of priority treatment (freedom of outer space, liability, allocation of radio frequencies, avoidance of interference between aircraft and spacecraft, identification and registration of space vehicles and co-ordination of launchings, re-entry and landing of space vehicles) and other legal problems (determination of outer space, contamination, exploration of celestial bodies, avoidance of interference between spacecraft and additional questions such as space meteorology). See also Introduction by Eilene Galloway, *op. cit.* at xiii.

[8] *Ibid.* at 1269.

[9] *Id.* para. 23 at 1270.

matter of such agreements foreshadowed the attitude of States as to the privileged status of astronauts and space vehicles in distress.[10]

ad 2. With respect to the question of identification of space vehicles[11] the Ad Hoc Committee recommended that suitable means (e.g., individual call signals and orbital characteristics), should be provided for the identification of individual space vehicles. In addition, appropriate markings should be displayed on space vehicles. It also recommended the registration, notification and co-ordination of launchings, without, however, expressly indicating who the responsible State should be.

In assessing the problems connected with liability for injury or damage caused by space vehicles, the Report posed the question whether the liability of the *launching State* should be unlimited in amount.[12] This clearly shows that according to the Report of the Ad Hoc Committee, liability and jurisdiction are linked to the launching State. The Report did not refer to the possibility that the launching State and the State of registration of the space vehicle could be different and that the latter could also be held liable or exercise jurisdiction.

Finally, the Report touched upon the problem of the sphere of validity (*ratione loci*) of rules governing the exercise of State jurisdiction. The Report Stated:

> Under the terms of existing international conventions and customary international law, States have complete and exclusive sovereignty in the air space above their territories and territorial waters. The concurrent existence of a region in space which is not subject to the same regime raises questions as where air space ends where outer space begins. It was noted that these limits do not necessarily coincide.[13]

The passage quoted implies that the Report recognizes two distinct legal regimes: That of airspace and outer space. It pointed out that under international law the subjacent State exercised sovereignty, hence jurisdiction, in the superjacent airspace and that outer space "is not subject to the same regime."[14]

[10] The Report also recommended in a tentative form the application of "certain substantive rules of international law ... concerning rights and duties with respect to aircraft and airmen landing on foreign territory through accident, mistake or distress ... in the event of similar landings of space vehicles." *Id.* para. 22.

[11] *Id.* paras. 17–20 at 1269.

[12] *Id.* para. 10 at 1268.

[13] *Id.* para. 23 at 1270. Legal problems not susceptible of priority treatment were discussed under paras. 23–33 at 1270.

[14] The Report made several tentative suggestions as to the delimitation of jurisdictional competencies. These included: the setting of a not loo low and not too high range "within which the limits of air space and outer space would be assumed to lie".

III. THE SESSIONS OF THE LEGAL SUB-COMMITTEE OF THE UNCOPUOS

Before the first session of the Legal Sub-Committee was convened, the General Assembly of the U.N. had unanimously adopted Resolution 1721 (XVI) of December 20, 1961 on *International Co-operation in the Peaceful Uses of Outer Space*. It commended two principles to States for their guidance:

> International law, including the Charter of the United Nations, applies to outer space and celestial bodies . . . ;
>
> Outer space and celestial bodies are free for exploration and use by all States in conformity with international law and are not subject to national appropriation.

From the first principle it follows that the concept of State jurisdiction is also applicable to outer space and celestial bodies. Since, however, the resolution provides for application and not automatic extension, it remains for the law-determining agencies to establish how the doctrine of State jurisdiction shall apply in particular cases. Part B of the Resolution gives some guidance as to how the U.N. General Assembly interprets the said principle with respect to registration, provision of information and public registration of launchings. Paragraph 1 of Part B of the Resolution called upon "States launching objects into orbit or beyond" to furnish information to the U.N. This is the first instance when a U.N. General Assembly resolution declared that the launching State is presumed to exercise jurisdiction over its spacecraft and presumably over astronauts therein.

The subsequent review of the activities of the Legal Sub-Committee will reveal how the Member States interpreted the principle that part and parcel with international law and the U.N. Charter the concept of State jurisdiction applies in outer space.

1. The First Session of the Legal Sub-Committee

The draft proposals submitted by the United States, the Soviet Union and India during the first session[15] contain references to the question of

It also recommended that international agreement should determine the permissibility of the space activity, altitude, "vertical" position, trajectory and flight mission, as well as instrumentation and other functional characteristics of the vehicle. According to the Report it would be premature to delimit outer space and airspace now. *Ibid.*, at 1270.

[15] The first session of the Legal Sub-Committee took place in Geneva from 28 May to 20 June, 1962. The statements have been summarized in U.N. Doc. A/AC.105/C.2/SR.1–15. Membership in the Legal Sub-Committee included the following States: Albania, Argentina, Australia, Austria, Belgium, Brazil, Bulgaria, Canada, Chad, Czecho-

jurisdiction. They may be regarded as indicating the opinion of the various States relating to the specific aspects of the exercise of State jurisdiction over space activities.

a. The Soviet Draft Proposal on the Basic Principles (Re launching State)

After declaring the principle of non-appropriation of outer space (Para. 2) and confirming the principle of applicability of international law to outer space (Para. 4) the Soviet draft proposal did not leave any doubt as to the extension of State jurisdiction over spacecraft and personnel therein.[16]

Paragraph 7 stated *inter alia* that "the sovereign rights of States to the objects they launch into outer space shall be retained by them." Under Paragraph 9 astronauts "as envoys of mankind" would enjoy privileged treatment in case of emergency landing anywhere on the earth "beyond the limits of the launching State." The privileged treatment would consist of the return of the astronaut as well as the space objects to the launching State.

Thus, it is clearly shown that in the situation contemplated in Paragraph 7 the *launching State* would exercise exclusive jurisdiction while under Paragraph 9 its jurisdiction would be concurrent with the local sovereign. The Soviet proposal is silent as to the legal status of spacecraft and personnel which land under circumstances other than those of emergency. However, Paragraph 8, declaring "the use of artificial satellites for the collection of intelligence information in the territory of foreign states . . . is incompatible with the objectives of mankind in its conquest of outer space," seems to suggest the exclusive jurisdiction of the local State in such cases.

b. The Soviet Draft Proposal on Rescue and Return

The Soviet draft proposal[17] spells out in greater detail the meaning of jurisdiction with respect to rescue. Every State would have authority and be bound (1) to render assistance (Article 1) without discrimination (Article 5), (2) to notify the launching State whose spacecraft or astronauts meet with accident (Article 2), (3) to notify the launching State and render assistance if the emergency landing took place on the territory of the Contracting State

slovakia, France, Hungary, India, Iran, Italy, Japan, Lebanon, Mexico, Mongolia, Morocco, Poland, Romania, Sierra Leone, Sweden, USSR, United Arab Republic, United Kingdom and the United States of America.

[16] *Declaration of Basic Principles Governing the Activities of States Pertaining to the Exploration and Use of Outer Space* A/AC.105/C.2/L.1. For text see *Report* of the Legal Sub-Committee on the work of its first session, A/AC.105/C.2/3 (10 June 1962) at 3–4.

[17] *International Agreement on the Rescue of Astronauts and Spaceships making Emergency Landings* A/AC.105/C.2/L.2. For text see *ibid.*

concerned (Article 3), and (4) to cooperate in the rescue operation on the high seas if the launching State so requested. The above-mentioned provisions make it clear that with respect to rescue on the high seas, the launching State would have the right to exercise both prescriptive and prerogative jurisdiction (exclusive jurisdiction of the launching State), and on the other hand, the territorial jurisdiction of the Contracting States is not affected, save for the case of return of astronauts and space vehicles to the launching State (Article 6).

It was the principle of exclusive jurisdiction of the launching State over its spacecraft and astronauts making emergency landings on the high seas, that was strongly criticised on humanitarian grounds. Likewise, the conditions of return (Article 7) were questioned by the United States and other Western countries in the Legal Sub-Committee, who claimed that should such provision be accepted, it would give free hand to the State within whose territorial domain astronauts and space vehicles make emergency landings, to exercise its jurisdiction in excess of reasonable limits.[18] In sum the Soviet proposal may be regarded as making a rigid attempt at infusing the concept of territorial jurisdiction into space law.

c. *The U.S. Draft Proposal on Assistance and Return*

The U.S. draft proposal[19] provides for unconditional return in laconic terms. (Para. 2) The salient features of the proposal are: (1) any type of space vehicle should be returned without exception as to its mission, (2) in addition to States, international organizations have the competence to claim the return of space vehicles for whose launching they are responsible, and (3) no request (authorization) by the launching State to another State for rendering assistance on the high seas is necessary. It appears from this early proposal that the U.S. did not intend to modify the concept of jurisdiction as established in international law. It showed, however, willingness to accept the complementary jurisdiction of a third State with respect to rescue operations on the high seas.

It is interesting to note that no mention was made in the above draft proposals about military spacecraft as such, although the question of peaceful *v.* military uses of outer space has been the subject of prolonged debate.

[18] The Soviet draft proposal contained two positive conditions: (a) display of identification marks, and (b) official announcement of the launching by the launching State; and one negative condition, prohibiting the collection of intelligence information. It is interesting to note that the Soviet draft did not mention military spacecraft either as a positive or as a negative condition.

[19] *Assistance and Return of Space Vehicles and Personnel* A/AC.105/C.2/L.3. For text, see *ibid.* at 5–6.

We are left in doubt, therefore, as to whether the analogy of military vessels and aircraft is applicable to military spacecraft.

d. The U.S. Draft Proposal on Liability

The U.S. proposal also confirmed[20] that the launching State and international organizations may exercise jurisdiction over space vehicles for whose launching they are responsible, by attaching international liability to them for damage caused by their spacecraft [Para. 3(a)]. The U.K. Representative suggested that in the case of joint space projects the test for liability might be "jurisdiction in the sense of effective control over the space vehicle, rather than ownership."[21]

No agreement has been reached on any of the proposals submitted to the Legal Sub-Committee during its first session.

e. The Indian Proposal

India submitted a proposal to the effect[22] that additional subjects should be taken up by the Legal Sub-Committee at its subsequent sessions. In this connection, other representatives suggested that *inter alia* the problem of "jurisdiction and law applicable to men in outer space and manned stations on celestial bodies"[23] should also be examined.

2. *The Second Session of the Legal Sub-Committee*

During the second session[24] the U.S. and the Soviet Union resubmitted and amended their previous draft proposals. In addition, the Sub-Committee considered a draft declaration of the U.S. on general principles,[25] as well as proposals by the United Arab Republic[26] and the United Kingdom[27] on the same subject.

[20] *Liability for Space Vehicle Accidents* A/AC.105/C.2/L.4. For text see, *ibid.* at 6–7.

[21] A/AC.105/C.2/SR.10 at 5. Cf. also para. 3 of the *Belgian Working Paper*... A/AC.105/C.2/L.7.

[22] Cf. A/AC.105/C.2/L.5 Corr. 1, *id.* at 7.

[23] A/AC.105/C.2/3 at 8. The second session of the Legal Sub-Committee took place in New York from 16 April to 3 May, 1963. The statements have been summarized in U.N. Doc. A/AC.105/C.2/SR. 16–28. Cf. also *Report of the Legal Sub-Committee.* U.N. Doc. A/AC.105/12 (6 May 1963).

[24] *The USSR Draft Declaration of the Basic Principles* A/AC.105/L.2. *The USSR Draft International Agreement on Rescue* A/AC.105/L.3. *The U.S. Draft Proposal on Assistance* A/AC.105/L.4. *The U.S. Draft Proposal on Liability* A/AC.105/L.5.

[25] *U.S.A. Draft Declaration of Principles Relating to the Exploration and Use of Outer Space* A/AC.1/881. For text see *Report of the Legal Sub-Committee* A/AC.105/12 (6 May 1963) Annex I.G. at 9–10.

[26] *U.A.R. Draft Code for International Cooperation in the Peaceful Uses of Outer Space* A/5181. For text see, *ibid.* Annex I.E. at 7–8.

[27] *United Kingdom. Draft Declaration of Basic Principles*... A/AC.1/879. For text see, *id.* Annex F at 8–9.

a. The U.S. and Soviet Draft Declarations on Legal Principles (Re Launching)

Paragraph 7 of the U.S. draft declaration provides:

> Jurisdiction over a space vehicle while it is in outer space shall be retained by the State or international organization which had jurisdiction at the time of launching. Ownership and property rights in a space vehicle and its components remain unaffected in outer space or upon return to the earth.

This position, although somewhat ambiguous, is a significant first step towards working out an agreement on articulate legal rules governing jurisdiction in outer space. It complements the respective provision of the Soviet draft. The difference between the two provisions is, that the U.S. draft expressly provides that the launching State or international organization retain jurisdiction over their spacecraft "while it is in outer space". The revised Soviet draft proposal contains no such stipulation.[28] The second sentence of said paragraph refers to rights of ownership in spacecraft. Such rights are not affected by the presence of the space object in outer space or by its return to earth. The Soviet draft has moderated previous negative attitudes toward international organizations. Accordingly, States may undertake space activities through international organizations (Para. 7), but "Sovereign rights over objects launched into outer space" may be retained by States only (Para. 8). Thus, the question of jurisdiction of international organizations over space vehicles is far from being settled.

b. The U.K. and U.A.R. Draft Declarations (Re Launching)

The U.K. draft declaration and the U.A.R. draft code do not contain express reference to jurisdiction. However, the jurisdiction of the launching State over its spacecraft may be inferred from the context of provisions.

c. The Belgian Working Paper on Liability

The Legal Sub-Committee also considered briefly a Working Paper submitted by the Belgian delegation on the Unification of Certain Rules Governing Liability for Damage caused by Space Vehicles.[29] Article 2 of the Working Paper suggests three criteria for the designation of the liable State by the plaintiff. These criteria could at the same time represent four spheres of concurrent jurisdictions: (a) "the State on whose territory the space device was launched", (b) "the State whose flag the space device

[28] A/AC.105/L.2.
[29] A/AC.105/C.2/L.7. For text see A/AC.105/12 at 10–12.

flies", and (c) "the State or States claiming ownership or co-ownership of the space device."

The second session of the Legal Sub-Committee concluded without any normative agreement being reached. In his Report the Chairman of the Sub-Committee suggested "that contacts and exchanges of views should continue, on which further action by the Committee will depend." According to the U.S. Representative, one of the areas of agreement that was reached during the session of the Sub-Committee included the principle that "jurisdiction over a space vehicle and its personnel in transit were retained by the State or international organization in which ownership of the vehicle resided at the time of launching."[30]

3. *The Third and Fourth Session of the Legal Sub-Committee*

Prior to the commencement of the third session of the Legal Sub-Committee the U.N. General Assembly unanimously adopted an outstanding resolution on outer space entitled *Declaration of Legal Principles Governing the Activities of States in the Exploration and Use of Outer Space* on December 13, 1963. This resolution laid down the basic principles of international space law which, as widely believed, have force of international law.

Paragraph 7 of the Declaration provides:

> The State on whose registry an object launched into outer space is carried shall retain jurisdiction and control over such object, and any personnel thereon, while in outer space. Ownership of objects launched into outer space, and of their component parts, is not affected by their passage through outer space or by their return to the earth. Such objects or component parts found beyond the limits of the State of registry shall be returned to that State, which shall furnish identifying data upon request prior to return.

The second sentence of this paragraph corresponds to both the second sentence of Paragraph 8 of the revised Soviet Draft Declaration of Basic Principles[31] and to the second sentence of Paragraph 7 of the U.S. Draft Declaration of Basic Principles. The first sentence is also reminiscent of the U.S. draft declaration with the marked difference, however, that the concept of State of registry was substituted for the words "jurisdiction at the time of launching." Finally, the closing sentence has been borrowed from Paragraph 5 of the U.S. Draft Declaration of Basic Principles. It represents a

30 Cf. A/AC.105/C.2/SR.16, 4. The term "in transit" used by the U.S. delegate apparently means space vehicle in transit through outer space and not through national airspace.

compromise between the original Soviet and U.S. opinions, that is, between the conditional return of space vehicles and astronauts including the prohibition of reconnaissance in outer space and no conditions whatsoever.[32]

Since in our opinion the *Declaration of Legal Principles* is a source of space law, the relationship between Paragraph 7 of the *Declaration* and Article VIII of the *Space Treaty* will have to be discussed in the context of the sources of space law with respect to rules governing the exercise of State jurisdiction in outer space and on celestial bodies.

During the third[33] and fourth[34] sessions of the Legal Sub-Committee the questions most discussed were those of liability, rescue and return.

a. Draft Agreements on Liability

The draft agreements on liability submitted by Belgium, the United States and Hungary are in conformity with each other, inasmuch as all of them attach liability to the launching State, although the term "liable State" does not have precisely the same meaning in all of the drafts.[35] Liability subsumes jurisdiction and *vice versa.*

b. Draft Agreements on Rescue and Return

The elaboration of detailed rules relating to rescue and return of astronauts and space vehicles is another aspect of the allocation of competing spheres of jurisdictions. In the course of the first and second parts of the third session, the Soviet Union[36] and the United States[37] submitted draft

[31] See *supra* n. 16.

[32] Paragraph 5 of the U.S. Draft Declaration of Basic Principles reads as follows: "States shall return to the launching authority any space vehicle or part that has landed by reason of accident, distress or mistake. Upon request, the launching authority shall furnish identifying data prior to return."

[33] The first part of the third session of the Legal Sub-Committee took place in Geneva from 9 March to 26 March, 1964. The statements have been summarized in U.N. Doc. A/AC.105/C.2/SR.29–37. The second part of the third session was held in New York from 5 to 23 October, 1964. The statements have been summarized in U.N. Doc. A/AC.105/C.2/SR.38–40. See also *Report of the Legal Sub-Committee* ... A/AC.105/19 (26 March 1964) and A/AC.105/21 (23 October 1964).

[34] The fourth session of the Legal Sub-Committee took place in New York from 20 September to 1 October, 1965. Cf. U.N. Doc. A/AC.105/C.2/SR.41–56. See also *Report of the Legal Sub-Committee* ... A/AC.106/29 (1 October 1965).

[35] Articles, 2, 3 & 6 of the Belgian (A/AC.105/C.2/L.7 Rev. 1, Rev. 2 & Corr. 122), Articles I, II & III of the U.S. (A/AC.105/C.2/L.8 Rev. 1 & Rev. 2) And Articles VI & VII of the Hungarian draft (A/AC.105/C.2/L.9). For texts see, U.N. Doc. A/AC. 105/C.2/W.2 rev. 3 (1965). See the Japanese proposal to the effect that only such States should be entitled to claim the return of their space vehicles which assumed liability for damage. A/AC.105/C.2/ SR.29–37 at 64.

[36] A/AC.105/C.2/L.2 Rev. 1. & 2.

[37] A/AC.105/C.2/L.9.

proposals on the subject, and a joint proposal was also submitted by Australia and Canada during the second part of the third session.[38]

The negotiations concerning these draft proposals represent variations on the concepts of exclusive and concurrent jurisdiction. According to these draft agreements the exercise of jurisdiction may be assumed by (a) the State of registry or international organization responsible for the launching,[39] (b) the launching State or as later modified by the Soviet Union, (c) the State which officially announced the launching.[40] The spheres of operative force of the rules proposed in the above-mentioned draft agreements may be determined *ratione loci, ratione instrumenti and ratione personae.*

(i) *The Exercise of State Jurisdiction Ratione Loci with Respect to Rescue.*

1. The U.S. proposals provided for the *exclusive prerogative* jurisdiction of the territorial State conditioned by the duty to return space vehicles and personnel. The local sovereign may exercise *complementary jurisdiction* with the State of registry in case assistance by the latter is necessary. However, the priority of the jurisdiction of the former prevails. [Article 2(1)].

2. The Soviet draft proposal also provides for the *exclusive jurisdiction* of the local sovereign. *Optional complementary jurisdiction* with the launching State depends on the request of the local sovereign in case of necessity. (Article 3)

3. The Australian-Canadian joint proposal suggested *exclusive jurisdiction* of the local sovereign and *optional complementary jurisdiction* of the State of registry in case the necessary rescue operation cannot be carried out by the Contracting Party.

4. The U.S. proposal suggested automatic *concurrent jurisdiction* of the Contracting Parties, subject to the priority of the jurisdiction of the State of registry [Article 2(1)] where rescue is attempted on the high seas or Antarctica.

5. The Soviet draft proposal provided for the *exclusive* jurisdiction with respect to rescue or search on the high seas and Antarctica, and direction of operations, as well as *optional complementary jurisdiction* of those Contracting States which the launching State would request. (Articles 4, 5 and Article 4 of the revised draft.) The Soviet insistence on the exclusive jurisdiction of the launching State with respect to rescue operations on the high seas elicited sharp criticism. The crux of the matter was, what should be the

[38] WG.I/17 Rev. 1.

[39] The U.S. draft, Article 1; Joint Proposal of Australia and Canada, Article 2; Statement of the Japanese delegate, WG.I/23.

[40] USSR Proposal, Article 2. *Ibid.*

reasonable limit of jurisdiction of the launching State in an area not constituting part of its territorial domain? Moreover, the issue was also coloured by humanitarian considerations. The Soviet position appeared to indicate uncertainty as to where to draw the limits of national security interests. The original Soviet draft went as far as claiming the exclusive right for the launching State to carry out search and rescue "of astronauts and spaceships in a zone of the high seas designated by itself." (Article 5). This provision was later modified. The Soviet Union still reserved, however, the competence for the State which officially announced the launching to give recommendations and technical advice to which the rescue operations should conform. In the opinion of the Soviet representative, the right to give general coordination meant something quite different from "direction or giving orders",[41] however, he did not elaborate upon this point. By the closing of the fourth session of the Legal Sub-Committee a general agreement emerged as to the formulation of an article governing rescue on the high seas.

6. The joint Australian-Canadian proposal suggested *complementary jurisdiction* of any Contracting Party who is in a position to carry out search and rescue on the one hand, and between the former and the State of registry, on the other hand. The State of registry would retain exclusive jurisdiction with respect to the direction of such operation (Article 4).

(ii) *The Exercise of State Jurisdiction Ratione Personae*

1. The U.S. proposal provided as a general rule that the territorial State may exercise *exclusive prerogative jurisdiction* and is bound to return astronauts who make emergency landings. It also provided as a specific rule that the territorial State and the State of registry shall exercise *complementary jurisdiction*. There are no formal conditions required for the return of astronauts [Article 3(1)].

2. The Soviet draft proposal, in essence, provides for the *concurrent jurisdiction* of the States affected. It is interesting to note that in this context the drafters used the language "return to their own country" instead of return to the launching State, which is a deviation from the wording of other articles (Article 8). The grammatical interpretation of these words suggests that the State of nationality of the astronauts is meant here. Accordingly, the State of nationality of the astronaut and not the State of nationality of the spacecraft would determine to which State the space crew would be returned. This is nothing more than the reception of the nationality principle of general international law in space law. The Soviet draft

[41] A/AC.105/C.2/SR.45 at 3–4. Cf. also the Soviet statement *ibid.* at 7–8. French criticism *ibid.* at 9. For U.S. position see, *ibid.* at 5.

did not provide for any additional condition as to the return of astronauts, similarly to those required for the return of space vehicles, except that spaceships were to have been launched in accordance with the *Declaration of Legal Principles.* (Article 5 of the revised draft proposal)[42] The *raison d'être* of Article 5 is recognizable also in Article 1(1) of the revised Soviet draft, which requires that all possible assistance be rendered to the crews of spaceships whether or not the space object is launched in outer space in accordance with the *Declaration of Legal Principles.* Beyond the apparent humanitarian consideration, the real significance of this construction was made plain by the Soviet, Rumanian and Bulgarian representatives in the Legal Sub-Committee. These delegations contended that astronauts involved in activities violating the *Declaration of Legal Principles* threaten the security of the subjacent State, and by implication they should be treated as spies or prisoners of war.[43]

Thus, the absence of requirement of the observation of the *Declaration of Legal Principles* with respect to assistance in distress, and the imposition of observance of the same with respect to their return, was meant to serve the purpose that a Contracting State may acquire jurisdiction over foreign nationals within its territorial domain and subsequently to subject them to its criminal jurisdiction. The same rationale would be secured with respect to space objects *inter alia* by making their return conditional on the same basis.

One of the main objectives of contemporary Soviet legal strategy can be observed at the very foundation of this scheme: namely, the Soviet attempt to mould space law according to the precepts of the Soviet concept of the international law of "peaceful coexistence." The answer of the majority of Member States of the U.N. was specific and to the point.[44] The gist of the Western response was that the Soviet proposal would leave the door wide open to the unilateral determination by one State of the nature of space activities,[45] and that safeguards should be provided against such arbitra-

[42] Soviet statement A/AC.105/C.2/SR.47 at 3. Bulgarian statement *ibid.* at 3–4. Romanian statement A/AC.105/C.2/SR.47 at 5–6. Hungarian statement A/AC.105/C.2/SR.44 at 8.

[43] Article 8 of the previous Soviet draft proposal did not refer to the *Declaration of Legal Principles.* The obligation "to facilitate the earliest possible return" was restricted to astronauts "envoys of mankind" in outer space.

[44] On the Soviet attempt to codify international law *uno ictu* in general terms whose meaning may be different to the States, and on the Western pragmatist, step-by-step problem-oriented approach and its built-in safeguards for a viable international legal order see McWhinney, 86–90, 101–106.

[45] U.N. Doc. A/AC.105/C.2/SR.55. 3. Mexican compromise A/AC.105/C.2/SR.43 at 3, 5. Canadian statement A/AC.105/C.2/SR.47 at 3. Australian statement *ibid.* at 6–7.

riness through, for example, arbitration.[46] This, however, was unacceptable to the Soviet Union and no articulate agreement has been reached.[47]

3. The joint Australian-Canadian proposal provided for the *complementary jurisdiction* of the local sovereign and the State of registration over personnel rescued within and outside territorial domain. No conditions were provided as to return. Their privileged position probably does not amount to immunity from the jurisdiction of the territorial State in absolute terms.

(iii) *Exercise of State Jurisdiction Ratione Instrumenti*

1. The U.S. draft provides for *concurrent jurisdiction* of the local sovereign and the State of registration subject to an optional condition as to the return of the space object [Article 3(2)].

2. In essence, the Soviet draft proposal provides for *concurrent jurisdiction* with formal conditions as to the return of space vehicles. (Article 6)

3. The joint Australian-Canadian proposal also provides for *concurrent jurisdiction* of the territorial State and the State of registration with the optional conditions as to return (Article 6).

The contribution of the third and fourth sessions to the clarification of certain principles of State jurisdiction may be summarized as follows. It became an accepted principle that astronauts and spacecraft making an emergency landing in the territory of a foreign State enjoy a privileged status and must be returned to the launching State or the State of registration of the space vehicle. With respect to the terrestrial effects of space activities the concept of territorial jurisdiction is unfettered, except in the case of emergency landing and return of spacecraft.[48] No attempt was made to draw up provisions governing the exercise of state jurisdiction according to types and categories of space vehicles and astronauts. Had the Soviet proposition regarding the qualification of the nature of space launchings according to the *Declaration of Legal Principles* been unconditionally

[46] Mexican suggestion U.N. Doc. A/AC.105/C.2/SR.46 at 5.

[47] U.N. Doc. A/AC.105/C.2/SR.45 at 8.

[48] For example the Swedish delegate pointed out that "every State must have the right to refuse representatives of a foreign State entry to areas which were of military importance or vital to the security of the State". U.N. Doc. A/AC.105/C.2/SR.29–37 at 56. France submitted a proposal stating: "A Contracting State shall not oppose the departure from its territory of persons on board a spacecraft which has made an emergency landing and shall do its utmost to assist them in making travel arrangements. The present article shall not be constructed as preventing juridical or administrative proceedings, or the enforcement of measures resulting from such proceedings, instituted by reason of the deeds or words of such persons after the completion of operations relating to the emergency landing". (WG.I/21). France also suggested that the local sovereign might retain the space object subject to the concurrence of the launching State. (WG.I/22).

accepted, it could probably have exercised much effect on the development of rules regarding State jurisdiction. In fact, the principle in whose respect general consensus appears to have been reached do not indicate that the immunity of astronauts and space vehicles in distress would depend on types of categories. Indeed, there is evidence that the Legal Sub-Committee did not consider it practical to introduce definitions unnecessarily at that time.[49]

4. *The Sixth and Seventh Session of the Legal Sub-Committee*

The most notable result of the work of the Legal Sub-Committee of the UNCOPUOS was the elaboration of the Agreement on Rescue and Return by the end of 1967. The Agreement will be analysed in detail in Chapter IV, paragraph 2(V) above. Regarding the preparation of a Draft Agreement on Liability for Space Vehicle Accidents, the Sub-Committee was bogged down by several questions of detail and could not make the expected progress.[50] Consideration and completion of this draft agreement was expected in 1969. A text was agreed to during the sixth session of the Legal Sub-Committee relative to the presentation of claims by States or international organizations and in respect of natural or juridical persons. The accepted principles do not introduce any new element, and, in fact, restate the principle of personal and territorial jurisdiction. Accordingly:

1. A Contracting Party which suffers damage, or whose natural or juridical persons suffer damage, may present a claim for compensation to respondent.
2. Subject to the provision of paragraph 1, a Contracting Party may also present to a respondent a claim in respect of damage sustained by any natural or juridical person in its territory.
3. A Contracting Party may also present a claim for damage sustained by its permanent residents in respect of whom neither the State of nationality nor the State in which the damage was sustained has presented a claim or notified its intention of presenting a claim.

[49] Cf. in this respect the statement of the French delegate suggesting an article to provide that all or part of the convention on rescue and return should be applied to certain categories of persons. U.N. Doc. A/AC.105/C.2/SR.47 at 9.

[50] The sixth session of the Legal Sub-Committee took place at the U.N. Office at Geneva on from 19 June to 14 July 1967. Cf. U.N. Doc. A/AC.105/C.2/SR. 74–85. *Report of the Legal Sub-Committee on the Work of its Sixth Session,* U.N. Doc. A/6804 (27 September 1967) Annex III, pp. 75. The Sub-Committee also held a special meeting on 19 April 1967 at the U.N. Headquarters where Mr. Eugeniusz Wyzner (Poland) was elected Chairman to succeed Mr. Manfred Lachs, who had been elected to the International Court of Justice. The Legal Sub-Committee held a special session at the U.N. Headquarters on 14 and 15 December 1967. Cf. U.N. Doc. A/AC.105/C.2/SR. 86–89. *Report of the Legal Sub-Committee on the Work of its Special Session . . .*, U.N. Doc. A/AC.105/43 (15 December 1967). The Legal Sub-Committee

4. No claim may be presented under this Convention with respect to the nationals of the respondent.[51]

a. *Questions Relative to the Definition of Outer Space*

No consensus has been reached in the UNOPUOS since 1958 regarding the definition and delimitation of outer space. The Legal Sub-Committee took up the issue of the definition of outer space at its sixth session. A general debate was held in plenary session on the agenda item and the scientific and Technical Sub-Committee was also consulted. France and Italy submitted draft recommendations concerning the questions relative to the definition and utilization of outer space.[52] France invited the Scientific and Legal Sub-Committee (i) to draw up a list of scientific criteria that could be helpful to the Legal Sub-Committee in its study relative to a definition of outer space, (ii) to give its views on the advantages and disadvantages of each scientific and technical criteria, (iii) to draw up a list of outer space activities which would appear to be in need of regulation, bearing in mind the specific requirements of the activities and their effects both on land and in airspace, and in outer space including celestial bodies, and (iv) to consider the order of priority for the study of such activities and their regulation.

The Italian draft recommendation requested the Scientific and Legal Sub-Committee to pass upon the following questions: (i) whether it is scientifically possible to determine accurately the line or zone of demarcation between airspace and outer space, (ii) and if so, at what altitude above sea level that line or zone of demarcation may be placed, (iii) whether it would be scientifically impossible or difficult to determine accurately such line or zone of demarcation, and (iv) whether it would not be preferable to establish it arbitrarily, and in that case at what altitude "having regard both to such physical data and practical considerations as may promote the development of activities in outer space and broader co-operation in this field among the States of the earth, without jeopardizing their right to freedom and their territorial security."

held its seventh session at the U.N. Office at Geneva from June 4th to 28th 1968. Cf. U.N. Doc. A/AC.105/C.2/SR. 90–110. *Report of the Legal Sub-Committee on the Work of its Seventh Session ...*, U.N. Doc. A/AC.105/45 (11 July 1968).

For developments regarding the Draft Agreement on Liability until the time of writing, see pp. 3–19 and Annex I., pp. 91 in the *Report of the Legal Sub-Committee on the Work of its Seventh Session.*

[51] *Ibid.* at 7.

[52] For the text of the proposals, see *International Cooperation in the Peaceful Uses of Outer Space, Report of the Committee on the Peaceful Uses of Outer Space,* U.N. Doc. A/6804 September 27, 1967) Annex III, at 73–75.

The Report of the Scientific and Technical Sub-Committee noted that there was consensus in the Sub-Committee "that it was not possible at the present time to identify scientific or technical criteria admitting a precise and lasting definition of outer space." It held the view that a definition of outer space "is likely to have important implications for the operational aspects of space research and exploration."[53]

The question of definition of outer space was again put on the agenda of the seventh session of the Legal Sub-Committee, only to decide in Resolution II to recommend to the UNCOPUOS "to place consideration of the study of questions relative to the definition of outer space on the agenda of the next session of the Legal Sub-Committee."[54]

b. Registration of Objects Launched into Outer Space

The Legal Sub-Committee considered a "Draft Convention concerning the registration of space objects launched into outer space for the exploration or use of outer space" by France under the agenda item of definition and utilization of outer space during its seventh session. No agreement was reached "on the inclusion in the resolution (of the Legal Sub-Committee) of the wording concerning (the) draft convention." It was then decided that the subject should be considered at the eighth session of the Legal Sub-Committee under the item of the agenda entitled "Study of questions relative to the utilization of outer space and celestial bodies, including the various implications of space communications."

The French Draft Convention drew attention to reference to registration in the Space Treaty and the advantages "at the international level, of the establishment of common rules governing the registration of objects launched into space for the exploration or use of outer space." Under the Convention every space object should be inscribed in a register "kept by a service under the supervision of one or more Government Parties to this Convention." Registration could be transferred (Article 1). The procedures of registration would be determined by the Governments maintaining the service. However, as a minimum requirement the registration should include (i) the registration number, (ii) the name of the object, where applicable, (iii) the name and address of the governmental or intergovernmental agency or non-governmental entity procuring the launching,

[53] *Ibid.* at 3–4.

[54] For the Czechoslovak and French proposals recommending to further consideration of the subject during the eighth session of the Legal Sub-Committee, see, U.N. Doc. A/AC.105/C.2/L.46 and L.50 Rev. 1 respectively *Ibid.* in Annex II, at 4–5. For Resolution II of the Legal Sub-Committee, see *Report of the Committee on the Peaceful Uses of Outer Space*, 1968. U.N. Doc. A/7285 at 136.

(iv) external specifications of the object (total weight, shape, dimensions and external component parts, and (v) the law applicable to the object and personnel if entities referred to above other than a State procures the launching (Article 2). The Parties to the Convention would be bound to provide information to each other, and also the registration would be accessible to the public. Article 3 provides detailed rules regarding the composition of the registration number. Articles 4 and 5 deal with procedural matters.

CHAPTER IV

THE *LEX LATA* REGARDING THE EXERCISE OF STATE JURISDICTION IN OUTER SPACE

In this Chapter we intend to state the law as it appears to be applicable today regarding the exercise of State jurisdiction over activities in outer space, including celestial bodies. Having examined the concept of State jurisdiction in general international law from the viewpoint of its applicability to space law, and analysed the U.N. practice regarding the jurisdictional aspects of liability, rescue and return, we still have to define the contribution of the Space Treaty to the concept of State jurisdiction in space law.

I. THE "SOURCES"

The *lex lata* regarding State jurisdiction over spacecraft and astronauts can be determined from the following "sources" of international space law: (a) international conventions; (b) international custom; (c) the general principles of law, and (d) General Assembly Resolution 1962 (XVIII) on the Declaration of Legal Principles.

1. International Conventions

The *Treaty Banning Nuclear Weapons Tests in the Atmosphere, in Outer Space and Under Water* of August 5, 1963,[1] and the Space Treaty of January 27, 1967 contain fundamental provisions regarding the exercise of State jurisdiction in outer space and on celestial bodies.[2]

[1] For the text of the Moscow Test Ban Treaty see Appendix III. See generally, Egon Schwelb, "The Nuclear Test Ban Treaty and International Law," 58 A.J.I.L. 643 (1964). I. G. Usachev, "Moskovskii dogovor o chastichnom zapreshchenii ispytanii iadernogo oruzhiia i mezhdunarodnoe pravo," *Sovetskoe Gosudarstvo i Pravo,* No. 3. 1964 pp. 72–78. G. P. Zhukov, "Iadernaia Demilitarizatsiia Kosmosa," *ibid.* at 80.

[2] For the text of the treaty see *Appendix II.* See also *Analysis and Background Data – Staff Report* (1967) 84 pp. As of March 1, 1967, the treaty had been signed on behalf

Article I of the *Test Ban Treaty* provides:

1. Each of the Parties to this Treaty undertakes to prohibit, to prevent, and not to carry out any nuclear weapon test explosion, or any other nuclear explosion, *at any place under its jurisdiction or control:*

(a) in the atmosphere; beyond its limits, *including outer space;* ... [Emphasis added.]

This provision of the Treaty subsumes that *inter alia* outer space may be an area which could be subjected to the jurisdiction or control of a Contracting Party.[3] This provision at first glance seems to be at variance with the principle of non-appropriation of outer space which was declared by General Assembly Resolution 1721 (XVI) of December 20, 1961, and later confirmed by the Declaration of Legal Principles. This provision is also a cardinal rule of the Space Treaty. We have pointed out above that State jurisdiction on the high seas is not jurisdiction over the high seas as such. This conclusion *a fortiori* applies to outer space and celestial bodies. Would it be true, then, that this provision of the *Test Ban Treaty* is in conflict with Article II of the Space Treaty which provides that "outer space, including the Moon and other celestial bodies, is not subject to national appropriation by claim of sovereignty, by means of use or occupation, or by any other means?"

In our opinion the answer is definitely no. A treaty must be interpreted "in

of 72 governments. The treaty has not yet entered into force. For the debates regarding the provisions of the *Space Treaty* see the summary records of the fifth session of the Legal Sub-Committee of the UNCOPUOS; A/AC.105/C.2/SR. 57–73. The *Space Treaty* was approved by United Nations General Assembly Resolution 2222(XXI) of December 19, 1966. *Report of the Legal Sub-Committee on the Work of its Fifth Session* Annex III, pp. 45 in the *Report of the Committee on the Peaceful Uses of Outer Space* U.N. Doc. A/6431 (22 September 1966). See also *Report of the Legal Sub-Committee on the Work of its Fifth Session* A/AC.105/35 (16 September 1966). For text of the Treaty see *inter alia,* 4 *U.N. Monthly Chronicle* 42–46 (January 1967). Concerning developments regarding the *Space Treaty* see, 3 *U.N. Monthly Chronicle* 5 (February 1966); *ibid.* 25 (May 1966); *ibid.* 48, 93–122 (October 1966); 4 *U.N. Monthly Chronicle* 34–46 (January 1967); *ibid.* 9 February 1967). The *N.Y. Times,* December 9, 1966 p. 18; Leavitt, W., "The Proposed Space Treaty: Is There Less There Than Meets the Eye?," 50 *Air Force and Space Digest* 43–45 (January 1967); Betty Goetz Lall, "Cooperation and Arms Control in Outer Space," *Bulletin of the Atomic Scientists* 34–37 (November 1966). Statement by Arthur J. Goldberg, "U.S. Notes Progress of Negotiations on Peaceful Uses of Outer Space, the Moon, and Other Celestial Bodies," *Dep't State Bull.* 321–325 (August 29, 1966), cf. also *ibid.* 249 (August 15, 1966); for Soviet reflection on their draft proposal regarding the space treaty see, V. S. Vereshchetin, "Pravovoe formy mezhdunarodnogo sotrudnichestva SSSR v mirnom osvoenie kosmicheskogo prostranstva," *Sovetskoe Gosudarstvo i Pravo,* No. 1 68–73 (1967).

[3] See Egon Schwelb, *loc. cit. supra* at 643. As to whether the provisions of the *Test Ban Treaty* are applicable to the Moon see "The Law of Celestial Bodies," by the *present writer,* 6 I.J.I.L. 224–225 (1966).

good faith in accordance with the ordinary meaning to be given to the terms of the treaty in their context *in the light of its object and purpose.*"[4] Consequently, it may be stated with certainty that it was the purpose of the framers of the *Test Ban Treaty* to prohibit any nuclear explosion in any place as provided in the Treaty, whether or not such place was under the jurisdiction or control of any of the Contracting Parties at the time when the Treaty was concluded. The *Test Ban Treaty* may not have been intended to prejudice any eventual development as to the extension of State jurisdiction or control to new areas. Indeed, the Treaty subsumes that any place where nuclear weapon test explosions would be carried out would *ipso facto* be subjected to the jurisdiction or control of the state concerned, even if only for the period of the test or until its after-effects cease.

This conclusion seems sufficient to substantiate one of the main points of this study, namely that State jurisdiction may be exercised in areas or over territories of outer space and celestial bodies as such, notwithstanding the proscription of national appropriation of outer space.

This type of jurisdiction is commensurately limited relative to its *functional scope.* We suggest that this type of State jurisdiction in space law, that is comparable to the nature of jurisdictional claims regarding the exploitation of the resources of the sea-bed and subsoil beyond territorial jurisdiction, should be called *functional jurisdiction.* The concept of territoriality is not and cannot be the legal basis of *functional jurisdiction.* The effect of the *Moscow Partial Test Ban Treaty* on the exercise of State jurisdiction in outer space and on celestial bodies is, that the exercise of *functional jurisdiction* which would be tantamount to the explosion of nuclear devices in this environment is prohibited.

The provisions of the Space Treaty will be analysed in detail separately. The applicability of other international conventions to outer space, as regards jurisdiction among other aspects, may well have to be decided on a pragmatic, *ad hoc* basis in the light of current developments and needs.[5]

2. *International Custom*

The concept of nationality, the protective and universality principle, and the customary rules regarding State jurisdiction in national airspace are all applicable to the exercise of State jurisdiction over space activities. These customary rules govern the exercise of State jurisdiction over space activ-

[4] Article 27 of the *Draft Article on the Law of Treaties* prepared by the International Law Commission. 61 A.J.I.L. 271 (1967).

[5] Lachs, 46.

ities in the environment where the traditional sphere of their operation is. Customary rules of international law, in general, cannot be regarded as applicable to the exercise of State jurisdiction over activities in outer space proper, unless there is evidence showing that their applicability is in harmony with the principles of international space law and State practice. The rules and principles of customary international law regarding State jurisdiction that were surveyed above provide a general guide as to the applicable law at the present time.

3. General Principles of Law

The general principles of law bearing upon the exercise of State jurisdiction concern the status of aliens, self-preservation, vessels in distress and restrictions upon the exclusive jurisdiction of States.

The Rapporteur on the *Spanish Zone of Morocco Claims* (1923)[6] said that "the maintenance of internal peace and social order" is the prime object and duty of every State. This principle is expressed in the provision that the State of registration of the spacecraft exercises jurisdiction and control over its spacecraft and personnel thereof. It follows from this general principle that the jurisdiction of the State of registration must extend beyond the confines of the spacecraft, both with respect to its own astronauts and within reasonable limits also to foreign astronauts. The decision of the Mexican-U.S. General Claims Commission (1923) in the *Dickson Car Wheel Co. Case* (1931) stated that foreigners generally may not claim damages for injuries suffered in consequence of extraordinary measures resorted to by States in order to save themselves from imminent dangers.[7] Since extraordinary and imminent dangers must be reckoned with in connection with space activities, it stands to reason to conclude that States would assume jurisdiction in order to avoid or prevent such situations, and if damage is caused to other States it may not necessarily involve the liability of the former State.

The Hoff (The Rebecca) Case (1929) stated the principle that vessels in distress enjoy a certain degree of immunity from territorial jurisdiction. The case also proved that it is basically the principle of self-preservation that permits a person to have recourse to extraordinary measures to save himself. The same principle justifies the privileged treatment of astronauts and space vehicles making distress landings in the territory of a foreign State.

[6] Rapport III (1924) 2 UNRIAA, p. 615, at 642.
[7] Op. of Comm. 1931 p. 175, at 192–193.

The line of reasoning behind the Dissenting Opinion of Judge Moore in *The Lotus* Case (1927),[8] the decision in the case of the *Le Louis* (1817)[9] and the oral argument of the U.S. counsel in the *Fur Seal Arbitration* of 1893,[10] is evidence that States have a right to interfere with the navigation of other States on the high seas for the purpose of "repelling injury."[11] We think this principle is applicable to space law. Consequently, a State may assume jurisdiction to interfere with the space activities of another State in the following cases: if there is grave suspicion that a spacecraft is equipped with nuclear weapons or other weapons of mass destructive effect in violation of international law or if a space device goes out of control and represents an imminent danger to the safety of space navigation; or where in consequence of a violation of international space telecommunications regulations, the broadcast of radio signals from outer space causes continuous interference with space communications.

The principle of territorial jurisdiction also imposes certain obligations on the local sovereign. The authorities of the State in whose territory foreign astronauts or spacecraft make a distress landing are liable to protect them against injurious acts by individuals from within its territory. However, international law does not impose upon States greater responsibility for the safety of astronauts and spacecraft within their territory than do their own laws regarding aliens.

The ruling of the Permanent Court of Arbitration in the *North Atlantic Coast Fisheries Case* (1910)[12] sheds light on the interdependence of rights and treaty obligations, as well as on the principle of good faith. This may be cited as another precedent supporting our arguments regarding the legal basis of the concept of "functional jurisdictions." The Permanent Court of Arbitration held that the treaty obligations of Great Britain to allow inhabitants of the United States to maintain fishing righs in certain of her territorial waters, did not affect Great Britain's other rights, i.e., her right to issue regulations regarding the protection and preservation of fisheries. On this analogy it may equally be said that the obligation of States not to appropriate outer space or celestial bodies in any way does not affect their other rights, original or derived, to legislate for the protection of their lawful interests, the preservation of resources in outer space and to issue regulations "desirable or necessary on grounds of public order and

[8] P.C.I.J. Series A, 10, p. 69.
[9] 2 Dods., p. 210, at 243.
[10] G. B./U. S. . . . 1 Moore, I. A., p. 755.
[11] The *Le Louis* (1817) *ibid.* at 246.
[12] I.H.C.R., p. 141, at 169.

morals"[13] without unnecessarily interfering with the principle of the freedom of outer space. Thus, it may be argued that States can assume "functional jurisdiction" over certain areas of the Moon surrounding their space stations, installations, locations of scientific experiments and eventually over mining areas. The balance between the treaty obligation as to non-appropriation of outer space and eventual claims to exercise "functional jurisdiction" in outer space would seem at present to rest basically on the principle of good faith. In the same decision the Permanent Court of Arbitration added:

> The line in question is drawn according to the principle of international law that treaty obligations are to be *executed* in perfect good faith, therefore excluding the right to legislate *at will* concerning the subject-matter of the treaty, and *limiting the exercise of sovereignty of the State bound by a treaty with respect to that subject-matter to such acts as are consistent with the treaty.*[14]

This passage shows that the inherent measure of good faith is reasonableness. We claim that the proposed concept of "functional jurisdiction" accords with the principle of good faith. The aim that the proposed concept is capable of fulfilling, we think, is to serve pragmatic needs that will arise as soon as the exploitation of outer space and the Moon becomes feasible, necessary and economical. Consequently, "functional jurisdiction" would by implication and prescription satisfy the standard of reasonableness. Thus we came a full circle demonstrating that the proposed concept is compatible also with one of the general principles of law.

4. *The Provisions of the Declaration of Legal Principles*

The Space Treaty is an international convention whose legal binding force cannot be challenged. What role, if any, can the Declaration of Legal Principles play after the entry into force of the Space Treaty?[15] The Declaration may remain or become a relevant legal document relative to Member States which either did not adhere to the Treaty on Outer Space, or would later withdraw from it under article XIV thereof. There are States who for one reason or another did not become Parties to the Treaty. Further, any State Party to the Treaty may later withdraw from it.[16] Now two questions may be asked: can States which are not Parties to the Space Treaty be regarded as being bound by the Declaration of Legal Principles, or must we

[13] *Ibid.* at 171.

[14] *Ibid.* at 169. Quoted from Cheng, *General Principles of Law,* 124. Emphasis supplied by Cheng.

[15] Cf. Article XIV.

[16] Cf. Article XVI.

fall back completely on the plane of general international law? These questions may be treated from two aspects. The first one concerns the legal nature of the Declaration of Legal Principles, and only after having solved this formal question can we examine what contribution the Declaration itself makes to the substantive rules governing State jurisdiction over space activities.

ad 1. The literature regarding the legal status of the General Assembly resolutions in general, and the status of the Declaration of Legal Principles in particular, has grown to sizeable proportions.[17] The analysis of the legal nature of General Assembly resolutions is not within the limited scope of this work. We have dealt with this question in greater detail elsewhere.[18] It will suffice here to refer to our conclusion argued in previous publications, according to which the Declaration of Legal Principles is a "formal declarative source" of international space law. There is a school of thought advocating that the U.N. General Assembly resolutions as such, have no legal force, because they are only recommendations subject to the exceptions stipulated by the U.N. Charter itself. This opinion, however, has been at-

[17] Jenks, 186. Cheng, "United Nations Resolutions on Outer Space: 'Instant' International Customary Law?," 5 I.J.I.L. 23–48. Csabafi, "The Law of Celestial Bodies," 6 I.J.I.L. 217 (1966). Vlasic, "The Growth of Space Law 1957–65: Achievements and Issues," *Yearbook of Air and Space Law,* (Mankiewicz ed.) 374–380 (1965). See generally, Rosalyn Higgins, *The Development of Customary International Law Through the Political Organs of the U.N.* (1963). Oscar Schachter, "The Development of International Law Through the Legal Opinions of the U.N. Secretariat," 25 B.Y.I.L. 91–125 (1948). Skubiszewski, "Forms of Participation of International Organizations in the Law-making Process," 18 *International Organization* 790–805 (1964), Jenks, "The Impact of International Organizations on International Law," 37 *Grotius Society Transactions* 23 (1951). F. B. Sloan, "Recommendations of the General Assembly," 2 *Columbia Journal of Trans-National* Law 210 (1965). Johnson, "The Conclusions of International Conferences," 35 B.Y.I.L. (1959). Eagleton, *International Government,* 197 (1948). Schwarzenberger, *A Manual of International Law,* 124 (1947). *International Law,* vol. I (2nd ed., 1949) pp. 539 *et seq.* Goodrich and Hambro, "Charter of the U.N.," 96 (1946). Kunz, "The Nature of Customary International Law," 47 A.J.I.L. 662 (1953). Fenwick, "The Sources of International Law," 16 *Mich. L. Rev.* 393–395 (1918). Pollock, "The Sources of International Law," 2 *Colum. L. Rev.* 511 (1902). F. A. Vallat, "The Competence of the United Nations General Assembly," 97 *Hague Recueil* 203 (1959). F. B. Sloan, "The Binding Force of a 'Recommendation' of the General Assembly of the United Nations," 25 B.Y.I.L. 37 (1948). For Soviet literature see, M. U. Yanovsky, "Soviet Science on the Legal Force of U.N. General Assembly Resolutions," (In Russian with summary in English at 121–122.) S.Y.I.L. 1964–1965 111–121 (1966). G. I. Tunkin, *Droit International Public,* 101–112 (1965). – "Remarks on the Juridical Nature of Customary Norms of International Law," 49 *Calif. L. R.* 419 (1961). Zhukov, *op. cit. supra* at 80. G. S. Stashevskii, "Sputniki sviazi i mezhdunarodnoe pravo," S.G.iP. No. 12. (66) (1964).

[18] Csabafi, "The General Assembly Resolutions on Outer Space as Sources of Space Law," VIIIth Colloquium 337–361. For favourable reflections see, John Michael Kemp, *op. cit. supra;* Markoff, *op. cit. supra.*

tacked in the theory of international law,[19] and it has also been shaken to its very foundations by the U.N. practice relative to the progressive development of international space law.[20]

This writer's opinion may be summarized as follows: The positive rule-making practice of the United Nations General Assembly regarding the peaceful uses of outer space should be considered as a unique case, rather than a breakthrough in international legislative technique. In the light of contemporary developments, such as membership in the U.N. and financing the organizations expenses, it would seem doubtful if the permanent members of the Security Council would choose to live by this precedent.

The *travaux préparatoires* (i.e., the summary records of the fifth session of the Legal Sub-Committee of the UNCOPUOS) prove that the Declaration of Legal Principles was regarded by Member States as expressing the *lex lata*.[21]

[19] See especially, Richard A. Falk, "On the Quasi-Legislative Competence of the General Assembly," 60 A.J.I.L. 782–791 (1966). "New Approaches to the Study of International Law," 61 A.J.I.L. 487 *et seq.* (1967). Cf. also *ibid.* at 630–631. McWhinney, 166.

[20] For the illustration of the U.N. practice see the statements of the U.S., the Soviet and the U.K. delegates made on the occasion of the adoption of the *Declaration of Legal Principles*. The U.S. Representative to the United Nations said:

> ... we believe these principles reflect international law as it is accepted by the Members of the United Nations. The U.S. for its part intends to respect these principles. We hope that the conduct which the resolution commends to nations in the exploration of outer space will become the practice of all nations.

U.N. Doc. A/PV. 1284 at 38–40.

The Soviet Representative to the United Nations said:

> The U.S. considers that these legal principles reflect international law as it is accepted by the Members of the U.N. and that on its part the U.S. intends to respect these principles. The Soviet Union will also respect the principles contained in this declaration.

U.N. Doc. A/AC.1/P.V. 1342 at 27–46. Cf. also U.N. Doc. A/AC.105/C.2/SR. 48, 10–11.

The U.K. Representative to the United Nations said:

> My Government intends to respect these principles and believes that the conduct they enjoy will become the practice of every State and thus serve to ensure the exploration and use of outer space for peaceful purposes.

U.N. Doc. A/AC. 1284 at 36–40. Cf. Also the statement of the Canadian delegate: A/C.1/SR 1346 at 189. The Indian delegate's statement U.N. Doc. A/AC.105/C.2/SR.22, 10. But see the notorious statement of the French delegate denying the binding nature of General Assembly resolutions 1721(XVI) and 1962 (XVIII)A/AC.105/PV.3 at 48. For the Communist Chinese position, see Hungdah Chiu (assisted by R. R. Edwards) "Communist China's Attitude Toward the United Nations: A Legal Analysis", 62 A.J.I.L. 28–32 (1968).

[21] See the following statements: Bulgaria: U.N. Doc. A/AC.1005/6. 2/SR.61, 4; Romania: *ibid.* at 6; USSR: *id.* SR. 62, 11; Mexico: *id.* at 7–8; Brazil, *id.;* Poland: *id.* at 6; UAR: *id.* at 2, 3, 4; Czechoslovakia: *id.* at 12 U.S.A.: *id.* SR. 63 at 5; USSR: *id.* at 6; Hungary: *ibid.* SR.64 at 3; U.S.A.: *ibid.* SR.64 at 10 India *id.* at 10; Japan: *ibid.*

Thus the answer to the first question may be summed up as follows. The obligations assumed by States in the Declaration of Legal Principles are similar to those which they assumed in the Space Treaty. It is less relevant whether the declaration itself has a declaratory or law-making nature, than the recognition that the fundamental principles the Declaration states are binding upon Member States of the U.N. The preceding circumstances of the adoption of the Declaration of Legal Principles prove our point. The legal principles it enunciates are based on the practice of States and not merely on negotiations among them. Resolutions 1721 (XVI) and 1962 (XVIII) together provide sufficient ground to regard them as evidence of customary international law.[22]

There is no appreciable difference between the proceedings attending the Declaration of Legal Principles and those characteristic of treaty making. Vlasic pointed out that international debate, governmental consultations, drafts, controversy, compromise and finally voting were the constitutive stages leading to the *opinio juris communis*.[23] The expressed intention of States to make these principles "declaratory of legal obligations"[24] and the unanimity of their adoption make up for the absence of formal signature of ratification. Why then did the States, supposedly intentionally, use the form of General Assembly resolutions to develop the law of outer space? It may be argued that the speed with which such consensus could be achieved and the built-in safeguards of the U.N. machinery were reasons of primary consideration. In retrospect, the history of the U.N. practice regarding the progressive development of space law admits of the conclusion that the special requirements of man's conquest of outer space could adequately be satisfied through the use of this unique law-making process.

ad. 2. Since, in our view, the legal principles enunciated by the Declaration have a force of international law we may now proceed to examining the legal relationship between two states of whom at least one is not party

SR.64 at 13; Canada: *ibid.* SR.65 at 3; U.K.: *id.* at 5; Argentina: *ibid.* SR.66 at 3; Hungary: *id.* at 4; India: *id.* at 6; U.S.A.: *id.* at 8; India: *id.* at 10; U.S.A.: *id.* at 11; USSR: *ibid.* SR.70 at 3.

[22] The Permanent Court of International Justice stated in *The Lotus Case* (1927) that the *opinio juris* is an inference from all the circumstances. In the *West Rand Central Gold Mining Co. v. R.* [1905], 2 K.B. 391 at p. 407, it was held that a customary rule must be of a nature that it hardly could be supposed that "any civilised State would repudiate it." The International Court of Justice held in the case, *Right of Innocent Passage over Indian Territory* (Portugal/India) (I.C.J. Reports (1960), 6.) *Inter partes* customary rule can also be created by particular practice and mutual acceptance of the States concerned. Cf. Cheng, *op. cit. supra.*

[23] *Ibid.* at 377.

[24] *Id.* at 378.

to the Treaty on outer space. If we recognize the legal nature of the Declaration and the principles contained therein, then it accords with logic to argue that, such being the case, the juridical relationship between State A and B, of whom at least one is not party to the Space Treaty, is governed by the Declaration of Legal Principles. It remains to ask whether the legal principles of the Declaration and the Space Treaty respectively regarding State jurisdiction are different from each other in substance. If they are identical then it makes no difference in terms of legal rules whether the Declaration of Legal Principles or the Space Treaty governs the exercise of State jurisdiction in outer space. A comparison of the provisions of the Declaration and the Space Treaty shows that the principle of State jurisdiction over spacecraft and astronauts has been stated in almost identical words in both instruments. Still, the relevant provisions of the Space Treaty differ from those of the Declaration in the following aspects:

1. The Declaration of Legal Principles has been addressed to all States; the Space Treaty is binding only upon States Parties to it.

2. The Treaty specifically stipulates that the State of registration of the space vehicle retains jurisdiction over such objects also "on a celestial body." This modification does not make any substantial difference.

3. Ownership is also extended by the Treaty to include "objects landed or constructed on a celestial body."

4. The principle of returning to the State of origin any space objects or parts found beyond its territory and the principle that the State of origin must furnish identifying data prior to the return of such objects applies to all States under the Declaration, while under the Treaty these principles apply only to States Parties to it.

5. Article XII of the Space Treaty provides for open access to "all stations, installations, equipment and space vehicles on the Moon and other celestial bodies." The Declaration contains no comparable provision. This is a basic difference, because with respect to the States Parties to the Treaty *inter se* the principle of exclusive quasi-territorial jurisdiction has been put aside. Thus, it follows that under the Declaration of Legal Principles the jurisdiction of the State of registration over its installations, etc., on celestial bodies is unfettered. A State not a Party to the Treaty is under no legal obligation to open its stations on the Moon to representatives of other States. It follows from the Declaration that the principle of quasi-territorial jurisdiction overrides the principle of personal jurisdiction. The situation is the reverse in cases where the Space Treaty applies; namely, the quasi-territorial jurisdiction of the State of registration of the spacecraft

yields to the personal jurisdiction of the State whose nationals the observers are.

6. The Declaration of Legal Principles does not contain a provision comparable to that of Article IV of the Space Treaty. This Article provides that "the Moon and other celestial bodies shall be used . . . *exclusively for peaceful purposes.*" (Emphasis added.) This means that "the establishment of military bases, installations and fortifications, the testing of weapons and the conduct of military maneuvers on celestial bodies" are forbidden. The scope of this provision is specifically restricted to celestial bodies. The military uses of outer space are not prohibited except that the launching into outer space or the installation on celestial bodies of nuclear weapons and weapons of mass destruction is prohibited. There is a marked difference between the status of outer space and celestial bodies, inasmuch that celestial bodies are set aside *exclusively* for peaceful purposes. On the other hand, it is also clear that the conduct of military manoeuvres in and military uses of outer space is not prohibited if such activities are carried out in accordance with international law and the U.N. Charter in general, and are not aggressive, in particular. The jurisdictional consequence of the examples mentioned above seems to be that States Parties to the Treaty on Outer Space could not claim immunity for their installations located on a celestial body solely on the analogy of the immunity of man-of-war in general international law. Such claims could, however, be maintained under the Declaration of Legal Principles which does not demilitarize celestial bodies in the sense the Space Treaty does. One final observation in this context should still be made. The exclusion of the analogy of men-of-war regarding the exemption of spacecraft on celestial bodies would not foreclose the analogy of public vessels as well.

Having first proved that the Declaration of Legal principles has legal binding force and, second, pointed out in what manner its provisions differ from those of the Space Treaty, we may now conclude by stating that the Declaration of Legal Principles can substitute and complement the provisions of the former although the scope of the provisions of the two instruments is not identical.

II. THE EFFECT OF ARTICLE VIII OF THE SPACE TREATY ON THE CONCEPT OF STATE JURISDICTION

1. The Relationship between Article VIII and the General Principles of International Space Law

The Treaty on *outer space* codified the *opinio juris* regarding outer space of Member States of the United Nations which evolved during the past decade.[25] The Treaty was hailed as an important step towards peace, complementing the examples set by the 1959 Antarctic Treaty and the 1963 limited Test Ban Treaty.[26] The Soviet representative said *inter alia* that the treaty was the fruit of a collective effort of many delegations.[27] The Chairman of the Legal Sub-Committee pointed out that with the adoption of the treaty, international law would acquire a new dimension.[28] The delegations to the U.N. generally recognised that the treaty extended the rule of international law into the realm of outer space and guaranteed the rights of all States regardless of their technological capabilities. The hope was expressed that a favourable climate had been created for an agreement on the non-proliferation of nuclear weapons and the banning of nuclear tests in all environments.

The representative of France drew attention to the fact that the provisions of the Space Treaty "constituted an innovation from the standpoint of traditional international law based on the sovereignty of states."[29] This would cause difficulties, he claimed, in the implementation of the Treaty and he therefore suggested that the question of definition and delimitation of outer space and the questions relative to the utilization and exploitation of outer space and celestial bodies should be studied urgently. The representatives of Burma, Ceylon, India, Kenya, Mexico, Pakistan and the United Arab Republic expressed their dissatisfaction with the wording of Article IV because, they claimed, it would by implication permit military uses of outer space.[30]

[25] The stages of the evolution of *opinio juris communis* were marked by the resolutions of the U.N. General Assembly on outer space.

[26] Cf. "Peaceful Uses of Outer Space: Assembly Adopts Three Resolutions", 4 *U.N. Monthly Chronicle* 34–46 (January 1967). For the U.S. representative's statement see, *ibid.* pp. 39, 41.

[27] *Id.* at 40, 41.

[28] *Id.* at 39.

[29] *Id.* at 40.

[30] *Id.* at 40. For a summary of statements regarding the *Space Treaty,* see *id.* at 39–42.

a. The Fifth Session of the Legal Sub-Committee

The question of State jurisdiction over space vehicles and astronauts was one of the issues regarding which agreement could easily be achieved in the first part[31] of the Legal Sub-Committee's fifth session.[32] Article 5 of the Soviet and Article 7 of the U.S. draft treaties are almost identical.[33]

The U.S. draft proposal was modified and brought into harmony with the Soviet draft with respect to the geographical scope of the provisions governing both outer space and celestial bodies.

Arthur J. Goldberg, the U.S. Representative to the United Nations, pointed out that the two articles were based on paragraph 7 of the Declaration of Legal Principles. He stated that the Soviet text, with a few changes, would be acceptable to the United States.[34]

Gotlieb, the Canadian Representative, said in turn that the jurisdiction and control of the State of registration would apply not only to personnel occupying the space vehicle, but also to astronauts leaving the object

[31] Statement by Arthur J. Goldberg, U.S. Ambassador to the United Nations before the Legal Sub-Committee of the UNCOPUOS at Geneva, Switzerland, on August 3, 1966, U.S./U.N. press release 4899 dated August 5, 1966. See also, "U.S. Notes Progress of Negotiations on Peaceful Uses of Outer Space, the Moon, and other Celestial Bodies", 55 *Dept. State Bull.* 321–325 (August 29, 1966).

[32] The first part of the Legal Sub-Committee's fifth session took place at Geneva from 12 July to 4 August and the second part in New York from 12 to 16 September 1966. Cf. U.N. Doc. A/AC.1005/C.2/SR. 57–70 and 71–73 respectively. *Report of the Legal Sub-Committee ...* A/AC.105/35 (16 September 1966). *Interim Report by the Chairman* A/AC.105/C.2/L.16 (6 September 1966).

[33] Article 5 of the Soviet draft treaty reads as follows:

> A State Party to the Treaty on whose registry an object launched into outer space is carried shall retain jurisdiction and control over such object, and over any personnel thereon, while it is in outer space or on a celestial body. Ownership of objects launched into outer space, including objects delivered to or constructed on a celestial body, and of their component parts, shall not be affected by their presence in outer space or on a celestial body or by their return to earth. Sub objects or component parts found beyond the limits of the State Party to the Treaty on whose registry they are carried shall be returned to that State, which shall, upon request, furnish identifying data prior to their return.

Article 7 of the U.S. draft treaty provides:

> A State may exercise control over its facilities and persons participating in its activities on a celestial body. Ownership of objects shall not be affected by their being landed, constructed or used on a celestial body.

[34] A/AC.105/C.SR.66 at 11. The U.S. Representative proposed the following changes:

> deletion of the words "it is" in the phrase "while it is in outer space or on a celestial body" in the English text of Article V of the Soviet draft. The words "delivered to" in part of the second sentence of Article V which read "including objects delivered to or constructed on a celestial body" could be replaced by the word "landed". The words "shall not be affected" in that same sentence could be replaced by the words "is not affected".

whether in outer space or on a celestial body.[35] Morozov, the Soviet Representative, expressed his support for the suggestion of the Canadian delegation and reaffirmed that the text of Article V of the Soviet draft treaty covered both the object launched into outer space and its crew, whether they are inside or outside the object.[36]

The French delegate expressed his doubt as to the desirability of including provisions regarding terrestrial effects of jurisdiction, when neither of the two draft treaties contained any other provision relating to terrestrial activities.[37] The Italian delegate drew attention to the fact that besides States, international organizations might also engage in space activities, and consequently the language of Article V of the Soviet draft should be changed accordingly.[38]

After this short debate Article VIII was agreed upon in the Working Group of the Legal Sub-Committee at its first meeting on July 27, 1966.[39]

b. State Jurisdiction over Spacecraft and Astronauts

Article VIII provides:

> A State Party to the Treaty on whose registry an object launched into outer space is carried shall retain jurisdiction and control over such object, and over any personnel thereof, while in outer space or on a celestial body. Ownership of objects launched into outer space, including objects landed or constructed on a celestial body, and of their component parts, is not affected by their presence in outer space or on a celestial body or by their return to Earth. Such objects or component parts found beyond the limits of the State Party to the Treaty on whose registry they are carried shall be returned to that State Party, which shall, upon request, furnish identifying data prior to their return.

Three related concepts are mentioned in this article:
(i) jurisdiction and control; (ii) ownership, and (iii) return.

ad (i) Jurisdiction and Control. The concept of jurisdiction and control has four constitutive elements: the State of registration, the object, the personnel of the spacecraft, and the *locus* of jurisdiction and control. The State of registration is supposed to be a State Party to the Treaty. Article

[35] *Id.*
[36] *Id.*
[37] *Id.*
[38] "The Parties to the Treaty" should be substituted for "A State Party to the Treaty," *id.*
[39] Interim Report by the Chairman of the Legal Sub-Committee, A/AC.105/C.2/L.16. WC/L.1 and Corr. 1. *Ibid.* Annex I. 2.

VIII does not *expressis verbis* provide that States other than the State of registration of the space vehicle may also retain jurisdiction and control. There is evidence in the U.N. practice that States were opposed to the idea that only the State of registration should be held liable for damage caused by such spacecraft.[40]

(i) Article VII of the Treaty stipulates the liability of the State that launches or procures the launching, or the State from whose territory or facility the launching took place. The third sentence of Article VIII provides that the object found beyond the territorial limits of the State on whose registry such object is carried shall be returned to that State. The Space Treaty does not make the registration of space vehicles compulsory. Article VIII refers to a national registry similar to the Declaration of Legal Principles. The provision of General Assembly Resolution 1721 (XVI) regarding the registration of space launchings with the U.N. Secretariat has no counterpart in the treaty.[41] Thus, if a Contracting Party does not enter the object in its national registry of space objects, the determination of the State of jurisdiction or the State of liability can only be based on the above-mentioned criteria of Article VII. The wording of the article seems to allow States involved in a joint space project to decide for themselves on whose registry the object should be carried.[42] It may be inferred from the reference in Article VIII to the State on whose registry an object is carried that dual or multiple registration is excluded. Quite clearly the registration of a space object in a national registry cannot be considered the constitutive factor for the exercise of State jurisdiction over such objects. Registration constitutes only *prima facie* evidence for State jurisdiction. As of the time of writing there is no evidence to the effect that the registration of space objects would be any different from the procedure established for the registration of ocean-going ships.

The reference in Article VIII to "a State Party to the Treaty on whose registry an object launched into outer space is carried" (hereafter referred to as "State of registration") is reminiscent of the theory of "floating territory," or "theory of property." It is an established rule that the State under whose flag a ship is sailing has jurisdiction over such a ship. The fiction of territoriality on which this law is based has been challenged both before

[40] Annex II of U.N. Doc. A/AC.105/21.

[41] Para. 7 of the *Declaration of Legal Principles.* Appendix, The U.N. registry of space launchings is based on the voluntary information of Member States.

[42] Article 18 of the Tokyo Convention on Offences Committed on Board aircraft, 1963. See *supra* at 48 *et seq.*

municipal courts[43] and in effect also by the Permanent Court of International Justice in *The Lotus* case.[44]

Article VIII did not bring about any change with respect to rules of nationality. It remains for municipal law to regulate on what condition a State's flag can validly be granted.[45] The *Nottebohm Case*[46] made it clear, however, that the granting of the flag cannot entirely be a matter of discretion of the State concerned. On this analogy there would seem to be no reason why the "link theory" could not be extended to spacecraft. It might well be argued that the combined use of the terms "jurisdiction and control"[47] would imply the acceptance of the "link theory." The connection, established in Article VIII between the "State of registry," on the one hand, and "jurisdiction and control," on the other hand, works both ways. Consequently, the registration of spacecraft should be made in the State which exercises control over the operation of the object launched into outer space. The legal effect of registration of spacecraft would be tantamount to a pledge on the part of the States Parties to the Treaty on Outer Space to recognize the validity of such registrations under municipal laws and regulations of the States concerned. Hence, contracting States may not contest the nationality of a spacecraft unless effective control over a disputed spacecraft is exercised by a State other than the State of registry. The

[43] Lord Atkin in *Chung Chi Cheung v. The King* [1939] A.C. 160 rejected the floating territory theory by saying *inter alia:*

> The truth is that the enunciators of the floating island theory have failed to face very obvious possibilities that make the doctrine quite impracticable when tested by the activities of life on board ship and ashore . . .

[44] P.C.I.J., Series A, No. 10 (1927) p. 25. Cf. Judge Finlay in his dissenting opinion described the acceptance of the floating island theory by the Court as:

> 'a new and startling application of a metaphor' which 'appears to be based on a misconception of the proposition that a ship on the high seas may be regarded as part of the territory of the country whose flag she flied . . .'.

He regarded a ship as a movable chattel and not a place. *Ibid.* at 52–53.

[45] It was stated in *The Muscat Dhows* case that:

> the granting of the French flag to subjects of his Highness the Sultan of Muscat in itself constitutes no attack on the independence of the Sultan. However, these subjects do not enjoy in consequence of that fact any right of extra-territoriality, which could exempt them from the sovereignty, especially from the jurisdiction, of His Highness the Sultan of Muscat.

U.N. Rep., vol. XI, p. 83 (1905).

[46] I.C.J. Reports (1955), 4.

[47] About the meaning of the term "control" Lachs said,

> Though *sensu stricto* not a legal term, it strengthens the former [jurisdiction]. It may be interpreted as implying the obligation of the other States not to interfere with the direction, supervision and all technical arrangements necessary for the object to fulfill its mission of exploration and use of outer space.

Op. cit. supra at 58.

effect of recognition of registry of spacecraft is restricted to the relations of States Parties to the Treaty *inter se.*[48]

In contrast to Article 17 of the Chicago Convention on International Civil Aviation of 1944, Article VIII did not mention the nationality of spacecraft. Ordinarily, however, registration confers upon the vessel the nationality of the State in which the registration took place.[49]

The Space Treaty did not give a solution regarding the problem of jurisdiction of international organizations over spacecraft. Article 7 of the Geneva Convention on the High Seas also left this question open. The International Law Commission dealt with the question in 1955.[50] Its suggestions are valuable and may provide a pattern of analogy for space law. Basing his arguments on the decision of the International Court of Justice concerning the *Reparation for Injuries* case, the Special Rapporteur to the Eighth Session of the International Law Commission stated that the U.N. certainly has the right to own and operate ships, otherwise it could not "effectively discharge its functions." He pointed out that the problem of jurisdiction could not be solved by creating a "United Nations registration." The legal status of vessels, whether on the high seas, in territorial waters or in a port, and the applicable law aboard such ships, would be problematical, because the United Nations, similar to other international organizations, cannot offer guarantees equivalent to those offered by States. To remedy this situation, it was suggested that "Member States of the U.N. recognize a special U.N. registration which entitles the ship to fly the U.N. flag and to special protection by the United Nations."

In addition, the U.N. would enter into a "special agreement with one or more of the Members by which these Members would allow the vessels concerned to fly their flag in combination with the U.N. flag." Such ships would be assimilated to the ships of these Member States which concluded a special agreement with the Secretary General of the U.N. Finally, Member

48 See Articles 17 and 18 of the Chicago Convention, 1944 on International Civil Aviation.

49 Under United States law the American flag can be flown both by a ship of American registry and American ownership: *The Alliance,* U.N. Rep., vol. IX, p. 140 (1903). It appears that the law of the State of the owners' nationality may also extend to vessels. See *The Chiquita,* 19 F. 2d. 417 (1927); *U.S. v. The Pirates,* 5 Wheat 84 at p. 199 (1820); *U.S. v. Jenkins,* 26 Fed. Cas. No. 15473a, (1838); *The Alta,* 136 Fed. 513 at p. 519 (1905); Under British law the nationality of British ships is determined by the nationality of their owners. Temperley's Merchant Shipping Acts, (5th ed., 1954) p. 3. Quoted from Bin Cheng, *The Law of International Air Transport* (Stevens – Oceana, 1962) pp. 129–130. See also Articles 4, 5, and 6 of the Geneva Convention on the High Seas, April 29, 1958.

50 See, U.N. Doc. A/CN.4/103; The ILC's report, A/2934. See also the letter of the Legal Council of the United Nations relating to the flag and registry of ten fishing vessels owned by the United Nations, A/CN.4/SR.320, para. 68.

States of the U.N. were supposed to recognize the special agreements and to "extend to the United Nations all international agreements relating to navigation to which they are a party."[51]

The jurisdiction with respect to the determination of the nationality of spacecraft has two aspects. First, on the analogy of maritime jurisdiction, the State of registry would be entitled to determine whether the spacecraft might claim its nationality. Secondly, a third State could claim competence within the bounds of reasonableness to ascertain whether the identification and documents of a space vehicle or station, etc., are true and in proper order.[52]

When comparing maritime jurisdiction concerning occurrences on board a ship on the high seas with Article VIII, a liberal reception of the rules regarding maritime jurisdiction affords itself. Accordingly, the law of the flag or the law of the State of registry governs matters of the nationality of the actor.[53] Since international law does not prohibit jurisdiction on board foreign vessels while in international waters, the municipal law likewise is valid on board a foreign space vehicle.[54]

Article VIII did not make clear what the effect on the exclusiveness of the State of registry's jurisdiction over the personnel of moon stations would be in case exchange of crews took place. Considerations should be given to the phrase, "personnel thereof." Would jurisdiction be unlimited with respect to every category of space personnel or should there be different categories? We suggest that three categories of persons be distinguished:

(a) visiting personnel for shorter periods of time;

(b) permanent crew and exchange personnel participating in joint experiments, and

(c) representatives of Contracting Parties inspecting the space station of another Contracting Party. It may be argued that category (a) and (b) should also be considered as falling into the category of "any personnel" of the moon station. If this proposition is accepted, there still is another problem to be solved, namely that of the time when the space personnel in question is to be considered for certain purposes to become subject to the jurisdiction of the State of registry of the "host" station. No doubt, the

[51] For the text see U.N. Doc. A/CN.4/103. See also ICAO Panel of Experts on Article 77 of the Chicago Convention, 1944, PE-77 / Working Draft No. 4 (18/5/60) pp. 2–3.

[52] See, however, *The Virginius Incident* (1873), 2 Moore, D., pp. 895 *et seq.;* See also British and Foreign State Papers (1873–1874), pp. 98–229.

[53] *The Queen v. Carr* (1882), 10 Q. B.D. 76, at p. 85.

[54] *Gerradin v. United Fruit Co.,* 60 F. 2d. 927 (1932).

physical presence of foreign astronauts in moon stations is sufficient and necessary reason for the State of registration to claim jurisdiction over them. It may well be that the criterion of physical presence within the object shall later have to be interpreted *sensu largo,* including the area adjacent to an installation.

Under Article VIII the jurisdiction and control of the launching State is not exclusive while the object and personnel thereof is not in outer space or on a celestial body. On the other hand, it is a matter of municipal law to ascribe the right to a State to legislate for acts or events occurring on board a vehicle carried on its registry. The *lex loci delicti* for the purpose of action in tort, may, however, be the local law.[55]

In case of concurrent jurisdiction the State of registry of the object seems to have prior claim, unless the States concerned agree otherwise.

(ii) The "instrumental" scope of jurisdiction and control is not defined in detail. "An object" launched into outer space is supposed to be registered. Component parts of such objects, as well as objects landed or constructed on a celestial body, would seem to fall also into the category of "objects" for the purpose of Article VIII. Article IV refers to "equipment or facility necessary for peaceful exploration." Thus, the term "object" should be given a broad interpretation allowing the inclusion of any object launched into outer space.

(iii) *Ratione personae* Article VIII governs "any personnel" of the spacecraft. Thus, the quasi-territorial jurisdiction of the State of registration overrides personal jurisdiction. In case of a multinational crew the personnel would be subject to the jurisaction and jurisfaction of the State of registry, and also to the jurisaction of the State of nationality should this State differ from the State of registry.

(iv) Regarding the sphere of application of the rule, it is provided that the State of registration shall "*retain* jurisdiction and control over such object, and over any personnel thereof, *while in outer space or on a celestial body.*" (Emphasis added.) It clearly follows that, since jurisdiction is "*retained*" the State of registry *a fortiori* has jurisdiction over its spacecraft while it is on the high seas, the polar areas or even in the territorial domain of a third State.

The wording of the first sentence shows that the contracting parties did not want to stipulate what changes, if any, the concept of territorial jurisdiction should undergo regarding the concurrent jurisdiction over foreign spacecraft in the territory of a third State. Thus, the applicability of the rules of general international law regarding the exercise of jurisdiction over

[55] *Mackinnon v. The Iberia Shipping Co.,* I.L.R., 1954, p. 126.

foreign space vehicles in territorial domain seems to be supported by Article VIII.

a. Accordingly, if a space vehicle enters the territorial domain of a third State, it becomes subject to the jurisdiction of that State in the fullest sense of the term. The question is whether different kinds of space vehicles are to be treated differently, or space vehicles automatically enjoy a certain measure of privileged treatment. The exercise of jurisdiction has always been asserted by States to be in accordance with international law. In this sense State practice is indicative of international law. The United States practice is to claim plenary jurisdiction; the French practice bases its claim on the criteria of peace, order and good government of the port. The Soviet Union, in effect, similar to the United States, adopts the criterion of "state security."

b. The analogy of jurisdiction in ports may shed some light on the rules governing jurisdiction over landing sites, or space overhaul, service and rescue stations. International law allocates jurisdiction in ports according to three contingencies of national interests:

(i) matters of internal concern of the ship, (ii) matters of interest to the host State, and (iii) interest of the community of nations. The vessel enjoys immunity from the jurisdiction of the State of the port if it enters the port due to distress, subject to the conditions that:

(1) the distress was urgent;
(2) the distress was of grave necessity;
(3) the danger was such that it caused "apprehension in the mind of an honest and firm man";
(4) the distress was not created by the claimant himself;
(5) the state of distress is proved by the claimant "in a clear and satisfactory manner."[56]

c. Under Article V of the Space Treaty the privileged treatment of astronauts as "envoys of mankind" is limited to the event of "accident, distress, or emergency landing on the territory of another State Party or on the high seas." As a rule, the extent of immunity must correspond to its purpose. Consequently, when the entry of a space vehicle and astronauts is not voluntary but due to distress, the purpose of immunity is to put the distressed subject into the same situation with respect to submission to the jurisdiction of the local authorities, as it or they would be were they not

[56] *The Eleanor* (1809), Edw. 135 at p. 161.; As to the objective scope or apprehension see, *The New York,* 3 Wheat 59 (1818); as to the nature of distress see, *The 'May' v. The King* [1931] 3 D.L.R. 15. at p. 23.

forced to enter foreign territory. The immunity is proportional, and in case of dispute should be subject to strict interpretation.

As to the content of immunity, in maritime law the privileged position means immunity from arrest and from paying local duties. Immunity does not allow of the flouting of local laws.[57] Further, it would seem that under this analogy space vehicles and astronauts engaged in an illegal activity against the State on whose territory they are forced to make an unintentional landing, could not be exempted from local criminal jurisdiction.

The global interests represented in the generally acclaimed principle of free and orderly navigation in outer space would require that States not exercise municipal legislative powers in a manner that would negate this principle. Mention should be made of the status of reconnaissance satellites and the crew manning such space objects. As the glaring example of the *Pueblo* incident shows, an eventual rescue operation involving a spacecraft which is claimed to have performed an espionage mission can easily lead to serious conflicts. The Soviet Union's position does not seem to have taken a reverse turn since she continues to regard space reconnaissance over Soviet territory as both international delinquency and a violation of Soviet municipal law. Until evidence to the contrary is produced, States which hold different views will have to risk exposing their craft and astronauts to the hazards of being charged with espionage and handled accordingly. Only common sense and the principle of reciprocity may temper excessive measures. This is, of course, a far cry from a regime of public order based on the rule of law.

d. The right of innocent passage of spacecraft through foreign national airspace is not recognized. Maritime analogy is thus irrelevant.

ad (ii) Ownership. Article VIII of the Treaty on Outer Space provides that "ownership of objects launched into outer space, including objects landed or constructed on a celestial body, and of their component parts, is not affected by their presence in outer space or on a celestial body or by their return to the Earth." Rights of ownership in space objects are internationally recognized and protected. The "owner" is not defined by Article VIII; but it would follow that either the launching State or the State of registration of the object is its owner until proof to the contrary. The owner and the State of jurisdiction need not necessarily be identical. Conditions and requirements of ownership of space objects is a matter of internal concern of every State. The Treaty provision is similar to that of paragraph 7 of the Declaration of Legal Principles with two differences:

[57] *Cushin and Lewis v. R.* (1935), L.R. Ex. C.R. 103; *U.S. v. Eagle Indemnity Co.,* 18F. 2d. 1935 (1926); *U.S. v. Sullivan,* 26F. 2d 606 (1928).

first, the scope of Article VIII extends only to the Contracting Parties, and second, special reference is made therein to installations on celestial bodies.

ad (iii) Return. The law governing the return of space objects recovered outside the territory of the launching authority by Contracting Parties to the Agreement and Rescue and Return is dealt with in Section 5 below.

2. *The Basic Principles of Space Law*

In this paragraph we will analyze how the concept of State Jurisdiction, as regulated in Article VIII, tallies with the other provisions of the Treaty on Outer Space.

Article I of the Treaty provides that space activities shall be carried out for the "benefit of mankind," in the "interest of all countries," on the basis of equality, "without discrimination," and in accordance with international law. Outer space has been declared the "province of mankind" where there is "free access" to all areas subsuming the freedom of scientific investigation. These fundamental principles *ipso jure* determine the limits and patterns of the exercise of State jurisdiction in outer space.

As a general principle, it should be pointed out here that State jurisdiction may not be exercised in an abusive manner, which would lead to the creation of monopoly positions by certain States *vis-à-vis* the international community. This is without prejudice to the fact that States are their own masters also in this "province of mankind" and deal with each other as sovereign equals. Reference in Article I to the principle of sovereign equality and the framework of contemporary international law instantly sets the entire Treaty on the sobering basis of realism. It is this approach, rather than the lofty principles of the Preamble, that will shape State practice.

3. *The Principle of Non-Appropriation (Article II)*

The principle of non-appropriation of outer space and celestial bodies is the cardinal principle of international space law. Article II provides:

> Outer space, including the Moon and other celestial bodies, is not subject to national appropriation by claim of sovereignty, by means of occupation, or by any other means.

This principle may be regarded as the "antithesis" of the principle of absolute and exclusive sovereignty, and its corollary the principle of national appropriation accepted in general international law. The principle of non-appropriation of outer space is one of the pillars of international space law. As a result, the whole body of rules of space law acquires a new orientation. The principle of non-appropriation also leads to a change in the legal basis of the concept of State jurisdiction. The principle proscribes territorial acquisition in outer space, but provides that States retain jurisdiction over objects launched into outer space or landed or constructed in celestial bodies. It may be argued that the right to exercise jurisdiction over certain areas can also be inferred from the doctrine of State jurisdictions. The Space Treaty does not determine with great precision where the limit of State jurisdiction should be drawn, so as to avoid eventual conflicts between the principle of non-appropriation and the exercise of jurisdiction which might be claimed to amount to a violation of this principle. Perhaps there is no outright contradiction between Articles II and VIII of the Treaty on Outer Space, but we agree with the French Representative to the U.N. who pointed out that the definition of outer space and the study of rules relative to the exploitation of outer space should be studied. The tasks facing international lawyers could, however, be defined in more specific terms. Consequently, we propose that the gap between these two principles should be filled by secondary rules providing for a finer adjustment of the jurisdictional competencies of States in outer space.[58]

4. Relationship Between Article VIII and Articles II and IV

The principle of applicability of international law to space activities was stated in Article III of the Treaty on Outer Space. This provision has already been dealt with above. Article IV provides for the partial demilitarization of outer space. Paragraph 1 of said article reads as follows:

> States Parties to the Treaty undertake not to place in orbit around the Earth any objects carrying nuclear weapons or any other kinds of weapons of mass destruction, install such weapons on celestial bodies, or station such weapons in outer space in any other manner.

[58] Another aspect of this problem was emphasized in a brief note published in 16 I.C.L.Q. 555 (1967). The observation is quoted in full:

> Although the Treaty does not purport to be complete, it carries a built-in gap in Article II on territorial acquisition in space which may present especial difficulties. Given the 'control and jurisdiction" which States exercise over vehicles and installations and their international responsibility, to deny 'sovereignty' (whilst obviously in harmony with the tenor of the Treaty) and yet to put no proprietary right in its stead may create more problems than it will solve. The Antarctic Treaty has been quoted in this and other regards as providing a precedent for the successful operation of this kind of international co-operation. But the case, though similar, is not quite on all fours for in Antarctica territorial claims were frozen; in space there will be a gap.

The so-called non-aligned nations directed sharp attacks against this restricted demilitarization and urged that the whole of outer space should be accorded the regime that was agreed by the two space powers relative to the Moon and celestial bodies.

Paragraph 2 of Article IV provides:

> The Moon and other celestial bodies shall be used by all States Parties to the Treaty exclusively for peaceful purposes. The establishment of military bases, installations and fortifications, the testing of new types of weapons and the conduct of military maneuvers on celestial bodies shall be forbidden. The use of military personnel for scientific research or for any other peaceful purposes shall not be prohibited. The use of any equipment or facility necessary for peaceful exploration of the Moon and other celestial bodies shall also not be prohibited.

The legal status of outer space proper and celestial bodies is not identical. They differ from each other with respect to the degree of demilitarization. Military uses of outer space are not prohibited. This may entail a security minded attitude of the space powers intended to provide the maximum legal protection for the integrity and safety of the objects they launch into outer space. The quasi-territorial jurisdiction of the State of registration may be less exclusive and absolute with respect to stations on the Moon than may be anticipated relative to objects launched into outer space.

5. *The Principle of Return of Astronauts (Article V) and the Agreement on Rescue and Return*

Article V of the Treaty on Outer Space provides:

> States Parties to the Treaty shall regard astronauts as envoys of mankind in outer space and shall render to them all possible assistance in the event of accident, distress, or emergency landing on the territory of another State Party or on the high seas. When astronauts make such a landing, they shall be safely and promptly returned to the State of registry of their space vehicle . . .

The Treaty creates an obligation for the Contracting Parties to render "all possible assistance" to the astronauts of another Contracting Party in conditions specified by the Treaty. Article V makes explicit two rules of State jurisdiction. Namely, that the territorial State exercises exclusive territorial jurisdiction within its boundaries, and that the State of registration exercises personal jurisdiction over the personnel of the spacecraft that is involved in an accident, distress or emergency landing. Attention should be drawn to the wording of Article V which makes mention of astronauts "as envoys of mankind *in outer space.*" (Emphasis added) Importance should be attached to this construction because it excludes any ambiguity as to the status of astronauts in law. Thus, astronauts may be regarded as "envoys of mankind" of a certain kind only in outer space, but not on earth, particularly on the territory of a third State. Consequently, astronauts could not claim privileges similar to those enjoyed by diplomatic representatives proper. It may fairly be said that Article V employs a figure of speech without the intention to attach to it literal legal consequences. Astronauts enjoy, of course, a special status and a hitherto untested limited immunity, but their right to exceptional treatment at the hands of third States Parties to the Treaty on Outer Space is something quite distinct from the immunity of diplomatic representatives.

Article V must be read together with Article VIII of the Treaty on Outer Space, because the return of space objects is handled separately in the latter Article. Since we have already dealt with the question of return of space vehicles in the context of ownership of objects launched into outer space, it will suffice here to state that Article VIII does not introduce the contingencies of accident, distress or emergency landing as causes of the duty and right to claim return. Rather, it simply mentions the fact of finding such objects beyond the limits of the State on whose registry they are carried. Since the Treaty on Outer Space did not set conditions as to the return of space objects, it would appear that the return is unconditional under the terms of the Treaty.[59]

It may be asked with justification whether the restriction of the scope of application of Article V to the cases of accident, distress or emergency landings is not logically implied in Article VIII as well. The treaty text and summary records of the debates of the Legal Sub-committee of the UN-COPUOS do not lend support to a restrictive interpretation of Article VIII, in the sense that the instances of presence of space objects beyond the territory of the State of registration should be exclusively those of accident, distress or emergency landing. It appears, then, that under Article VIII objects whose landing was planned, i.e. intentional, in contrast to unintentional landings (such as accidents, distress or emergency landings) that would be covered by the Treaty anyway, should also be returned to the State of registration. If such were the case, then there would have to exist a right for the Contracting Parties to use the territorial domain of other Contracting Parties as landing sites. Such a wholesale renunciation of the territorial prerogative was clearly not the intention of the Con-

[59] But, see the Comment of the Soviet Union Branch of the International Law Association, in Appendix VI.

tracting Parties. It is well to remember that not even the right of innocent passage of spacecraft through the airspace of a third State is recognized in international space law. For all practical purposes, therefore, Article VIII covers contingencies associated with unintentional landings of space objects in the territory of States other than the State of registration. In this respect there is no difference between Article VIII and Article V other than that of wording. The paucity of the *travaux préparatoires* of the Treaty on Outer Space leaves the door open for a more liberal interpretation as regards the return of space objects intentionally landed in areas on celestial bodies designated by a Contracting Party for landing, erection of installations or experiments. In this context the wording of Article VIII would afford broader applicability. In our opinion, Article VIII also places a clear-cut obligation on Contracting Parties to return space objects that are found within their designated areas on a celestial body.

Paragraph 1 of Article VII creates an exception to the principle of territorial jurisdiction by imposing the obligation on Contracting Parties to return "safely and promptly" astronauts who make a distress landing "to the State of registry of their space vehicle." The obligation is not unconditional, because the causes which give rise to the obligation are specified. The Treaty does not grant immunity to astronauts; their privileged treatment is restricted only to the event of return as a consequence of accident, distress or emergency landing.

Upon reading Article V it may be stated that the principles of territorial jurisdiction and quasi-territorial jurisdiction exist concurrently. The State exercising quasi-territorial jurisdiction over spacecraft also exercises personal jurisdiction over astronauts thereof. In outer space the situation is different, because the principle of quasi-territorial jurisdiction has an absolute applicability. On the other hand, when territorial jurisdiction and quasi-territorial jurisdiction collide with each other, in such case territorial jurisdiction takes precedence over the latter, unless an exception is made in an express stipulation, as in the case of the obligation relative to the return of astronauts. (Article V)

The Preamble of the Agreement on Rescue and Return states that the purpose of the Agreement is "to develop and give further concrete expression" to the duties provided for by Articles V and VIII of the Space Treaty. Special mention is made of international co-operation and "sentiments of humanity" that motivated the provisions of the Agreement.[60]

[60] For the preparation of the Agreement see, the *Report of the Legal Sub-Committee on the Work of its Sixth Session,* U.N. Doc. A/6804 (27 September 1967) Annex III, at 2–75. See also the *Report of the Legal Sub-Committee on the Work of its Special*

The Agreement provides for two sets of rules, one governing "the personnel of a spacecraft" (Articles 1–4), the other "space objects or their component parts." (Article 5) If, owing to accident, distress, emergency or unintended landing, astronauts land in the territory under the jurisdiction of a Contracting Party they will be subject to its territorial jurisdiction. Under Article 2 a Contracting Party in such situation "shall immediately take all possible steps to rescue them and render all necessary assistance," inform the launching authority and also the Secretary-General of the United Nations. The personnel of the spacecraft shall be "safely and promptly returned to representatives of the launching authority." (Article 4)

Article 6 defines the term "launching authority" as the State responsible for the launching, or "where an international inter-governmental organization is responsible for launching, that organization providing that that organization declares its acceptance of the rights and obligations provided for in this Agreement and a majority of States members of that organization are Contracting Parties to this Agreement" and the Treaty on Outer Space. By defining the "launching authority" with reference to "the State responsible for the launching" one cannot help inquiring further as to what State should be considered responsible for the launching at least for the purpose of the Agreement. The Agreement provides no guidance in this respect. But it may well be argued that a State Party to the Treaty on Outer Space on whose registry an object launched into outer space is carried is the "State responsible for the launching." This conclusion is supported by the stated objective of the Agreement "to develop and give further concrete expression" to the general duty of rescue and return provided for in the Space Treaty. The territorial jurisdiction of a Contracting Party under Article 2 is limited by the concurrent right of the launching authority to co-operate with the Contracting Party "with a view to the effective conduct of search and rescue operations." This restriction is, of course, rather nominal, because search and rescue operations are subject to "the direction and control" of the Contracting Party and no procedure is outlined as to who should determine "if assistance by the launching authority would help to effect a prompt rescue or would contribute substantially to the effectiveness of search and rescue operations." Contracting Parties have the right "to extend assistance in search and rescue operations" if astronauts alight on

Session, U.N. Doc. A/AC.105/43 (15 December 1967) pp. 6. Text of agreement is reproduced therein as well as in Appendix IV *infra.*

the high seas or in any other place not under the jurisdiction of any State which may eventually include celestial bodies as well.

It is not clear from the Agreement whether the assistance has to be invited first, or whether the Contracting Party may act on its own initiative if it is in a position to extend assistance "if necessary." The humanitarian motivation of the Agreement would require a flexible interpretation of Article 3. In any event, if security considerations required, the launching authority could prohibit undue interference with the object or personnel by a Contracting Party. Essentially similar provisions govern space objects or their component parts with the difference that the territorial State is bound to recover a space object that landed in its territory under the terms of the Agreement only upon request by and if necessary assistance from the launching authority. It may require the furnishing of identifying data by the launching authority. Article 5 governs space objects generally; no conditions as to their return are specified. Consequently, the return of space objects and their component parts found beyond the territory over which the launching authority has jurisdiction is unconditional under the terms of the Agreement.[61]

6. The Principle of International Responsibility of States for National Activities in Outer Space (Article VI)

Article VI subsumes that the national State is bound to exercise jurisdiction in order to ensure that "national activities are carried out in conformity with the provisions set forth in the . . . treaty." In other words, States Parties to the Treaty are under a legal obligation to exercise jurisdiction in outer space and on celestial bodies for the stated purposes. Such jurisdiction is exercised over "national activities" carried out by "governmental agencies or by non-governmental entities."[62] It follows that it is for the municipal laws to determine that activities in outer space are regarded as "national activities." It may also be concluded that States may exercise legislative jurisdiction relative to the activities of their nationals in outer space, even if their activity is considered by the municipal law of another State Party to the Treaty as being its "national activity." The exercise of this right as of any other right must be *bona fide.*

[61] See the comment of the Soviet Union Branch of the ILA in Appendix VI.

[62] The activities of non-governmental entities require "authorization and continuing supervision by the appropriate State Party to the Treaty". This is an example for the exercise of control in outer space. See Article VIII of the Space Treaty.

7. *Liability (Article VII)*

Article VII provides that the State which launches or procures the launching, or from whose territory or facility the space object is launched, is internationally liable for damage to another State. Liability, as a matter of logic, subsumes the right and duty to exercise jurisdiction over objects launched into outer space. We may add that with respect to installations on celestial bodies the owner may also be held liable and also may exercise jurisdiction over such object.

8. *The Principle of Co-operation (Article IX)*

Article IX provides that "States Parties to the Treaty shall be guided by the principle of co-operation and mutual assistance and shall conduct all activities in outer space, including the Moon and other celestial bodies, with due regard to the corresponding interests of all other States Parties to the Treaty." This rule is directly applicable to the exercise of State jurisdiction in outer space. Thus, States may not pass laws which would contravene the general principle of co-operation and mutual assistance.

9. *Tracking Facilities (Article X)*

Article X confirms the applicability of the principle of territorial jurisdiction with respect to the terrestrial effects of space research. It depends on the territorial State whether or not to grant facilities for tracking stations to be set up in its territorial domain by a third State. The nature and conditions as to the establishment of tracking facilities is a matter of negotiation and agreement between the parties concerned.

10. *International Organizations (Article XI)*

Article XI bears upon the competence of the U.N. regarding the dissemination of information about space activities. "On receiving (such information) the Secretary-General of the United Nations should be prepared to disseminate it immediately and effectively." Under Article XIII

> ... any practical questions arising in connection with activities carried on by international government organizations in the exploration and use of outer space ... shall be resolved by the States Parties to the Treaty either with the appropriate

international organization or with one or more States members of the international organization, which are Parties to the Treaty.[63]

Such practical questions may include *inter alia* jurisdictional conflicts. This principle applies when space activities are carried out by a single State, jointly with other States or in the framework of international intergovernmental organizations. (paragraph 1 of Article XIII)

11. The Principle of Open Access to Moon Stations (Article XII)

"All stations, installations, equipment and space vehicles on the Moon and other celestial bodies shall be open to representatives of other States Parties to the Treaty." Article XII does not regulate under whose jurisdiction such representatives will be. This may give rise to concurrent and conflicting jurisdictions. It will be recalled that under Article VIII the State of registration of the space object retains jurisdiction and control over such objects "and over any personnel thereof" in outer space and on a celestial body. We suggest that observers should not be considered under the same category of the personnel of the space that they are supposed to inspect. The principle of immunity of such representatives can be inferred from Article VIII, Article XII and from the objectives of the Treaty. It still remains to be settled, however, whether the State of nationality or the State of registry of the space object may exercise jurisdiction over observers, should the two States be different,[64] or should this question arise when representatives participate on behalf of an international organization. The exercise of jurisdiction over scientific exchange personnel constitutes another category which also has to be settled in time. We believe that the application of the Antarctic analogy would provide a good solution with less controversy than in Antarctica. It is clear, however, that the State of registration exercises exclusive jurisdiction with respect to the safety and normal operation of such objects.

III. THE LEGAL BASIS OF STATE JURISDICTION IN SPACE LAW

Having analysed the concept of State jurisdiction in general international law and examined its status in space law, we may now conclude as follows. The concept of State jurisdiction in general international law is

[63] Paragraph 2 of Article VIII of the Antarctic Treaty. Cf. *supra* at 76.

[64] Paragraph 1 of Article VIII of the Antarctic Treaty which provides that scientific exchange personnel, members of their staff and observers are subject "only to the jurisdiction of the Contracting Party of which they are nationals."

derived from the principles of territoriality and sovereignty. The concept of State jurisdiction in space law is derived from the principles of sovereign equality of States, non-appropriation and the general principles of space law as declared by the Space Treaty. Comparing the two "formulae" of the concepts of State jurisdiction we may see that the notion of territoriality does not form part of the concept of jurisdiction in space law. Consequently, due regard is to be given to this proposition when rules governing the exploitation of outer space and celestial bodies in general and the protection of lawful interests and legal titles in particular are drawn up.

CHAPTER V

OBSERVATIONS *DE LEGE FERENDA*

We wish to conclude this study with two brief observations *de lege ferenda* regarding our proposed concept of "functional jurisdiction". We also wish to include certain statements which may be found in the White Paper on A Domestic Satellite Communication System for Canada of 28 March 1968, and two preceding reports prepared by the Science Council of Canada and the Science Secretariat in February and July 1967 respectively. As will be seen, these documents bear out the possibility that the proposed concept may one day become a practical instrument in the hands of a government to pave the way towards the accommodation of a commensurate claim to exercise exclusive jurisdiction over certain zones of outer space, and by analogy over certain designated areas on celestial bodies for a functionally determined purpose.

I. A PROPOSAL: THE CONCEPT OF "FUNCTIONAL JURISDICTION"

Why should a new concept of jurisdiction be introduced into space law? There are two reasons, of which the first, the formal one, should now be taken for granted had not North American legal scholarship generated an instant distrust toward theoretical concepts. A reference to Kant, Schopenhauer and Kelsen, or for that matter even to Marshall McLuhan, should provide an answer; but perhaps it should be added that the great utility of concepts consists in the fact that the original material of knowledge is easier to handle, survey, order and communicate. The second reason why a new look at the exercise of State jurisdiction is deemed necessary is substantive. As the foregoing analysis showed, international law contains a fair number of applicable rules and principles regarding territorial jurisdiction, jurisdiction over nationals and quasi-territorial jurisdiction. The Treaty on Outer Space and the Agreement on the Rescue of Astronauts, the Return of Astronauts and the Return of Objects Launched into Outer

Space, as approved by U.N. General Assembly Resolution 2345 (XXII) of December 19th 1967, partly reaffirmed the applicable rules of international law and partly supplemented them with new principles and rules on the exercise of State jurisdiction. As a result, we are left with a handful of general legal principles and rules and several areas which are inadequately covered by them. Foremost of these problems is the complex of *lege ferenda* rules regarding the exploitation and uses of outer space resources spatial, natural and frequency resources included.

Here reference to the applicability of international law and the U.N. Charter is of no avail, because binding rules cannot be discovered even with a magnifying glass. Article II of the Treaty on Outer Space frees outer space, including the Moon and other celestial bodies, from claims of national appropriation. This rule should, however, be read and applied in the context of Article I of the Treaty, whose wording displays a painstaking effort to strike a fair balance between global community interests and those of the individual states engaging in space activities. The outcome is that paragraph 1 of Article I declaring that the exploration and use of outer space shall be carried out for the benefit and in the interest of all countries, irrespective of their degree of economic or scientific development, and that outer space shall be the province of mankind, is untranslatable into legal obligations and rights, as of now. On the other hand, we come across a cardinal principle in Paragraph 2, namely that outer space shall be free for exploration and use by all states without discrimination of any kind, *on the basis of equality and in accordance with international law,* and there shall be free access to all areas of celestial bodies. The principle of equality of states, in other words, means sovereign equality.

It may be well to point out here, that Article II of the Treaty on Outer Space does not altogether banish the principle of sovereignty from space law, since under Article I States continue to deal with each other as sovereign entities, as it is understood in contemporary international law. Hence the maxim *par in parem non habet imperium* remains a valid principle as regards the forbearance of the exercise of jurisdiction by one state over space vehicles and stations registered by another state. The principle of sovereign equality by its nature, however, works both ways: namely, both in favour of the community of the underdeveloped, developing or simply nations not active in space exploration, on the one hand, and especially for those exploring and using outer space, on the other hand. This is, of course, another way of saying what the Chapman Report on Canadian Space Program so aptly expressed: "Ultimately one realizes that, while science is 'open', technology is 'closed'."[1] Bearing in mind the politico-economic realities prevailing in our contemporary world community one cannot but sympathize with the dramatic efforts demonstrated by the developing nations to write more tangible safeguards into the law-books of international space law, so that they can achieve something more than bare legal equality. Whether or not international legislation of the kind we have now is the adequate instrument to achieve, instead of registering and concretizing changes brought about by politico-economic developments in our global village, which after all law by its very nature is meant to reflect one way or another, is another vexing question that we cannot go into here.

The thorny problem which international legal scholarship, the UNCOPUOS and the U.N. Ad Hoc Committee on the Seabed and Ocean Floor[2] have to tackle is not only to spell out in legal terms the meaning of the phrases outer space, the celestial bodies, the seabed and the ocean floor as provinces of mankind; but much more what would be an effective and acceptable legal régime for these spaces affording an equitable sharing of the wealth and natural resources to be found therein among states exploiting these resources and third states. The search for new rules is somewhat burdened by the fact that the enquiry must be carried out as a matter of fact with deference to the present structure of international law. In the vernacular of McLuhan this is "rear-view-mirrorism" on a global scale. Since the chief feature of contemporary international law is the existence of sovereign nation States, it would be impossible to ask them to subordinate their immediate tangible interests to objectives of ideal blueprints conjuring up a world system which is not yet born. No wonder that the outcome of a search for new rules and principles to govern the exploitation and distribution of the natural resources of international spaces[3] may be one replete with compromises and general principles, as exemplified by the Treaty on Outer Space. The situation is not completely hopeless, because we may comfort ourselves with two findings. First, with the Hegelian maxim, namely, that what is real is rational and what is rational is real. It would be fallacious to attempt to write law imposing obligations on individual nation States, which they are not willing to undertake in favour of a non-existing global community. Until mankind *per se* assumes legal personality

[1] *Chapman Report* at 95.

[2] See, 62 A.J.I.L. 955–965 (1968).

[3] The term *international spaces* was first used by Dr. J. F. Kish, now instructor in international law at St. John's College, Cambridge, England, in *A Nemzetközi Térségek Jogállása* (The Legal Status of International Spaces) Közdok, Budapest, 1944, pp. 104. For a review of the book by the *present writer*, see 33 *Journal of Air Law and Commerce* 506–507 (1967).

under transnational law, sovereign nation states and organizations created by them continue to be the carriers of international rights and obligations. Consequently, full credit must be given to the lawful interests of states engaging in the exploration and exploitation of the natural resources of international spaces, because it is only they who are capable and willing to allocate financial and intellectual resources, develop technologies and employ manpower for its exploration and exploitation.

Secondly, international law is a supple tool which has been serving states in all seasons. Clive Parry's words aptly describe the potential inherent in international law. In writing about the rise of the doctrine that a state may lay exclusive claim to at least the continental shelf adjacent to its shores, though some thirty years ago it was assumed that the sea-bed was as free as the superjacent seas, Professor Parry concludes:

> The academic problem whether an international court may even be compelled to pronounce a *non liquet*, to confess itself unable to decide a question laid before it because there is no law applicable to that question, has, we may note, ceased to be even an academic problem. Increasingly it is recognized that the general principles of law constitute an inexhaustible well from which new rules or new interpretations to fit new situations may be drawn. International law, in effect, has come of age; or, as we may prefer to put it, things have come full circle and a "modern law of nature" has come to be recognized to continue to discharge that role the antique conception of the law of nature discharged in first giving birth to international law.[4]

Thus, if we rely on the continuing needs of sovereign nation states and draw upon the "inexhaustible well" of international law, we may be best equipped to devise a legal régime for international spaces, and at the same time to make as much concession to global community interests as is presently possible.[5]

[4] C. Parry, "The Function of Law in the International Community", in *Manual of Public International Law,* 47 (Sørensen ed. 1968).

[5] The following passage is an interesting illustration of two extreme positions, one of which regards the internationalization of the sea-bed and the ocean floor a threat to the exploitation of the sea resources, while the other demands instant returns in the billion dollar range for states who are passive onlookers: David A. Loehwing, "Wealth of The Sea, The Oceanography Industry Has Begun to Tap It." *Barron's* December 30, 1968, p. 15, col. 1:

> Sharks and the extreme pressures of the underwater environment are not the only hazards with which aquanauts must contend. Potentially more serious is the threat by the United Nations to claim sovereignty over the ocean floor beyond the limits of national jurisdiction. The Maltese delegation has introduced a resolution providing that all the wealth derived from the seas beyond the continental shelf be devoted to aid for the underdeveloped nations.
>
> A fortnight ago, the issue threatened to delay adjournment of the U.N. General Assembly, as Malta dangled before the eyes of under-developed countries a promise of $ 6 billion annually in aid derived from the ocean depths. In the final days

Returning now to Articles I and II of the Treaty on Outer Space, we may determine our task to consist of making explicit what is implicit in the above articles by bridging the two with specific rules as to the exploitation and uses of outer space and celestial bodies. Exploitation and uses are unimaginable without the extension of state authority or jurisdiction to the areas or spatial zones affected. Whatever these specific rules will be, we think they will have to satisfy two standard requirements: first, the principle of prohibition of national appropriation of outer space and celestial bodies, and second, the principle of freedom of outer space and equality of sovereign states.

Since, as we said, the exercise of jurisdiction looms large in the context of exploitation of outer space, it is the concept of state jurisdiction, we propose, that has a key position. Let us examine the nature of the concept of State jurisdiction as regards the exploitation of the resources of outer space, including the Moon and other celestial bodies. For the sake of legal shorthand we shall call the kind of State jurisdiction we are about to explain *functional jurisdiction*. One qualifying explanation is thought to be necessary, though, right at the outset in order to clarify what we mean by the proposed term. We did not overlook the possible objection that every form of State jurisdiction is by its very nature "functional". True as such a hypothetical objection may be, the use of the adjective "functional" in the term is warranted because of the following reason. The exercise of State jurisdiction in outer space and on celestial bodies is based on the principle declared by Article II of the Treaty on Outer Space, which proscribes national appropriation thereof. Consequently, sovereignty, territoriality and occupation cannot validly substantiate a claim by a state to exercise jurisdiction in outer space and on celestial bodies. These three concepts have, however, played a constitutive role in the development of the doctrine of State jurisdiction as it is now established in contemporary international law relative to the traditional terrestrial environment. This points out the difference between the concept of State jurisdiction in traditional international law and the concept of State jurisdiction in space law regarding outer space and celestial bodies.

Therefore, when a state exercises jurisdiction in outer space or on a celestial body, it always has to bear in mind that the area or zone thus subjected to its authority is not an object of its sovereignty or part of its territory. The right to claim jurisdiction in such instances and the reason why such claims merit recognition under international law may be based on the

of the session, however, the Maltese resolution was withdrawn and delegates voted to put aside for further study the whole matter of international control.

principle of freedom of outer space in general, and on the permissibility of one specific kind of space activity in particular. Thus, this kind of jurisdiction is functional in the sense that its permissibility is tied up with the lawfulness of a particular form of exploitation of outer space and celestial bodies. *Functional jurisdiction* is thus distinguished by three features. First, that State jurisdiction is claimed and exercised with respect to a certain spatial zone or area in outer space or celestial bodies, as the case may be (international space). Second, that *functional jurisdiction* is not based on titles derived from such concepts as sovereignty, territoriality and occupation (new concept of State jurisdiction in international space law). Third, that *functional jurisdiction* is justified by the need to render protection for the safe and orderly carrying out of an activity (element of function).

The term may be defined in the following words: *functional jurisdiction* means the right of a state in international law to regulate rights of persons, to affect property, things, events and occurrences in designated zones in outer space or areas on celestial bodies, whether by legislative, executive or judicial measure to the extent and for the period of time that is necessary to safeguard and secure its right to explore and exploit outer space including celestial bodies. It follows from the nature of *functional jurisdiction* that claims to this kind of State jurisdiction must be founded on the requirements of and contained by the inherent nature of a specific activity. In other words, the substance of the jurisdiction is determined by the safeguarding functions it is invoked to perform. Also, there must exist a close link between the physical element (spatial zone or area) and the activity of the claimant state. For the present time there are no standards according to which such links could be identified. Another feature of *functional jurisdiction* follows from the requirement that the claims staked to exercise it are to be subjected to strict interpretation. Namely, no title can be acquired by a state to exclusive control in outer space for an indefinite or infinite period on the strength of the fact that it is exercising or exercised *functional jurisdiction*. The right to exercise *functional jurisdiction* is not only "functionally" defined, but it is also limited in terms of time. The right to exercise *functional jurisdiction* ceases to exist when activity is halted or when the cause is consummated or the link breaks up.

One may ask whether the proposed concept of *functional jurisdiction* is unique, or whether precedent can be found through analogies in international law. Upon examining the development of the law of the sea, we may state that a suprisingly great number of precedents exist, which have not been viewed in the light of demands which current technological developments pose for the international law of the sea and space law. The random survey of state practice that follows will show that certain elements of the proposed concept of *functional jurisdiction* can be spotted in diverse international agreements regarding the extension of State jurisdiction to the high seas and ocean floor, for the purpose of securing the exploitation of natural resources or simply to protect certain terrestrial interests from interference beyond territorial limits.

That the cardinal principle of the freedom of the sea was not interpreted in the sense that it would bar the possibility of appropriating a limited portion of the bed of the open sea, may be illustrated by the case of extended State jurisdiction over pearl and sedentary fisheries. While the bed of the sea, as opposed to the subsoil, cannot be appropriated because it would affect the freedom of navigation, "a limited portion of the bed of the open sea is capable of occupation by individual states" points out Colombos "for well-defined purposes and [the occupation is] entitled to recognition by other States."[6] Pearl fisheries of the coasts of Ceylon and the Persian Gulf belong to Great Britain "by immemorial usage and effective occupation."[7] British claims to the Ceylonese and Bahrein pearl fisheries extend to a distance of from 12 to 20 miles from the land. The exercise of sovereign rights and jurisdiction over pearl banks was considered to be compatible with the principle of the freedom of the seas. Thus, Vattel in the eighteenth century wrote: "who can doubt that the pearl fisheries of Bahrein and Ceylon may be lawful objects of ownership."[8] Westlake pointed out the peculiarity of the case of pearl fisheries jurisdiction and brought into his argument the notion of "physical connection with the stable element of the locality."[9]

The general rule seems to be that the use of the sea-bed is regulated by international agreements.[10] Of further interest is the Anglo-French agreement of August 2, 1839, which set up a Mixed Commission with the responsibility of preparing a set of regulations for the guidance of fishermen

[6] Colombos, 67–68.

[7] *Ibid.* at 68.

[8] Vattel, *Droit des Gens,* vol. I, Chapter XXIII. See also, Colombos, 159; Sir Cecil Hurst, "Whose is the Bed of the Sea?," B.Y.I.L. 40 (1923–1924); Conforti, *Il regime juridico dei mari* 284–287 (1957); Papandreou, *La situation juridique des pêcheries sédentaires en haut mer,* 100–109 (1958); Hackworth, vol. ii, pp. 674–680.

[9] Westlake, vol. I, pp. 190–191. For an analysis of British municipal legislation and adjudication see, Colombos, *op. cit. supra* at 160.

[10] See for example the Declaration signed by Great Britain and France on September 29, 1923, regarding the regulation of oyster fisheries in the open sea adjacent to their territorial waters. (Treaty Series, /1923/, No. 31 /Cmd. 1966/.); Treaty between Venezuela and Great Britain of February 26, 1942, regarding the division between the two countries of both the sea-bed and the subsoil of the Gulf of Paria.

of the two countries in the seas lying between the coasts of Great Britain and France. It was followed by the Anglo-French Declaration of June 23, 1843, which reserved oyster fishing within specified areas for British and French subjects respectively. The joint declaration empowered the ships of the parties to arrest vessels infringing the rules of the Declaration and to bring them into port. But the jurisdiction to decide on the violation of the rules was reserved exclusively for the tribunals of the flag State.[11]

[11] A British Order-in-Council issued on August 23, 1843 (6 & 7 Vict. c. 79, s. 6) and the "sea Fisheries Act" of 1868 (31 & 31 Vict. c. 45) contain provisions regarding the regulation of valuable oyster beds outside territorial waters. See in this respect, Colombos, 403; Lewis M. Alexander, "Off-Shore Claims and Fisheries in North-West Europe," *The Yearbook of World Affairs,* 236–259 (1960). Further examples include *The Foyle Fisheries Act* (Northern Ireland), 1952, c. 5, and *The Foyle Fisheries Act* (Irish Republic), No. 5, of 1952 regarding the preservation of the valuable salmon fisheries in the Foyle River which is divided between Northern Ireland and the Irish Republic.

For British legislation regarding the Antarctica see the following statutes:
Antarctic Treaty Act 1967 (c. 65)

This Act enables effect to be given to measures for the conservation of Antarctic fauna and flora which have been or may hereafter be recommended for approval by contracting parties to the Antarctic Treaty signed at Washington on December 1, 1959.

S. 1 provides that it is an offence while in Antarctica to wilfully kill, injure, molest or take any native mammal or native bird or to gather any native plant within a specially protected area or drive any vehicle within such an area, or to bring into any part of Antarctica any animal or plant of a species which is not indigenous to Antarctica. S. 2 deals with exemptions from s. 1 by virtue of a permit or in cases of extreme urgency; s. 3 with the issue of permits; s. 4 with penalties; s. 5 with the application of the criminal law to observers and exchanged scientists; s. 6 with the power to make further provisions for giving effect to measures recommended for approval by contracting parties; s. 7 with further powers exercisable by Order in Council; s. 8 with proceedings and evidence; s. 9 with extension of the Act to the Isle of Man, any of the Channel Islands, and any colony; s. 10 with interpretation and supplementary provisions; and s. 11 with short title.

The Act received the Royal Assent on July 27, 1967, and came into force on that date.

Antarctic Treaty (Contracting Parties) Order 1968 (No. 887) [4d.], made on June 7, 1968, under the Antarctic Treaty Act 1967 (c. 65), s. 7 (1); certifies for the purposes of the 1967 Act who are the contracting parties to the Antarctic Treaty.

Antarctic Treaty (Specially Protected Areas) Order 1968 (No. 888), made under the Antarctic Treaty Act 1967, s. 7 (2) (*b*); operative on July 1, 1968; designates as specially protected areas for the purposes of the 1967 Act certain areas of the Antarctic in pursuance of art. IX (1) of the Antarctic Treaty.

Antarctic Treaty (Specially Protected Species) Order 1968 (No. 889) [4d.], made under the Antarctic Treaty Act 1967, s. 7 (2) (*a*); operative on July 1, 1968; designates fur seals and the ross seal as specially protected species for the purposes of the 1967 Act in pursuance of art. IX (1) of the Antarctic Treaty.

Antarctic Treaty Act 1967 (Appointed Day) Order 1968 (No. 886 (C. 11) [4d.], made June 7, 1968 under the Antarctic Treaty Act 1967 (c. 65), s. 10 (5); appoints July 1, 1968 as the appointed day for the purposes of the 1967 Act.

See also, *International Convention for the Unification of Certain Rules Concerning the Immunity of State-Owned Ships,* signed at Brussels, April 10, 1926. British Shipping

The characteristics of the international practice of states regarding the above-mentioned cases exhibit certain pertinent analogies regarding the eventual exercise of *functional jurisdiction* in outer space. First, the international agreements regarding the use of the seabed did not assert rights of sovereignty. They reaffirmed the rights of passage and navigation in the high seas over areas of the seabed claimed for exclusive exploitation. Second, claims were staked by other interested States for specific and functionally well-defined uses of the seabed and were granted recognition. Third, the state practice in question indicates that states usually set a pattern for the extension of their jurisdiction over areas that are international spaces. Accordingly, the limitation of rights implicit in the principle of the freedom of the seas, in the sense of reserving the exercise of a particular right within a designated area only for a single state rather than for the community of states, was never attempted to be achieved through "omnibus claims," but only by claims restricted both geographically and functionally to a specific form of the exploitation of sea-resources.

It is against this background that we propose to introduce the concept of *functional jurisdiction*. This concept may prove helpful in the creation of an integrated system of law governing the exploitation of resources not only in outer space but generally in what we call international spaces.

Finally, the international agreements to which we referred above recognize the lawfulness and priority of claims of those states that have tangible vested interests either on account of "rights . . . in uninterrupted and undisputed proprietorship," or a physical connection and also have the capability and preparedness to exploit the resources. Treaty practice in the field shows that the allocation of the resources of the seabed can be lawfully secured through agreements between the states concerned. The recognition of such transactions by third states may be assumed to follow, if claims are reasonable both in respect of the claimant state and to the extent it affects the freedom of navigation. There is evidence to the effect that in exceptional cases (e.g. pearls, sponges, oysters, coral, amber, chanks, etc.) the legal position of the sea-bed can be regulated by means other than express international agreements. This brings out what we have said above in sharper contrast.

The legal régime of the continental shelf is an illustration of the exten-

Laws 8 (London, 1963) p. 1121. *International Convention relating to the Arrest of Seagoing Ships,* signed at Brussels, May 10, 1952. *ibid.* at p. 1126. *International Convention on Certain Rules Concerning Civil Jurisdiction in Matters of Collision,* signed at Brussels, May 10, 1952. *id.* at p. 1131. *International Convention for the Unification of Certain Rules relating to Penal Jurisdiction in Matters of Collision or Other Incidents of Navigation,* signed at Brussels, May 10, 1952. *id.* at p. 1134.

sion of State jurisdiction beyond the zone of the territorial sea. The exercise of State jurisdiction over the continental shelf means that the principle of non-appropriation of the sea-bed is not an absolute one, and is subject to interpretation according to changing conditions and requirements with due deference to the principle of the freedom of navigation.[12] The *modus operandi* relative to the establishment of jurisdiction over the continental shelf was announcement by states of unilateral claims. In many cases these declarations were not followed by actual exploitation of the sea-resources. Thus, legal titles were only created on the strength of which exclusive sovereign rights and jurisdiction were exercised.[13]

Article 2 of the Convention on The Continental Shelf confers sovereign rights to the coastal State over the continental shelf, but only "for the purpose of exploring it and exploiting its natural resources."

The legal régime of the continental shelf does not prejudice the freedom of the seas. Under Article 2(2) the rights of the coastal State are exclusive. The coastal State is entitled to decide according to its discretion whether or not to explore the continental shelf or to proceed with the exploitation of its resources. It alone has the right to dispose of this right. It may give concessions or reject claims by third states. The right of the coastal state need not be backed up by "effective or national occupation." Article 4 vests on the coastal State the "right to take reasonable measures" necessary to safeguard its interests in the continental shelf as well as secure "the laying and maintenance of submarine cables or pipelines on the continental shelf." The limits of reasonableness as to exercising jurisdiction over the continental shelf are identified by Articles 4 and 5. Accordingly, the coastal State may not impede the laying of submarine cables or pipelines, unjustifiably interfere with navigation, fishing or conservation of the living resources of the sea nor with fundamental oceanographic or other scientific research. The coastal State is entitled to construct, maintain and operate installations and to create safety zones extending to 500 metres around such installations. Ships of third States must respect such safety zones.

The Continental Shelf Convention bears out the fact that inroads have been made into the centuries-old traditional principle of the freedom of the high seas, thereby rendering it a qualified principle. While the basic freedoms are reaffirmed, the extension of State jurisdiction towards the high seas goes along with the progressive development of technology, economic, political and defense requirements of coastal States. Although

[12] For an analysis of the claims to the sea-bed and subsoil of the continental shelf see Auguste, *The Continental Shelf,* 105–1065 (1960).

[13] Colombos, 74, 75–76.

the legal régime of the continental shelf cannot be said to have reached its final stage because even its meaning continues to be a major contentious issue, several characteristic features can be identified that mark the balance between the principle of the freedom of navigation and exclusive State jurisdiction.

Thus, installations in the continental shelf are under the jurisdiction of the coastal State, but do not possess the status of islands and do not effect the delimitation of the territorial sea of the coastal State. The presence of installations in the continental shelf cannot alter the international nature of the high seas and no claims may be based on the existence of such installations that would bring about the same effect. No installations or safety zones may be established if interference is likely to be caused to international navigation. The coastal State is bound to give warning of the establishment and presence of such installations and safety zones, remove the installations if they are disused or abandoned and undertake in the safety zone the appropriate measures for the protection of the living resources of the sea from harmful agents. Finally, the consent of the coastal State is necessary for any research relating to the continental shelf. The coastal State may not normally deny to grant its consent, but it has the right to participate or be represented in such activities.

An additional point is worthy of consideration. The Continental Shelf Convention and municipal laws do not confer title of sovereignty to any part of the high seas to the coastal State. The coastal State is merely entitled to sovereign rights for the purpose of exploring the continental shelf and exploiting its natural resources. From the fact that the Continental Shelf Convention and municipal laws do not confer on States and what Articles I and II of the Treaty on Outer Space expressly provide, we may draw the logical conclusion that the Treaty on Outer Space cannot be interpreted in a sense that would foreclose specific rules conferring rights and obligations on States regarding the exploration and exploitation of outer space including celestial bodies. In our opinion it will be necessary to prepare an international agreement which would define certain specific cases when a state, being able to show a "particular and distinctive interest", may claim the right to exercise *functional jurisdiction* in a designated zone of outer space or area on a celestial body.

Thus, Canada, for example, could by an Act of Parliament designate a section of a stationary orbit for a Canadian communications satellite within which it could exercise *functional jurisdiction.* Such zones or areas could be referred to as "designated areas." Canadian law would be applicable with respect to any act or omission which takes place in a "designated area" or in any other place, whether or not under the jurisdiction of third States, and which would, if taking place in the State that lawfully established such "designated area," constitute an offence under the law in force in that State. Canadian courts would have jurisdiction with respect to questions arising out of acts and omissions taking place in a "designated area." Such "designated areas" could be created by unilateral legislation, if the tests required by the doctrine of *functional jurisdiction* are duly satisfied. The boundaries of a "designated area" and certain technical questions, such as the avoidance of radio interference, should be negotiated and regulated by the interested States and international organisations.[14] As a point of final observation we should like to recall that the already extensive literature on the legal régime of the deep sea bed and subsoil reflects trends of ideas favouring the conception of State jurisdiction which is similar to the proposed *functional jurisdiction.*[15] The Treaty on Outer Space is frequently referred to as an example of internationalization that may provide guidelines for the emerging law of the ocean floor and subsoil.

In all fairness, it should be admitted that space law at present has little to offer in terms of explicit rules. Analogy is justified only to a certain extent, namely, inasmuch as the principle of freedom and non-appropriation of outer space is concerned. Beyond this point neither the UN-

[14] For an analogy see the *British Continental Shelf Act,* 1964, Eliz. 2, Ch. 29; *Continental Shelf (Designation of Areas) Order,* No. 697, May 12, 1964; *Continental Shelf (Jurisdiction) Order,* No. 930, 1964. See also the Anglo-Norwegian Agreement of March 10, 1965, regarding the division of the North Sea continental shelf; Proclamation of the Federal German Government of January 24, 1964, asserting sovereign rights over the continental shelf and its resources and the declarations of the Netherlands of December, 1964, and Denmark of March, 1966, relative to the control of all installations on the subsoil of the North Sea.

[15] For literature on the proposed régime of the ocean floor and subsoil see *inter alia* the following works and references therein: Lewis A. Alexander (ed.) *The Law of the Sea* (The Ohio State University Press, 1967) pp. 321; J. E. Carroz and A. G. Roche, "The Proposed International Commission for the Conservation of Atlantic Tunas," 61 A.J.I.L. 673–702 (1967); Richard Young, "The Legal Regime of the Deep-Sea Floor," 62 A.J.I.L. 641–653 (1968); "Sea Bed and Ocean Floor," *ibid.* at 955–965; Oliver L. Stone, "United States Legislation Relating to the Continental Shelf," 17 I.C.L.Q. 103–117 (1968). For an inquiry into the applicable law governing the exploitation of off-shore resources and common petroleum deposits, see William T. Onorato, "Apportionment of an International Common Petroleum Deposit," 17 I.C.L.Q. 85–102 (1968); Colin Warbrick, "Off-Shore Petroleum Exploitation in Federal Systems: Canadian and Australian Action," 17 I.C.L.Q. 501–513 (1968). Further reference is made in this context to the resolutions passed by the U.N. General Assembly: Res. 2172 (XXI), December 8, 1966; Res. 2340 (XXII), December 18, 1967; See also the Maltese proposal regarding the legal régime of the seabed and the ocean floor, U.N. Doc. A/6695, August 18, 1967. For texts of draft resolutions submitted by the U.S.S.R., India, the United States and the Republic of Tanzania, see 62 A.J.I.L. 960–965 (1968).

COPUOS nor space legal scholarship deal extensively with the question of applicable law governing exploitation and the sharing of common space resources. Ironically, the literature on the régime of the ocean floor and the sea bed is more advanced and has so far produced a fair number of schemes describing how these questions could be solved. These suggestions are well known and fall outside the scope of the present study. Nevertheless, Professor Young's reminder that "it is prudent to make haste slowly" is apt to be recalled here because care and circumspection are required in the formulation of legal rules for both the ocean space and outer space. "To be durable and satisfactory," argues Professor Young, "a regime for deep-sea bottom resources must be based on a solid knowledge of geographical facts, of technological capabilities present and anticipated, and of political and economic realities. It is believed that the analysis and synthesis of these elements have not yet advanced to the stage where decisions of a permanent character can be made with wisdom." [16]

The problem of apportioning international resources in outer space including celestial bodies appears perhaps to be somewhat academic. The existence of such shared deposits has been, as yet, very slight indeed. There is to this writer's knowledge, only one such field which may become subject of international negotiation and settlement of conflicting rights of exploitation. This field involves the use of a designated section of a stationary communications satellite's orbit. The proposed concept of *functional jurisdiction* would ensure that States could proceed in order to protect their interests regarding parking locations, as a matter of right. If in fact, this theory, complemented with an acceptable measure of international control and regulation by specialized international bodies or mixed commissions were to prevail, it would undoubtedly make an equitable exploitation of outer space between interested Governments considerably easier to agree on, as a legal title would thus be determined prior to the commencement of actual exploitation and sharing. Consequently, specific rules regarding the exploitation of space resources could gradually be developed to effect security of legal title over resources claimed, maximum efficiency and economy of exploitation according to an international standard, and the mutual benefit of all states having common interest.

II. REFLECTIONS ON THE JURISDICTIONAL ASPECTS OF THE ESTABLISHMENT OF A CANADIAN DOMESTIC SATELLITE COMMUNICATION SYSTEM

With regard to whether or not there is useful precedent for a unilateral

[16] Richard Young, *loc. cit. supra* at 651.

claim to the exercise of exclusive jurisdiction in a designated belt of outer space, the answer here is clearly positive. The securing of rights inherent in the international status of the high seas through unilateral claims is by no means an untried practice. Turning from these relevant analogies which we examined on the previous pages to evidence bearing more directly on the problem, it is useful at this point to consider actual State policies on apportionment of common spatial resources. There is to this writer's knowledge, only one instance which indicates that one government already seriously considers the necessity and advantages of a unilateral claim regarding the exercise of exclusive jurisdiction in a limited zone of outer space. The problem of exploitation of outer space including celestial bodies and the way and means of safeguarding commensurate legal titles of states individually concerned has been and will continue to be of far greater interest than limited actual evidence reveals.

It will be well to recall here the earlier reference to the inquiries conducted on behalf of the Canadian government into the desirability of securing parking locations on a synchronous orbit between longitudes 75° W and 115° W suitable for Canadian domestic satellites. The White Paper on A Domestic Satellite Communication System for Canada of 28 March 1968 points out with a sense of urgency that frequencies and parking space for Canadian domestic satellites are limited and adequate measures should be taken to secure both for Canada. The number of suitable parking locations is limited to perhaps six or seven at the most, since a separation of about six degrees between satellites on geostationary orbit is thought to be practical. The *White Paper* reminds us that:

> efficient and fair exploitation of those limited resources, frequencies and parking locations in synchronous orbit [require] a considerable measure of technical consulation and coordination between the countries responsible for the various satellite communication systems.[17]

The *White Paper* reflects uncertainty as to the law relative to the establishing of rights in outer space:

> Parking spaces and frequencies are essentially international, in the sense that they cannot be claimed by one country. The procedures for establishing rights of first occupation are not yet fully defined.[18]

The *White Paper,* however, did not fail to point to the fact that:

> In most instances of radio frequency use, formal international recognition

[17] White Paper on Domestic Satellite Communication System for Canada, The Honourable C. M. Drury, Minister of Industry, 28 March 1968, p. 66. Hereafter this document will be referred to as *White Paper.*

[18] *Ibid.*

of a country's requirements tends to be achieved on a first-come, first-served basis. There is, therefore, a degree of urgency that planning for the Canadian domestic system should proceed apace.[19]

The *White Paper* was preceded by two separate studies which provide more detailed insights into this most interesting case. As will be seen, these documents deserve special attention because they reflect a decision-making process which may very well set a precedent which other states may come to regard as a standard of conduct. To be sure, no formal claim has yet been staked by the Canadian government for designated parking locations for Canadian communications satellites and one cannot be sure if the Canadian government will ever consider such a course of action the only possible means to safeguard Canadian interests. There are other ways to achieve the same goal: for example, through negotiation and co-ordination of activities with other interested States on a regional basis. But the decisive point is the fact that the Canadian government, or for that matter any government, should be able to dispose of its claim to exercise exclusive jurisdiction over parking locations as a matter of right, rather than restraint based on *ad hoc* bargaining. A closer look at the documents in question will reveal an implicit trend towards the proposed concept of *functional jurisdiction.* It will be well to recall here again that the concept of *functional jurisdiction* puts states in the position from which they can negotiate on the basis of an explicit right to extend their jurisdiction to designated areas and zones in outer space for a functionally determined purpose. Whatever action the Canadian government will finally decide to take, an eventual forbearance of the exercise of exclusive jurisdiction should be considered as a commendable example of moderation, rather than deference to a supposed prohibitive rule of international space law.

1. The Sources

A. The Royal Commission on Government Organization called attention to the fragmentation of governmental non-military space research and suggested that it be consolidated into a single agency in January, 1963. Following this early consideration of the problems of Canadian involvement in space research, the Science Secretariat of the Privy Council Office commissioned in May, 1966, the first comprehensive study of Canadian upper atmosphere and space programs. The study group consisting of Dr. J. H. Chapman, Defense Research Board (Chairman), Dr. P. A. Forsyth, University of Western Ontario, Dr. P. A. Lapp, de Havilland Aircraft of Canada Ltd., and Dr. G. N. Patterson, University of Toronto, submitted

[19] *Id.*

its report to the Science Secretariat at the end of 1966. It was published in February, 1967, as Science Secretariat, Special Study No. 1, *Upper Atmosphere and Space Programs in Canada.*[20] It became known as the *Chapman Report* and is so referred to in this study.[21] The *Chapman Report* is an initial source of background information relating to Canadian space research. It reflects the consolidated view of universities, industrial corporations, government departments and agencies, technical associations and professional persons. Hearings were held in several cities of Canada and visits were made to the headquarters of the National Aeronautics and Space Administration in Washington, as well as to European and Japanese space facilities. The study group examined scientific, technological, economic, and other benefits from space science. Particular attention was given to questions of "make or buy."

The Report pointed out Canada's "unique geographical position"[22] and stressed the need "to develop competitive technologies, to train and educate scientists and engineers, and to resist firmly the erosion of national control over the essential fabric of our (Canadian) national structure" if Canada is to retain "an independent identity" and provide "an acceptable standard of living for its people."[23]

The Report reflects three areas of consensus, namely:

(i) The need for a central organization for space activities in Canada;

(ii) The need for Canadian satellites for domestic telecommunications by 1970 or 1971;

(iii) The growing need for a Canadian satellite launching capability.[24]

B. The *Chapman Report* was considered at the meetings of the Science Council of Canada in January, March, May, and June, 1967. In turn the Science Council published its findings and recommendations in July, 1967, under the title *A Space Program for Canada.*[25] It is referred to as *Science*

[20] Science Secretariat, Special Study No. 1, *Upper Atmosphere and Space Programs in Canada* by J. H. Chapman, P. A. Forsyth, P. A. Lapp, G. N. Patterson. (Science Secretariat Privy Council Office, February, 1967) pp. 258.

[21] The *present writer* felt free to draw heavily on the text of the three documents which are discussed in this chapter. For the responsibility of the Science Council of Canada under the Science Council of Canada Act, see *Chapman Report* at 2–3.

[22] *Ibid.* at 4.

[23] *Id.* the *Chapman Report* consists of three parts. The first part describes current and projected government, university, and industrial programs for the 1961 to 1971 period. The second part is devoted to Canadian international space programs. Part three of the report is in the nature of an appendix to the first part, presenting the Harp-McGill University research program.

[24] Science Council of Canada, Report No. 1, *A Space Program for Canada* (July 1967), pp. 31.

[25] See note above.

Council Report in this study. The *Science Council Report* has taken fully into account the comments and recommendations of the *Chapman Report* but has not formally endorsed them.[26] This document consists of three parts, namely: Introduction, Findings and Recommendations, and Canadian Activities in Upper Atmosphere and Space. The Report deals with the following questions: Canadian Space Agency, Space Facilities, Satellite Communications, Resource Exploration by Satellite, Satellite Launching Systems, Industrial Development, University Space Research Programs, Space and the Law.[27]

C. Subsequent to the *Science Council Report* the Government appointed a Task Force[28] in July, 1967, "to study and advise on the question of satellite communications in the Canadian context". The previously mentioned *White Paper* is the outcome of the recommendations of this Task Force, which may be considered the last although not final pronouncement of the Canadian Government on the question. The Government's conclusion is "that a domestic satellite communication system is of vital importance for the growth, prosperity, and unity of Canada, and should be established as a matter of priority."[29] The *White Paper* consists of seven chapters, appendices and a useful glossary of terms. The first chapter describes the significance and technique of communication by satellite. The second chapter is devoted to international cooperation in the field of telecommunication by satellites. Chapters three to seven deal with Canadian capabilities and needs, the nature of the domestic satellite communication system and international implications of the establishment of the system. The recommendations are summarized in Chapter Seven.

[26] *Ibid.* at 3.

[27] It is of interest to quote from the Science Council Report the passage explaining the term upper atmosphere and space as used in the Council's findings:

> The terms upper atmosphere and space are used, usually together, to refer to the continuum to which the scientific activity under discussion is directed. There is no definite boundary between upper atmosphere and space. The combination is the earth-bound region in which phenomena of space merge with phenomena of the earth and its atmosphere ... Roughly speaking the upper atmosphere is just above the levels currently used by high-flying aircraft and above the zone in which phenomena that constitute the weather occur ...
>
> ... space used by itself should be given the same meaning: that is, it includes upper atmosphere. Any more specific meaning for *space* is suitably qualified, for example, *outer* space, *inter-planetary* space, etc.

Id. at 4.

[28] The Task Force was created by the Prime Minister of Canada on July 14, 1967. It interviewed interested parties both inside and outside the Government as well as abroad. The findings of the Task Force and its recommendations were submitted to the Federal Government early in November, 1967. Cf. *White Paper* at 78 *et seq.*

[29] *White Paper* at 8.

2. *Basis of the Recommended Claim, or the Substance of the Term "Canada's Particular and Distinctive Requirements"*

A. For the purposes of the *Chapman Report* the term domestic satellite communications via satellites means "traffic originating from points within Canada and destined for other points within Canada, but may also include internal extensions of external circuits."[30] The principal uses for domestic satellite communications in Canada (hereafter referred to as DOMSATCOM) would be:

(a) for telephone, telegraph and data communication with remote communities in Canada which are not presently served by landlines or terrestrial radio relay facilities. Satellite ground stations would also be capable of receiving TV and radio programs for retransmission through local broadcasting or over a cable distribution system;

(b) for distribution of TV and radio programs from central satellite ground transmitters, beamed from satellite to receiving stations which would receive the signals and feed them to local TV and radio transmitters or distribution cables. This would not be a direct broadcasting system. This system would provide coverage as far north as 78°. For the first time it would be possible to provide a truly national TV and radio program service to people in all parts of Canada. Communities having a population of not less than 300 could be economically linked to the system. Because of Canada's vast expanses in the east-west direction, it would be necessary to broadcast the English language TV and radio programs in 6 time zones and French language programs in at least 3 time zones, with a possible future need to provide French programming in 6 time zones;

(c) for long-distance general telecommunications traffic in an east-west direction. A satellite communication system of this nature could provide bulk service between major Canadian cities;

(d) for direct broadcast to homes and schools. There is a growing demand for educational television (ETV) channels in Canada. Direct broadcasting to home TV receivers from satellites is still some time off but the possibility is much greater that direct broadcasting of FM radio programs to homes and automotive receivers may be introduced within a few years.[31]

The establishment of DOMSATCOM would require geostationary satellites in an equatorial orbit.[32] The provision of DOMSATCOM to provide

[30] *Chapman Report* at 17.

[31] *Ibid.* at 17–19.

[32] The *White Paper* gives the following definition of synchronous (stationary or geostationary) orbit:

> A satellite in such an orbit appears to be stationary from any point on the earth, although its velocity is about six thousand nine hundred statute miles per hour. In such an orbit a satellite passes around the earth in approximately twenty-four hours corresponding to the rotation of the earth. A synchronous satellite must have

both telecommunications to isolated areas and a truly national TV coverage in both French and English is strongly recommended by the *Chapman Report* to be a major aim of the Federal Government.

After an examination of the growth and needs of the Canadian communications industry the Report estimates that 12 to 20 TV channels from satellites will be needed for domestic Canadian use by 1980.

The most decisive part of the whole complex of DOMSATCOM is the question of ownership or control of Canadian satellites. Should Canada own its own domestic satellites or rent them from COMSAT. Here the *Chapman Report* touches on the crux of the problem. In the words of the Report:

> The principal factor in this question is that the space 22,300 miles above the equator along a belt approximately of 18,000 miles long (20° either side of 95°W longitude), is available to any country for operation of a synchronous satellite for domestic TV transmissions.[33]

Space law, points out the Report, "would seem to permit Canada the right to lay claim to a piece of this sky as a location for satellites for Canada's particular needs."[34] The Report considers Canada's needs modest in relation to those of INTELSAT, the U.S. and South American countries.

Accordingly, the *Chapman Report* concludes:

> The sky territory for location of Canada's satellites is valuable. If given over to the U.S., or any other country, this territory could be lost forever. Staked in the near future, it could be used to fulfill *Canada's particular and distinctive requirements*. Ownership of this property would give Canada due bargaining power in the evolution of an overall domestic satellite service for all of North and South America. This territory should be treated as prudently as Canada's water resources. It should be shared, rented or sold only on terms that are good for Canada.[35] (Emphasis supplied)

Accordingly, the Report concludes that the ownership and operation by Canada of the Canadian DOMSATCOM is "most vital."[36]

The Report does not, however, overlook the necessity of concluding bilateral agreements with the U.S. in order to regulate the positioning and frequency sharing of Canadian and U.S. communications satellites. A Ca-

an average altitude above the earth of approximately twenty-two thousand three hundred statute miles.

at 94.

[33] *Chapman Report* at 86.

[34] *Ibid.*

[35] *Id.*

[36] *Id.*

nadian satellite would most likely be positioned between two U.S. satellites and they would use the same frequency band under present frequency assignments. The *Chapman Report* also urges that frequencies above 10,000 Mc/s and below 14,000 Mc/s should be reassigned for communications satellite use on an exclusive worldwide basis and also that frequencies for direct satellite-to-home transmission (470 to 890 Mc/s) should be reserved.

Obviously, of considerable importance for Canada is who will ultimately provide the space segment required for DOMSATCOM.[37] The following passage from the *Chapman Report* is quoted for its directness illustrating the national implications of the significance of legal rules, which can provide adequate safeguards regarding national interests in outer space and also that a State gets its due:

> The provision of satellites for Canadian use is a commercial operation which requires technical and managerial skill and competence, and which includes an element of risk. It would be unfortunate if this package, including substantial profits, were to go to a foreign corporation, since the technical competence and capability to build this family of satellites now exist in Canadian industry.
>
> The outlook for the communications industry clearly will be much brighter if a Government decision were made to assign responsibility for provision of the space segment of future Canadian communications to a Canadian agency and to authorize a Canadian Communications satellite program.[38]

B. The *Science Council Report* describes "Canada's particular and distinctive requirements" in a fashion similar to that of the *Chapman Report.* Thus, it points out the necessity and "tremendous advantage" of DOMSATCOM for Canada[39] and stresses the fact more than once, that "there is only one orbit for geostationary satellites, and in due course it could become overcrowded."[40] The *Science Council Report* even amplifies the warning of the previous report to the effect that the national interest of Canada regarding at least a fair participation in the provision of the space segment and in the sharing of benefit of the discovery and development of the resources, requires "a much more dynamic policy" and "a strong sustained national effort."[41]

C. The *White Paper,* by introducing new ideas, in a way complements the above-mentioned two reports by explaining "Canada's particular and distinctive requirements." Thus the *White Paper,* while stressing the geo-

[37] The term "space segment" means all those aspects of a system which are concerned with the creation, launching and control of the satellite. *White Paper* at 92.

[38] *Chapman Report* at 89.

[39] *Science Council Report* at 29–30.

[40] *Ibid.* at 28.

[41] *Id.* at 7.

graphical factor, adds that "communication by satellite represents a revolution which will profoundly affect the whole future pattern of national and international communications." DOMSATCOM "would not be simply a marginal improvement or addition to the present system." It would be "the only means to provide the 'jump' in the capacity needed to ensure the rapid expansion in the services now contemplated."[42] Communications satellites can span large areas in North-South and East-West distances. They can relay television and telephone signals to many widely separated points simultaneously and eliminate the need for costly relay stations. Estimates show that already over distances exceeding six hundred to a thousand miles satellite communications service is more economical than the terrestrial communications network.

Perhaps the most succinct definition of the term "particular and distinctive requirements," which we think would be sufficient to substantiate an eventual claim to *functional jurisdiction* over a designated section of a geostationary orbit, can be found in Chapter I of the *White Paper:*

> The significance of this revolutionary technique to Canada with its enormous areas of difficult terrain and its widely distributed population is fundamental and obvious. It offers the first opportunity to provide, economically, television and reliable telephone service to the North and other sparsely populated areas. It provides dramatic and far reaching opportunities to increase the distribution of French and English TV programmes from coast to coast; for it allows Canadians, wherever they are, to benefit from the simultaneous transmission of television programmes in both languages. Wherever it is justified, a modest receiving station and television transmitter can be installed to serve any locality.[43]

The technique, which the *White Paper* describes extensively, deserves attention in order to be able to appreciate the "functional" element of an eventual exercise of *functional jurisdiction.* After describing what a stationary satellite is the *White Paper* states:

> It is this type of "stationary" or "synchronous" satellite which is now favoured by most countries for communication purposes. It would carry a somewhat directional antenna, limiting its coverage to the area it is designed to serve. A satellite located in a stationary orbit over the equator, between 80°W and 120°W longitude would be "visible" from any point in Canada, including the far North up to 78° latitude. The most suitable position would be approximately midway between these two points, at roughly the same latitude as Winnipeg. From this position its antenna would provide coverage for the whole of Canada.[44]

The limited number of available parking locations for Canadian communications satellites continues to be a grave concern also for the *White*

[42] *White Paper* at 10.
[43] *Ibid.* at 14.
[44] *Id.* at 14.

Paper:

The number of possible communication satellites which may be placed in such an orbit is limited. There is a natural limit imposed by the number of suitable frequencies that are available in the electro-magnetic spectrum, requiring satellite separation to avoid interference between satellite transmission beams. At this time the necessary separation between satellites using the same frequencies is considered to be about six degrees of longitude.[45]

The *White Paper* declared that "Canada has an established need for a domestic satellite communication system . . . and that the technique is a natural one for the Canadian environment."[46] It was pointed out that East-West general communications requirements were growing at a rate of about twenty per cent per year.[47] Consequently, an early start must be made implying "that agreements should be obtained, as soon as possible, for the coordinated use of radio frequencies which have been assigned by the ITU and of satellite locations needed for a Canadian domestic satellite communication system."[48]

3. *The Legal Nature of the Recommended Claim*

That a formal claim should be made by the Canadian Government to a designated belt of a synchronous orbit was most explicitly expressed in the *Chapman Report*. The Report formulated its recommendation in the following words:

The space available for locating synchronous communications satellites is limited, and Canada has a clear claim to a reasonable number of positions for domestic communications satellites.

Therefore it is recommended:

(c) that Canadian rights to station satellites in synchronous orbit locations between 75°W and 115°W longitude be established by international agreement and taken up by occupation within a reasonable time.[49]

The *Chapman Report* also drew attention to the unsatisfactory international assignment for Canada of radio frequencies. Therefore it recommended:

(d) that consideration be given to reassignment by ITU of frequencies for communications satellites to increase the bandwidth available, to remove the limitations due to interference with the present radio-relay services in Canada,

[45] *Id.* at 15–16.
[46] *Id.* at 32.
[47] *Id.* at 34.
[48] *Id.* at 36.
[49] *Chapman Report* at 112.

and to provide frequencies for direct TV broadcast from satellites.[50]

The *Science Council Secretariat Report's* recommendation is almost a word for word replica of that of the *Chapman Report:*

> There is only one orbit in which satellites are stationary with respect to the earth. It is about three earth diameters above the equator, and it must serve all the nations of the world. Canada should press for international agreement on the use of this synchronous orbit, and should seek rights to station Canadian satellites in it at locations between longitudes 75°W and 115°W. Moreover, Canada should be prepared to demonstrate her intention to exercise these rights.[51]

Further, the *Report* stressed:

> The radio frequencies assigned by the International Telecommunications Union for satellite communications in North and South America are not satisfactory to most users . . . Canada should continue to press for a solution that would increase the bandwidth available and remove the limitations due to interference with the present radio relay services in Canada. It is also desirable to secure an early allocation of frequencies suitable for direct television broadcast from satellites.[52]

As is apparent, the tenor of the recommendation was not toned down although some changes were introduced into the wording. Thus, the word "occupation" disappeared in the *Science Council Report's* recommendation. Occupation is only one way to acquire rights and this mode of acquisition may not always be desirable or necessary. Whatever the motive behind the change in wording was, one should not overlook the fact that the recommendation to the effect that Canada "demonstrate her intention to exercise these rights, [i.e. to reserve parking locations] within a reasonable time" affords a wider choice of action and does not rule out the "demonstration of intention" through effective occupation. It would seem to the present writer that a formal claim to exercise *functional jurisdiction* relative to parking locations would be more in line with the general meaning of the *Science Council Report.*

The *White Paper* represents the authoritative opinion of the Federal Government of Canada. Government policy objectives are expressed generally in more complex, as opposed to the rather explicit language of the previous two documents. The *White Paper* makes mention of the Treaty on Outer Space and handles the question of DOMSATCOM in its international context. It observes that "the space segment of a satellite

50 *Ibid.*
51 *Ibid.* at 9–10.
52 *Id.* at 10–11.

communication system is international by its very nature," because "any synchronous satellite occupies a permanent position in the international domain of outer space."[53] It appears to be the Canadian Government's intention to settle conflicting claims to the same parking location through international agreement between the states concerned. Accordingly, the *White Paper* recommends that:

> In establishing a Canadian domestic system it will be necessary, therefore, to reach agreement with other Governments who might feel that they too have an interest in using the same part of outer space, either now or in the future.[54]

The absence in the *White Paper* of a recommendation that the Canadian Government lay an explicit claim to certain parking locations does not reflect the abandonment of the idea at all. In fact, in the *White Paper* the unclarified situation which reigns in space when the international nature of outer space comes in contrast with the exploitation of outer space by individual states. Thus, the *White Paper* does not attempt to solve this thorny legal problem. Instead, it reaffirmed the international status of outer space, stressed on numerous occasions the fact that the number of parking locations is limited to "six or seven [at] the most," and provided a substantiated presentation of Canada's requirements that can be met only by a fair sharing of the available locations. No leads were given as to what action the Canadian Government would take to secure the needed parking locations. The language of the *White Paper* is rightly non-committal, and only a general reference is made to the necessity of international negotiations and agreements with other Governments who may have similar claims. In this way the door is not shut, the Government is not committed to a specific policy and remains free to choose the course of action that will eventually best serve Canadian interest. It would be a rash conclusion to say that the recommendations of the previously examined reports are overruled by the findings of the *White Paper,* because the *White Paper* itself pointed out that "the procedures for establishing rights of first occupation are not yet fully defined."[55]

From the legal point of view the findings of the *Chapman* and the *Science Council Reports* amount to suggesting that Canada extend the exercise of *functional jurisdiction* to a designated parking location. The formal basis of the proposed claim we take to be "Canada's particular and distinctive requirements."

[53] *White Paper* at 62.

[54] *Ibid.*

[55] *Id.* at 66. It should be noted that the *White Paper* referred in this context to the fact that "in most cases of radio frequency use, formal international recognition of a country's requirements tends to be achieved on a first-come, first-served basis."

It goes without saying that Canada is entitled to launch its communications satellites in a synchronous orbit. This right clearly follows from Article 1, Paragraph 2 of the Treaty on Outer Space. Implicitly, Canada has a right to parking locations and also is entitled to expect other States to respect this right. Moreover, it may proceed under international and municipal law to provide adequate safeguards.

On the other hand, it stands equally clear that the principle of non-appropriation of outer space including celestial bodies declared by Article 2 of the Treaty on Outer Space is an imperative rule of international space law. The validity of an eventual claim by the Canadian Government, therefore, would depend on the purpose of the claim. Clearly no State could lawfully claim sovereignty over parking locations thereby extracting this belt from the common régime of outer space. If, however, the claim satisfies the requirements we outlined in the preceding pages on *functional jurisdiction,* then in our view it will be in conformity with the developing principles of international space law.

Indeed, the documents examined above draw attention to a delicate problem centering around the exploitation and uses of outer space. We saw the emergence of a new criterion, that of "particular and distinctive requirements" which was used as a shorthand for substantiating claims for parking locations in outer space. It would be, of course, too academic to embark upon guessing games as to the manner in which this criterion can be manipulated by governments; nevertheless it is prudent to register at least the existence of this phenomenon in Canadian policy.

The previous material may be summarised as follows: Although, as we pointed out above, there are no developed rules of international space law stemming from State practice with direct bearing on the question of apportionment of space resources in general and parking locations in particular, a synthesis of the principles declared in the Treaty on Outer Space and those of general international law would undoubtedly provide a body of law to apply to the case in point. At the very least, it can be said with certainty that in no case could any state proceed unilaterally with exploitation procedures based on unrestricted occupation of parking locations for a synchronous satellite to the prejudice of all other interested states. On the other hand, the protection of rights ensured by Article 1 of the Treaty on Outer Space through the exercise of *functional jurisdiction* would be soundly in keeping with the progressive development of international space law. Articles 1, 3 and 9 of the Treaty on Outer Space imposes the obligation of international cooperation on the Contracting States.

From this obligation and future experiences to be derived from the increasing use and exploitation of outer space, sufficient ground will be created for international codification of such practices and procedures. Thereafter, the role of inter-governmental bodies, in the form of specialised international regulatory committees or regional mixed commissions, may very well become of practical importance. Even until this stage of development is reached, continued individual initiative by States to co-operate appears to be the only realistic solution for the progressive development of international space law.[56] The law that will ultimately develop must be fair and equitable. It is therefore submitted in conclusion that only such a law as is founded on international co-operation, agreement, reasonableness, common sense and a system of efficient safeguards is likely to be acceptable for both space powers and prospective space users.[57]

[56] For the position of the Canadian Government regarding international cooperation and especially with ITU, see *White Paper* at 62 *et seq.* By way of analogy reference is made here, for example, to the intergovernmental sea fishery bodies and state practice regarding the sharing of international common petroleum deposits. Cf. J. E. Carroz and A. G. Roche, *loc. cit. supra;* William T. Onorato, *loc. cit. supra.* See also, Paper presented by the International Telecommunication Union entitled "Difficulties Liable to Arise from the Launching and/or Operation of a Space Object Through Non-Compliance with International Regulations Governing the Use of the Radio-frequency Spectrum", in *Report of the Committee on the Peaceful Uses of Outer Space,* (New York, 1968) U.N. Doc. A/7285 at 202–203. This paper is reproduced as Appendix III of this report at the request of the Canadian delegation.

[57] For further developments regarding the establishment of DOMSATCOM, see *inter alia* Bernard Kaplan, "Ottawa hunts data on satellite," *The Montreal Star,* January 12, 1968, p. 1, col. 1; Brian Upton, "Quebec wants say in programs," *ibid.,* at p. 1, col. 1 & p. 2, col. 6; "A satellite system for Canada", *The Montreal Star,* January 13, 1968, p. 9; Bernard Kaplan, "'Quebec comes first' Ottawa gets rebuff on French satellite," *The Montreal Star,* January 16, 1968, p. 1, col. 7; Steve Hendler, "Canada space program urged," *The Montreal Star,* February 22, 1968, p. 4, col. 6 & p. 5, col. 8; "All-Canada satellite network proposed in new legislation," *The Montreal Star,* April 2, 1968, p. 1, col. 3 & p. 4, col. 3; "Satellite program shared," *The Montreal Star,* August 17, 1968, p. 1, col. 8. "Satellite project agreed," *The Montreal Star,* January 24, 1969, p. 1, col. 1; "Confusion clouds Quebec-Paris talks," *The Montreal Star,* January 25, 1969, p. 1, cols. 4, 6 & p. 4, cols. 1–2.

CONCLUSION

The purpose of the foregoing pages was to assess the progressive development in the United Nations of the concept of State jurisdiction in international space law. It is important here to recall the earlier reference in the *Introduction* to the fact that the scope of enquiry of this work was intentionally limited to the U.N. practice. Thus, we endeavoured to illustrate on the basis of U.N. documents that the concept of State jurisdiction has undergone a process of modification in space law. It is no longer based on concepts of sovereignty, appropriation and territoriality.

In Chapter II the doctrine of State jurisdiction was described in general terms, the purpose being to provide some sort of a balancesheet. The terms of reference and the activity of the Legal Sub-Committee of the UNCOPUOS were then examined against this background.

Chapter III dealt with the actual contribution of the UNCOPUOS to the progressive development of the concept of State jurisdiction as illustrated by the Agreement on the Rescue of Astronauts, the Return of Astronauts and the Return of Objects Launched into Outer Space of 1967, and the draft of an agreement relative to the question of Liability for Damage Caused by the Launching of Objects into Outer Space as of June, 1968.

Chapter IV was devoted to the *lex lata* governing the exercise of State jurisdiction in outer space including celestial bodies.

Finally, in Chapter V we expounded in detail our proposal regarding the concept of *functional jurisdiction* and, as a matter of illustration, we also passed on the international jurisdictional implications of the establishment of a Canadian domestic communications satellite system.

We wish to conclude this study by emphasizing the organizational and administrative requirements that are necessary for the fulfillment of the objectives of the Treaty on Outer Space, notably that outer space including celestial bodies be used for peaceful purposes as well as exploited for the benefit of every country on the basis of international space law in the spirit of co-operation, co-ordination, a fair measure of international regulation and in accordance with the standards of economic efficiency. It is inevitable that some new universal or regional inter-governmental bodies will come into existence to attend to the business generated by increasingly regular space activities. In the face of this prognosis, the rationality and plausibility of which is widely acknowledged, it is somewhat disappointing to note that the already more than one-decade-old U.N. involvement in the progressive development of space law has not produced results. The blame, of course, should not be put in front of the door of the U.N., since it is the non-committal stance of the two space powers regarding the vesting of certain powers in international organizations that presently provides the major stumbling block.

Nevertheless, the U.N. Secretariat has been performing highly useful evidentiary and recording functions in pursuance of U.N. General Assembly Resolution 1721 (XVI) of December 20, 1961, and the Secretary-General of the U.N. is empowered to disseminate "immediately and effectively" information received from States regarding the nature, conduct, locations and results of space activities under Article XI of the Treaty on Outer Space. To be sure, these responsibilities carried out by the U.N. are based on the discretion and co-operation of Member States rather than on legally enforceable obligations on the latters' part. Beyond this point, no consensus as to the nature of international space administration can be unearthed from the U.N. practice. The question of the creation of an international space agency under the auspices of the U.N. has not been put on the agenda of the Legal Sub-Committee of the UNCOPUOS. The U.N. is, of course, not indifferent toward this question. The effect of the Treaty on Outer Space on international organizations was extensively discussed in the Legal Sub-Committee of the UNCOPUOS.[58] The Report of the UNCOPUOS to the General Assembly, as adopted at its 59th meeting, on October 18, 1968 bears evidence that the importance of the problem is growing. Accordingly, participants in the Conference on the Exploration and Peaceful Uses of Outer Space, held in Vienna from August 14 to 27, 1968, discussed suggestions regarding the extension of the role of the United Nations in the obligatory registration of the launching of objects into outer

[58] See U.N. Doc. A/AC.105/C.2/SR. 64 at 13 (India); A/AC.105/C.2/SR. 66 at 11 (Italy); *ibid.* at 12 (U.S.A.); *id.* (U.S.S.R.); *id.* (United Kingdom); *id.* at 13 (United Kingdom); *id.* (France); *id.* (Australia); *id.* at 14 (Romania); A/AC.105/C.2/SR.70 at 10 (Italy); *ibid.* at 12 (Sweden); *id.* at 14 (Canada) *id.* at 15 (France).

[59] *Report of the Committee on the Peaceful Uses of Outer Space,* A/7285, General Assembly, Official Records Twenty-Third Session, Agenda item 24. (United Nations, New York, 1968) p. 85.

space.[59] Clearly, the establishment of an international agency with full-fledged power to control, regulate and administer the exploration and uses of outer space is out of sight. Perhaps it should be added that our own feeling is that the creation of an international space agency with statutory power to carry out such wide responsibilities, if only it were currently feasible, would be highly advantageous, and would benefit the whole of mankind.

Be that as it may, rather than enter into self-defeating speculations, the main principles enunciated by the Treaty on Outer Space and the emerging need for secure titles and avoidance of "first come first served" tactics and the ensuing conflicts, could be fulfilled if regional inter-governmental organizations or mixed commissions were established to carry out evidentiary and recording functions. Attention is drawn in this context to facts of contemporary international relations. First, the International Telecommunication Union already performs a function similar to the one just mentioned. However, the ITU has only power to regulate the use of the valuable property of radio frequencies; it does not have power to allocate parking locations which is, as will be recalled, an equally important requirement for establishing a stationary satellite communications system. Secondly, the decision of the Soviet Union and other of its allies to go along with their own space communications network, called INTERSPUTNIK,[60] points to the rise of regional interests in outer space in general and relative to a satellite orbit belt in particular. The reluctance of the Soviet Union regarding the transfer of decision-making powers to international bodies, and the difficulties of sharing of control by member states over an eventual space organization, only make our suggestion to start with international regional bodies rather than a universal institution more realistic.[61]

60 See message from Soviet Premier Kosygin to the U.N. Conference on the Peaceful Uses of Outer Space. *Report of the UNCOPUOS* ... A/7285 (1968) pp. 24–25. Thomas J. Hamilton, "Soviet to establish space communications network to compete with Intelsat," *The New York Times,* August 15, 1968, p. 18; "Soviet space plans called duplication," *The New York Times,* August 17, 1968, p. 14. For suggestions and opinions regarding the role of international organizations relative to outer and ocean space, see Jenks, 131; Christol, 424–425; Jessup and Taubenfeld, 256–261. Alexander (ed.) *loc. cit. supra* at 282 *et seq.*

61 See closing statement by Dr. Kurt Waldheim, President of the U.N. Conference on the Peaceful Uses of Outer Space held in Vienna from 14 to 27 August 1968:

> International co-operation is likewise necessary and desirable. The needs and goals of the various geographical areas seem to be different. Whereas, for example, advanced countries might find it interesting to use satellites for the automatic transmission and exchange of data, developing countries might wish to give more weight to the use of satellites for agriculture, water management, education and training and the survey of earth resources. Regional co-operation is therefore of

Recalling the opening sentence of this study – that international space law has become a reality – we should like to conclude by saying that after the Treaty on Outer Space and the Agreement on Rescue and Return, international legal scholars may well be advised to turn their attention to the details and the less dramatic elaboration of a comprehensive, positivist doctrine of international space law. This requires a step-by-step method and well-timed work. It was this consideration that motivated this modest study.

great importance and can lead – as in the case of Europe – to the establishment of regional organizations.

Report of the UNCOPUOS ... 1968 p. 95.

DECLARATION OF LEGAL PRINCIPLES GOVERNING THE ACTIVITIES OF STATES IN THE EXPLORATION AND USE OF OUTER SPACE

Unanimously adopted by the General Assembly of the United Nations on December 13, 1963[1]

The General Assembly

Inspired by the great prospects opening up before mankind as a result of man's entry into outer space,

Recognizing the common interest of all mankind in the progress of the exploration and use of outer space for peaceful purposes.

Believing that the exploration and use of outer space should be carried on for the benefit of all peoples irrespective of the degree of their economic or scientific development,

Desiring to contribute to broad international co-operation in the scientific as well as the legal aspects of the exploration and use of outer space for peaceful purposes,

Believing that such co-operation will contribute to the development of mutual understanding and to the strengthening of friendly relations between states and peoples,

Recalling its resolution 110 (II) of November 3, 1947, which condemned propaganda designed or likely to provoke or encourage any threat to the peace, breach of the peace, or act of aggression, and considering that the aforementioned resolution is applicable to outer space,

Taking into consideration its resolutions 1721 (XVI) of December 20, 1961, and 1802 (XVII) of December 14, 1962, adopted unanimously by the States Members of the United Nations,

Solemnly declares that in the exploration and use of outer space States should be guided by the following principles:

1. The exploration and use of outer space shall be carried on for the benefit and in the interests of all mankind.
2. Outer space and celestial bodies are free for exploration and use by all States on a basis of equality and in accordance with international law.
3. Outer space and celestial bodies are not subject to national appropriation by claim of sovereignty, by means of use or occupation, or by any other means.
4. The activities of States in the exploration and use of outer space shall be carried on in accordance with international law, including the Charter of the

1 Resolution 1962 (XVIII).

United Nations, in the interest of maintaining international peace and security and promoting international co-operation and understanding.

5. States bear international responsibility for national activities in outer space, whether carried on by governmental agencies or by non-governmental entities, and for assuring that national activities are carried on in conformity with the principles set forth in the present Declaration. The activities of non-governmental entities in outer space shall require authorisation and continuing supervision by the State concerned. When activities are carried on in outer space by an international organisation, responsibility for compliance with the principles set forth in this Declaration shall be borne by the international organisation and by the States participating in it.

6. In the exploration and use of outer space, States shall be guided by the principle of co-operation and mutual assistance and shall conduct all their activities in outer space with due regard for the corresponding interests of other States. If a State has reason to believe that an outer space activity or experiment planned by it or its nationals would cause potentially harmful interference with activities of other States in the peaceful exploration and use of outer space, it shall undertake appropriate international consultations before proceeding with any such activity or experiment. A State which has reason to believe that an outer space activity or experiment planned by another State would cause potentially harmful interference with activities in the peaceful exploration and use of outer space may request consultation concerning the activity or experiment.

7. The State on whose registry an object launched into outer space is carried shall retain jurisdiction and control over such object, and any personnel thereon, while in outer space. Ownership of objects launched into outer space, and of their component parts, is not affected by their passage through outer space or by their return to the Earth. Such objects or component parts found beyond the limits of the State or registry shall be returned to that State, which shall furnish identifying data upon request prior to return.

8. Each State which launches or procures the launching of an object into outer space, and each State from whose territory or facility an object is launched, is internationally liable for damage to a foreign State or to its natural or juridical persons by such object or its component parts on the Earth, in air space, or in outer space.

9. States shall regard astronauts as envoys of mankind in outer space, and shall render to them all possible assistance in the event of accident, distress, or emergency landing on the territory of a foreign State or on the high seas. Astronauts who make such a landing shall be safely and promptly returned to the State of registry of their space vehicle.

1280th Plenary Meeting
December 13, 1963

APPENDIX II

TREATY ON PRINCIPLES GOVERNING THE ACTIVITIES OF STATES IN THE EXPLORATION AND USE OF OUTER SPACE, INCLUDING THE MOON AND OTHER CELESTIAL BODIES

Signed at Washington, London and Moscow, January 27, 1967

The States Parties to this Treaty,

Inspired by the great prospects opening up before mankind as a result of man's entry into outer space,

Recognising the common interest of all mankind in the progress of the exploration and use of outer space for peaceful purposes,

Believing that the exploration and use of outer space should be carried on for the betterment of mankind and for the benefit of States irrespective of their degree of economic or scientific development,

Desiring to contribute to broad international co-operation in the scientific as well as in the legal aspects of exploration and use of outer space for peaceful purposes,

Believing that such co-operation will contribute to the development of mutual understanding and to the strengthening of friendly relations between nations and peoples,

Recalling Resolution 1962 (XVIII), entitled "Declaration of Legal Principles Governing the Activities of States in the Exploration and Use of Outer Space," which was adopted unanimously by the United Nations General Assembly on 13 December 1963,

Recalling Resolution 1884 (XVIII), calling upon states to refrain from placing in orbit around the Earth any objects carrying nuclear weapons or any other kinds of weapons of mass destruction or from installing such weapons on celestial bodies, which was adopted unanimously by the United Nations General Assembly on 17 October 1963,

Taking account of United Nations General Assembly Resolution 110 (II) of 3 November 1947, which condemned propaganda designed or likely to provoke or encourage any threat to the peace, breach of the peace or act of aggression, and considering that the aforementioned resolution is applicable to outer space,

Convinced that a Treaty on Principles Governing the Activities of States in the Exploration and Use of Outer Space, including the Moon and Other Celestial Bodies, will further the Purposes and Principles of the Charter of the United Nations,

Have agreed on the following:

ARTICLE I

The exploration and use of outer space, including the moon and other celestial bodies, shall be carried out for the benefit and in the interests of all countries, irrespective of their degree of economic or scientific development, and shall be the province of all mankind.

Outer space, including the moon and other celestial bodies, shall be free for exploration and use by all states without discrimination of any kind, on a basis of equality and in accordance with international law, and there shall be free access to all areas of celestial bodies.

There shall be freedom of scientific investigation in outer space, including the moon and other celestial bodies, and states shall facilitate and encourage international co-operation in such investigation.

ARTICLE II

Outer space, including the moon and other celestial bodies, is not subject to national appropriation by claim of sovereignty, by means of use or occupation, or by any other means.

ARTICLE III

States Parties to the Treaty shall carry on activities in the exploration and use of outer space, including the moon and other celestial bodies, in accordance with international law, including the Charter of the United Nations, in the interest of maintaining international peace and security and promoting international co-operation and understanding.

ARTICLE IV

States Parties to the Treaty undertake not to place in orbit around the Earth any objects carrying nuclear weapons or any other kinds of weapons of mass destruction, install such weapons on celestial bodies, or station such weapons in outer space in any other manner.

The moon and other celestial bodies shall be used by all States Parties to the Treaty exclusively for peaceful purposes. The establishment of military bases, installations and fortifications, the testing of any type of weapons and the conduct of military maneuvers on celestial bodies shall be forbidden. The use of military personnel for scientific research or for any other peaceful purposes shall not be prohibited. The use of any equipment or facility necessary for peaceful exploration of the moon and other celestial bodies shall also not be prohibited.

ARTICLE V

States Parties to the Treaty shall regard astronauts as envoys of mankind in outer space and shall render to them all possible assistance in the event of accident, distress, or emergency landing on the territory of another State Party or on the high seas. When astronauts make such a landing, they shall be safely and promptly returned to the state of registry of their space vehicle.

In carrying on activities in outer space and on celestial bodies, the astronauts of one State Party shall render all possible assistance to the astronauts of other States Parties.

States Parties to the Treaty shall immediately inform the other States Parties to the Treaty or the Secretary General of the United Nations of any phenomena they discover in outer space, including the moon and other celestial bodies, which could constitute a danger to the life or health of astronauts.

Article VI

States Parties to the Treaty shall bear international responsibility for national activities in outer space, including the moon and other celestial bodies, whether such activities are carried on by governmental agencies or by non-governmental entities, and for assuring that national activities are carried out in conformity with the provisions set forth in the present Treaty. The activities of non-governmental entities in outer space, including the moon and other celestial bodies, shall require authorization and continuing supervision by the appropriate State Party to the Treaty. When activities are carried on in outer space, including the moon and other celestial bodies, by an international organization, responsibility for compliance with this Treaty shall be borne both by the international organization and by the States Parties to the Treaty participating in such organization.

Article VII

Each State Party to the Treaty that launches or procures the launching of an object into outer space, including the moon and other celestial bodies, and each State Party from whose territory or facility an object is launched, is internationally liable for damage to another State Party to the Treaty or to its natural or juridical persons by such object or its component parts on the Earth, in air space or in outer space, including the moon and other celestial bodies.

Article VIII

A State Party to the Treaty on whose registry an object launched into outer space is carried shall retain jurisdiction and control over such object, and over any personnel thereof, while in outer space or on a celestial body. Ownership of objects launched into outer space, including objects landed or constructed on a celestial body, and of their component parts, is not affected by their presence in outer space or on a celestial body or by their return to the Earth. Such objects or component parts found beyond the limits of the State Party to the Treaty on whose registry they are carried shall be returned to that State Party, which shall, upon request, furnish identifying data prior to their return.

Article IX

In the exploration and use of outer space, including the moon and other celestial bodies, States Parties to the Treaty shall be guided by the principle of co-operation and mutual assistance and shall conduct all their activities in outer space, including the moon and other celestial bodies, with due regard to the corresponding interests of all other States Parties to the Treaty. States Parties to the Treaty shall pursue studies of outer space, including the moon and other celestial bodies, and conduct exploration of them so as to avoid their harmful contamination and also adverse changes in the environment of the Earth resulting from the introduction of extraterrestrial matter and, where necessary, shall adopt appropriate measures for this purpose. If a State Party to the Treaty has reason to believe that an activity or experiment planned by it or its nationals in outer space, including the moon and other celestial bodies, would cause potentially harmful interference with activities of other States Parties in the peaceful exploration and use of outer space, including the moon and other celestial bodies, it shall undertake appropriate international consultations before proceeding with any such activity or experiment. A State Party to the Treaty which has reason to believe that an activity or experiment planned by another State Party in outer space, including the moon and other celestial bodies, would cause potentially harmful interference with activities in the peaceful exploration and use of outer space, including the moon and other celestial bodies, may request consultation concerning the activity or experiment.

Article X

In order to promote international co-operation in the exploration and use of outer space, including the moon and other celestial bodies, in conformity with the purposes of this Treaty, the States Parties to the Treaty shall consider on a basis of equality any requests by other States Parties to the Treaty to be afforded an opportunity to observe the flight of space objects launched by those states.

The nature of such an opportunity for observation and the conditions under which it could be afforded shall be determined by agreement between the states concerned.

Article XI

In order to promote international co-operation in the peaceful exploration and use of outer space, States Parties to the Treaty conducting activities in outer space, including the moon and other celestial bodies, agree to inform the Secretary General of the United Nations as well as the public and the international scientific community, to the greatest extent feasible and practicable, of the nature, conduct, locations and results of such activities. On receiving the said information, the Secretary General of the United Nations should be prepared to disseminate it immediately and effectively.

Article XII

All stations, installations, equipment and space vehicles on the moon and other celestial bodies shall be open to representatives of other States Parties to the Treaty on a basis of reciprocity. Such representatives shall give reasonable advance notice of a projected visit, in order that appropriate consultations may be held and that maximum precautions may be taken to assure safety and to avoid interference with normal operations in the facility to be visited.

Article XIII

The provision of this Treaty shall apply to the activities of States Parties to the Treaty in the exploration and use of outer space, including the moon and other celestial bodies, whether such activities are carried on by a single State Party to the Treaty or jointly with other states, including cases where they are carried on within the framework of international intergovernmental organizations.

Any practical questions arising in connection with activities carried on by international inter-governmental organizations in the exploration and use of outer space, including the moon and other celestial bodies, shall be resolved by the States Parties to the Treaty either with the appropriate international organization or with one or more states members of that international organization, which are Parties to this Treaty.

Article XIV

1. This Treaty shall be open to all states for signature. Any state which does not sign this Treaty before its entry into force in accordance with paragraph 3 of this article may accede to it at any time.
2. This Treaty shall be subject to ratification by signatory states. Instruments of ratification and instruments of accession shall be deposited with the Governments of the United States of America, the United Kingdom of Great Britain and Northern Ireland and the Union of Soviet Socialist Republics, which are hereby designated the Depositary Governments.
3. This Treaty shall enter into force upon the deposit of instruments of ratification by five governments including the governments designated as Depositary Governments under this Treaty.
4. For states whose instruments of ratification or accession are deposited subsequent to the entry into force of this Treaty, it shall enter into force on the date of the deposit of their instruments of ratification or accession.
5. The Depositary Governments shall promptly inform all signatory and acceding states of the date of each signature, the date of deposit of each instrument of ratification of and accession to this Treaty, the date of its entry into force and other notices.
6. This Treaty shall be registered by the Depositary Governments pursuant to Article 102 of the Charter of the United Nations.

Article XV

Any State Party to the Treaty may propose amendments to this Treaty. Amendments shall enter into force for each State Party to the Treaty accepting the amendments upon their acceptance by a majority of the States Parties to the Treaty and thereafter for each remaining State Party to the Treaty on the date of acceptance by it.

ARTICLE XVI

Any State Party to the Treaty may give notice of its withdrawal from the Treaty one year after its entry into force by written notification to the Depositary Governments. Such withdrawal shall take effect one year from the date of receipt of this notification.

ARTICLE XVII

This Treaty, of which the English, Russian, French, Spanish and Chinese texts are equally authentic, shall be deposited in the archives of the Depositary Governments. Duly certified copies of this Treaty shall be transmitted by the Depositary Governments to the governments of the signatory and acceding states.

IN WITNESS WHEREOF the undersigned, duly authorized, have signed this Treaty.

DONE in triplicate, at the cities of Washington, London and Moscow, this twenty-seventh day of January one thousand nine hundred sixty-seven.

(Signatures omitted)

APPENDIX III

TREATY BANNING NUCLEAR WEAPONS TESTS IH THE ATMOSPHERE, IN OUTER SPACE AND UNDER WATER

The Governments of the United States of America, the United Kingdom of Great Britain and Northern Ireland, and the Union of Soviet Socialist Republics, hereinafter referred to as the "Original Parties",

Proclaiming as their principal aim the speediest possible achievement of an agreement on general and complete disarmament under strict international control in accordance with the objectives of the United Nations which would put an end to the armaments race and eliminate the incentive to the production and testing of all kinds of weapons, including nuclear weapons,

Seeking to achieve the discontinuance of all test explosions of nuclear weapons for all time, determined to continue negotiations to this end, and desiring to put an end to the contamination of man's environment by radioactive substances,

Have agreed as follows:

Article I

1. Each of the Parties to this Treaty undertakes to prohibit, to prevent, and not to carry out any nuclear weapon test explosion, or any other nuclear explosion, at any place under its jurisdiction or control:

(a) in the atmosphere; beyond its limits, including outer space; or underwater, including territorial waters or high seas; or

(b) in any other environment if such explosion causes radioactive debris to be present outside the territorial limits of the State under whose jurisdiction or control such explosion is conducted. It is understood in this connection that the provisions of this subparagraph are without prejudice to the conclusion of a treaty resulting in the permanent banning of all nuclear test explosions, including all such explosions underground, the conclusion of which, as the Parties have stated in the Preamble to this Treaty, they seek to achieve.

2. Each of the Parties to this Treaty undertakes furthermore to refrain from causing, encouraging, or in any way participating in, the carrying out of any nuclear weapon test explosion, or any other nuclear explosion, anywhere which would take place in any of the environments described, or have the effect referred to, in paragraph 1 of this Article:

ARTICLE II

1. Any Party may propose amendments to this Treaty. The text of any proposed amendment shall be submitted to the Depositary Governments which shall circulate it to all Parties to this Treaty. Thereafter, if requested to do so by one-third or more of the Parties, the Depositary Governments shall convene a conference, to which they shall invite all the Parties, to consider such amendment.

2. Any amendment to this Treaty must be approved by a majority of the votes of all the Parties to this Treaty, including the votes of all of the Original Parties. The amendment shall enter into force for all Parties upon the deposit of instruments of ratification by a majority of all the Parties, including the instruments of ratification of all of the Original Parties.

ARTICLE III

1. This Treaty shall be open to all States for signature. Any State which does not sign this Treaty before its entry into force in accordance with paragraph 3 of this Article may accede to it at any time.

2. This Treaty shall be subject to ratification by signatory States. Instruments of ratification and instruments of accession shall be deposited with the Governments of the Original Parties – the United States of America, the United Kingdom of Great Britain and Northern Ireland, and the Union of Soviet Socialist Republics – which are hereby designated the Depositary Governments.

3. This Treaty shall enter into force after its ratification by all the Original Parties and the deposit of their instruments of ratification.

4. For States whose instruments of ratification or accession are deposited subsequent to the entry into force of this Treaty, it shall enter into force on the date of the deposit of their instruments of ratification or accession.

5. The Depositary Governments shall promptly inform all signatory and acceding States of the date of each signature, the date of deposit of each instrument of ratification of and accession to this Treaty, the date of its entry into force, and the date of receipt of any requests for conferences or other notices.

6. This Treaty shall be registered by the Depositary Governments pursuant to Article 102 of the Charter of the United Nations.

ARTICLE IV

This Treaty shall be of unlimited duration.

Each Party shall in exercising its national sovereignty have the right to withdraw from the treaty if it decides that extraordinary events, related to the subject matter of this Treaty, have jeopardised the supreme interests of its country. It shall give notice of such withdrawal to all other Parties to the Treaty three months in advance.

ARTICLE V

This Treaty, of which the English and Russian texts are equally authentic, shall be deposited in the archives of the Depositary Governments. Duly certified copies of this Treaty shall be transmitted by the Depositary Governments to the Governments of the signatory and acceding States.

IN WITNESS WHEREOF the undersigned, duly authorised, have signed this Treaty.

DONE in triplicate at the city of Moscow the fifth day of August, one thousand nine hundred and sixty-three.

For the Government of the United States of America: DEAN RUSK.

For the Government of the United Kingdom of Great Britain and Northern Ireland: HOME.

For the Government of the Union of Soviet Socialist Republics: A. GROMYKO.

APPENDIX IV

AGREEMENT ON THE RESCUE OF ASTRONAUTS, THE RETURN OF ASTRONAUTS, AND THE RETURN OF OBJECTS LAUNCHED INTO OUTER SPACE

The Contracting Parties,

Noting the great importance of the Treaty on Principles Governing the Activities of States in the Exploration and Use of Outer Space, Including the Moon and Other Celestial Bodies, which calls for the rendering of all possible assistance to astronauts in the event of accident, distress or emergency landing, the prompt and safe return of astronauts, and the return of objects launched into outer space,

Desiring to develop and give further concrete expression to these duties,

Wishing to promote international co-operation in the peaceful exploration and use of outer space,

Prompted by sentiments of humanity,

Have agreed on the following:

Article I

Each Contracting Party which receives information or discovers that the personnel of a spacecraft have suffered accident or are experiencing conditions of distress or have made an emergency or unintended landing in territory under its jurisdiction or on the high seas or in any other place not under the jurisdiction of any State shall immediately:

(a) notify the launching authority or, if it cannot identify and immediately communicate with the launching authority, immediately make a public announcement by all appropriate means of communication at its disposal; and

(b) notify the Secretary-General of the United Nations who should disseminate the information without delay by all appropriate means of communication at his disposal.

Article II

If, owing to accident, distress, emergency or unintended landing, the personnel of a spacecraft land in territory under the jurisdiction of a Contracting Party, it shall immediately take all possible steps to rescue them and render them all necessary assistance. It shall inform the launching authority and also the Secretary-General of the United Nations of the steps it is taking and of their progress. If assistance by the launching authority would help to effect a prompt rescue or would contribute substantially to the effectiveness of search and rescue operations, the launching authority shall co-operate with the Contracting Party with a view to the effective conduct of search and rescue operations. Such operations shall be subject to the direction and control of the Contracting Party, which shall act in close and continuing consultation with the launching authority.

Article III

If information is received or it is discovered that the personnel of a spacecraft have alighted on the high seas or in any other place not under the jurisdiction of any State, those Contracting Parties which are in a position to do so shall, if necessary, extend assistance in search and rescue operations for such personnel to assure their speedy rescue. They shall inform the launching authority and the Secretary-General of the United Nations of the steps they are taking and of their progress.

Article IV

If, owing to accident, distress, emergency or unintended landing, the personnel of a spacecraft land in territory under the jurisdiction of a Contracting Party or have been found on the high seas or in any other place not under the jurisdiction of any State, they shall be safely and promptly returned to representatives of the launching authority.

Article V

1. Each Contracting Party which receives information or discovers that a space object or its component parts has returned to Earth in territory under its jurisdiction or on the high seas or in any other place not under the jurisdiction of any State, shall notify the launching authority and the Secretary-General of the United Nations,
2. Each Contracting Party having jurisdiction over the territory on which a space object or its component parts has been discovered shall, upon the request of the launching authority and with assistance from that authority if requested, take such steps as it finds practicable to recover the object or component parts.
3. Upon request of the launching authority, objects launched into outer space or their component parts found beyond the territorial limits of the launching authority shall be returned to or held at the disposal of representatives of the launching authority, which shall, upon request, furnish identifying data prior to their return.
4. Notwithstanding paragraphs 2 and 3 of this article, a Contracting Party which finds that a space object or its component parts discovered in territory under its jurisdiction, or recovered by it elsewhere, is of a hazardous or deleterious nature may so notify the launching authority which shall immediately take effective steps, under the direction and control of the said Contracting Party to eliminate possible danger or harm.
5. Expenses incurred in fulfilling obligations to recover and return a space

object or its component parts under paragraphs 2 and 3 of this article shall be borne by the launching authority.

Article VI

For the purposes of this Agreement, the term "launching authority" shall refer to the State responsible for launching, or, where an international intergovernmental organization is responsible for launching, that organization provided that that organization declares its acceptance of the rights and obligations provided for in this Agreement and a majority of the States members of that organization are Contracting Parties to this Agreement and to the Treaty on Principles Governing the Activities of States in the Exploration and Use of Outer Space, Including the Moon and Other Celestial Bodies.

Article VII

1. This Agreement shall be open to all States for signature. Any State which does not sign this Agreement before its entry into force in accordance with paragraph 3 of this article may accede to it at any time.
2. This Agreement shall be subject to ratification by signatory States. Instruments of ratification and instruments of accession shall be deposited with the Governments of the United States of America, the United Kingdom of Great Britain and Northern Ireland and the Union of Soviet Socialist Republics, which are hereby designated the Depositary Governments.
3. This Agreement shall enter into force upon the deposit of instruments of ratification by five Governments including the Governments designated as Depositary Governments under this Agreement.
4. For States whose instruments of ratification or accession are deposited subsequent to the entry into force of this Agreement, it shall enter into force on the date of the deposit of their instruments of ratification or accession.
5. The Depositary Governments shall promptly inform all signatory and acceding States of the date of each signature, the date of deposit of each instrument of ratification of and accession to this Agreement, the date of its entry into force and other notices.
6. This Agreement shall be registered by the Depositary Governments pursuant to Article 102 of the Charter of the United Nations.

Article VIII

Any State Party to the Agreement may propose amendments to this Agreement. Amendments shall enter into force for each State Party to the Agreement accepting the amendments upon their acceptance by a majority of the States Parties to the Agreement and thereafter for each remaining State Party to the Agreement on the date of acceptance by it.

Article IX

Any State Party to the Agreement may give notice of its withdrawal from the Agreement one year after its entry into force by written notification to the

Depositary Governments. Such withdrawal shall take effect one year from the date of receipt of this notification.

ARTICLE X

This Agreement, of which the English, Russian, French, Spanish and Chinese texts are equally authentic, shall be deposited in the archives of the Depositary Governments. Duly certified copies of this Agreement shall be transmitted by the Depositary Governments to the Governments of the signatory and acceding States.

IN WITNESS WHEREOF the undersigned, duly authorized, have signed this greement.*

(Signatures etc. omitted)

* The Agreement was opened for signature on April 22, 1968, simultaneously in London, Moscow and Washington, and came into force on December 3, 1968.

APPENDIX V

DRAFT CONVENTION CONCERNING THE REGISTRATION OF OBJECTS LAUNCHED INTO SPACE FOR THE EXPLORATION OR USE OF OUTER SPACE

The Governments signatories of this Convention,

Considering that the registration or entry in a register of objects launched into outer space is mentioned in several provisions of the Treaty on Principles Governing the Activities of States in the Exploration and Use of Outer Space, including the Moon and Other Celestial Bodies,

Considering the advantages, at the international level, of the establishment of common rules governing the registration of objects launched into space for the exploration or use of outer space,

Have agreed on the following provisions:

ARTICLE I

Any object launched into space for the exploration or use of outer space shall be registered by entry in a register kept by a service under the supervision of one or more Governments Parties to this Convention. Each Government shall inform the Depositary Government of the establishment or termination of the services under its supervision.

There shall be only registration of each object, but the registration may be transferred from one service to another.

ARTICLE II

Each Contracting Party, acting separately or, in the case of a joint service, together with the other Contracting Parties exercising supervision over that service, shall determine the rules of law applicable to registration.

However, the entry in the register concerning each object shall include at least:

(a) the registration number;

(b) where applicable, the name of the object;

(c) the name and address of the governmental or inter-governmental agency or non-governmental entity procuring the launching;

* Reproduced from *Report of the Legal Sub-Committee on the Work of its Seventh Session (4–28 June 1968) to the Committee on the Peaceful Uses of Outer Space,* U.N. Doc. A/AC.105/45 (11 July 1968) Annex II.

(d) the external specifications of the object, such as total weight, shape, dimensions and external component parts;

(e) the law applicable to the object and to the persons carried in it when an inter-governmental agency or a group of natural or juridical persons, referred to in sub-paragraph (c) hereof, procures the launching.

Each Contracting Party undertakes to provide any other Contracting Party with any information requested by the latter regarding the particulars referred to in sub-paragraphs (a) and (c) of the preceding paragraph concerning any object registered by a service under its supervision, whether such supervision is exclusive or shared with other Governments.

The registers of services functioning in the territory of any State whose Government is a party to this Convention shall (so far as possible,) be accessible to the public.

Article III

The registration number shall be composed of:

(a) the letter C, followed by a dash;

(b) the mark of the registration service, chosen from among the symbols assigned by international telecommunications regulations as identifying radio call signals to the State or States exercising supervision over the service which keeps the register. This mark shall be followed by a dash;

(c) the registration mark, consisting of Roman capital letters, Arabic numerals or a combination of such letters and numerals. This mark must be clearly distinguishable from those reserved for aircraft or for distress or emergency signals.

This number shall be displayed in at least two places on the object and on opposite sides thereof, if the size of the object permits. It shall be repeated as frequently as possible in order to permit identification, in case of accident, of portions or component parts of the object. The height of the characters shall be determined by technical considerations. The number shall be shown on at least one identification plate inside the object. The processes and materials used for reproduction of the registration number and manufacture of the identification plate shall be such, having regard to the conditions in which the object will be used, as to provide the best possible guarantee that the registration number will be identifiable as speedily as possible if the object or its component parts are found.

Article IV

At (two-year) intervals, on the proposal of the Government Depositary of this Convention, a Conference shall be convened in order to consider in the light, *inter alia,* of scientific and technical advances, measures which could be adopted with regard to the questions dealt with in articles 2 and 3 of this Convention.

At such a conference, it may be decided by unanimous vote of the Contracting Parties represented and voting that the said common rules may at subsequent Conferences be adopted by a (two-thirds) majority of the Contracting Parties represented and voting and be binding upon all the Contracting Parties.

The first conference shall take place in the third year after the date of entry into force of this Convention.

ARTICLE V

Any Contracting Party may propose amendments to this Convention.

For this purpose, it shall transmit the text of the amendment to the Depositary Government, which shall communicate it to all the other Governments Parties. If at least one third of the latter state that they consider it necessary to discuss the proposal, a review conference shall be convened as soon as possible on the proposal of the Depositary Government.

Amendments adopted by the majority of the Contracting Parties represented and voting shall enter into force for the Governments (ratifying,) approving (or accepting) them (one) month(s) after one half of the Contracting Parties, at the date of adoption of the amendment by the conference, have deposited (the instrument of ratification or) the notification of approval (or acceptance) concerning them with the Government Depositary of this Convention. They shall enter into force for any other Government (one) month(s) after that Government has deposited the relevant instrument or notification.

If, after the Depositary Government has informed the other Governments Parties to this Convention of the text of a proposed amendment, at least two-thirds of the Contracting Parties intimate that the amendment can be adopted without the convening of a review conference, the said amendment shall enter into force, for those Contracting Parties, (one) month(s) after the last reply from one of them has reached the Depositary Government. The amendment shall enter into force for any other Contracting Party (one) month(s) after its reply has reached the Depositary Government.

ARTICLE VI

No reservation may be made in respect of this Convention.

(followed by the formal provisions)

APPENDIX VI

PROGRESS REPORT ON THE QUESTION OF THE LEGAL STATUS OF SPACECRAFT

by RENÉ H. MANKIEWICZ, *Rapporteur*

INTRODUCTION

1. At the 52nd Conference held in Helsinki, the Space Law Committee had before it a Questionnaire on the Legal Status of Spacecraft prepared by the undersigned Rapporteur of Working Group III. Lack of time prevented consideration of any part of the report. On the recommendation of the Committee, the Conference adopted the following resolution:

"The 52nd Conference of the International Law Association held in Helsinki in August 1966

(1) *Receives and notes* the Questionnaire on the Legal Status of Spacecraft presented to the Space Law Committee by the Rapporteur of Working Group III:

(2) *Invites* the Branches of the Association to comment on the Questionnaire and to suggest answers to the questions there stated; and

(3) *Request* the Space Law Committee

a. to continue the study of the subjects in the light of the comments and answers of the Branches, and

b. to present to the 53rd Conference recommendations for draft rules on the Legal Status of spacecraft or a progress report on its study, as the case may be."

2. Replies to, and comments on, the Questionnaire have been received from the German, Hungarian and Soviet Union Branches, from Professors Cocca, de La Pradelle, Lissitzyn and von Rauchhaupt, and from Messrs. Hewitson and Hubert.

At Helsinki, your Rapporteur suggested that the discussion be confined, at that stage, to the questions under I-General and II B, Responsibilities of and with respect to spacecraft. Comments of the German and Soviet Union Branches deal with all chapters of the Questionnaire; the other replies are concerned mainly with the questions listed under I of the Questionnaire. Professor von Rauchhaupt would like questions of administrative law to be included in the Questionnaire.

3. The Space Law Committee met in Paris on 16 September 1967 to study the replies received by that date, as well as a preliminary report by the undersigned Rapporteur. It considered a draft definition of space objects, but felt that the draft was not ready to be submitted for adoption to the Committee at

the forthcoming Conference.[1] On the other hand, the Committee adopted the following resolution with respect to registration:

"All space objects to be launched should be registered by a State or inter-governmental organization in accordance with its own regulations. All launches by a State or inter-governmental organization should be notified to the United Nations in a way which allows the identification of the launched space objects".

4. Events which have occurred since the Helsinki Conference may have a bearing on the answers to some of the questions listed in the Questionnaire. I am referring in particular to the adoption by the United Nations General Assembly of the Treaty on principles governing the activities of States in the exploration and use of outer space, including the moon and other celestial bodies (hereinafter referred to as "the Treaty on Exploration") and the Agreement on the rescue of astronauts, the return of astronauts and the return of objects launched into outer space (hereinafter referred to as "the Agreement on Rescue and Return").

a) Firstly, these instruments may be relevant with respect to terminology and definition. The Treaty on Exploration avoids the expressions "space vehicle" and "spacecraft" (except that the former is used in Articles V and XII); instead, the word "objects" is used, without any qualifying adjective. Moreover, the Treaty distinguishes between "objects" and "component parts" (Article VII) but a like regime applies to either of them.

Note: Article XII speaks of "stations", "installations", "equipment" and "space vehicles", but only when these happen to be on the moon or other celestial bodies. None of the expressions aforementioned is defined in either of the instruments.

The Agreement on Rescue and Return uses the expressions "spacecraft" in Articles 1, 2, 3 and 4, and "space object" in Articles 5 and 6. The latter is always followed by the words "or its component parts". In addition, the words "objects launched into outer space" are found in the title, the first clause of the Preamble and in Article 5, para. 3; in the latter instance it is followed by the words "or their component parts".

b) The Agreement on Rescue and Return contains a definition of the expression "launching authority" (Art. 6) The expression refers to "the State responsible for launching, or, where an inter-governmental organization is responsible for launching, that organization, provided that that organization declares its acceptance of the rights and obligations provided for in this Agreement and a majority of the States Members of that organization are Contracting Parties to this Agreement and to the (Treaty on Exploration)."

c) In accordance with United Nations Resolutions No. 1962, Article VIII of the Treaty on Exploration assumes that objects launched into space are registered in a State, without, however, specifying in what State they are to be registered or excluding *expressis verbis* registration in more than one State and/or with an international organization; in this regard please see II, para. 5 of the Questionnaire.

d) Articles VI and XII of the Treaty on Exploration deal with juris-

[1] It was to be reconsidered at a further meeting of the Committee, but it proved impossible to hold that second meeting.

diction over space activities and objects. Article VI obliges the Parties to the Treaty to exercise control over their national space activities, whether they are carried out by governmental agencies, by non-governmental entities or international organizations. Article XII, on the other hand, vests in the State of registry – whichever that State may be – jurisdiction over objects in space, on a celestial body or returning to earth. (In addition, it preserves the property rights of the owner – whoever that owner may be – over these objects and their component parts.)

II. ANALYSIS OF AND COMMENTS ON THE REPLIES

Terminology

5. The question of terminology has not been solved by the Treaty nor by the Agreement, for they use different expressions concurrently.

There seems to be general agreement in the comments submitted to the Rapporteur that the term to be used shall be all-embracing.

Contrary to the precedent established by the Treaties on Exploration, it appears to your Rapporteur that – for the present purposes – the word "object" cannot be used without any qualifying description. It is therefore noteworthy that, whenever the word "object(s)" appears in the Agreement on Rescue and Return, it is either preceded by the word "space" and followed by the words "or its component parts" (Article 5, para. 1, 2, 4 and 5), or followed by the words "launched into outer space".

The expression "object launched into space" being by itself a partial definition, more will be said thereto in paragraph 10, f, below.

6. The Hungarian Branch favors the expression "space object" as being the most comprehensive one. Professor de La Pradelle suggests the expression *engin spatial* ("space device"). It is the one used by the Rapporteur in his writings. Professor de La Pradelle notes that the word *engin* may evoke warlike activities, but does not consider this to be an impediment to the use of the expression. Your Rapporteur shares that view which is opposed by Professor Cocca who prefers the word "vehicle". The question arises, however, whether the word *engin* – or "vehicle" – could properly apply to, for example, space platforms. It should also be made clear that "engin" comprises any part detached therefrom during passage through air or outer space.

Alternatively, your Rapporteur suggests that consideration may be given to the word "device" which could be translated into French either by *dispositif* or *appareil*. Finally it seems fit to recall that the late Professor John C. Cooper used to prefer the word "instrumentality".

(i) General – Definition of Spacecraft

7. There appears to be general agreement that the definition should be all-embracing and might be followed by a classification according to both technical and legal criteria.

a) The German Branch proposes that the definition be formulated so as "to include the launcher (booster) debris and spent spacecraft". (They specify also that wild, malfunctioning and spent spacecraft should not be considered as "pirate" spacecraft.) Moreover, they propose that "the definition should be drafted so as to make the "instrumentality" a spacecraft from the beginning of its launching until its landing on earth or its disintegration, respectively . . . ."

b) The Soviet Union Branch "feels that the chief criteria of a definition of a space object should be its purpose, (namely) exploration and use of outer space, including the moon and other celestial bodies. Such definition should cover the space object from the moment of its being launched to the moment of its scientific dismantling or correspondingly of its disintegration. It "should also embrace the spent space objects . . . (and) cover artificial satellites of the earth, the moon or other celestial bodies, spacecraft, orbiting space platforms, interplanetary stations and laboratories, stations, installations, equipment on the moon and other celestial bodies, separate stages of the carrier rocket, space probes as well as detached parties of space objects and separate debris of spacecraft that disintegrated. Land stations (rocket launching sites, tracking and control stations, transmitting and receiving stations) should *not* be covered by the definition of "space object" though they can be subject to appropriate international legal arrangement".

c) Professor de La Pradelle expresses the view that "Il serait préférable d'adopter une définition à portée limitée qui pourrait être applicable aux fusées mais qui viserait essentiellement les capsules terminales et exclurait sans équivoque les installations terrestres fixes du tir spatial et de la poursuite du vol spatial".

d) Mr. Hewitson observes that "future technology is likely to soon render any such definitions out of date.

8. The Working Group may wish to consider, first, the scope of the definition, namely, whether it should apply to the "object" as soon as it is assembled on earth or only when it has been launched. There is little doubt that, while still on the earth's surface and before being launched, the "object" is a movable to which applies the local law of movable things. However, it should be examined whether it is desirable, as in the case of aircraft, to apply special rules (i) during and/or (ii) after the assembling of the object.

N.B. The definition of "aircraft" applies traditionally whether the aircraft is on the ground or in flight. In fact, many States apply special rules to aircraft under construction, and to finished aircraft, e.g. law of aircraft mortgages.

A further question is whether the special status should attach to the "object" after its return to earth from outer space, particularly when it lands or falls on foreign territory or on the high seas.

9. As already noted in the Questionnaire, a definition using the word "space" – e.g. object launched into, or being capable of moving through "space" – seems to require a definition of, at least, the lower limit of space. Therefore, the Committee may wish to explore the possibility of using the reliance of spacecraft on the physical laws of astronautical flight as criterion for its definition. But one must also bear in mind that, as has now been proved, spacecraft can be manoeuvred, while in space, by men (on board or on the earth). Hence, the criterion ought to be the "capability" of spacecraft to move under said physical

laws, or any more appropriate definition of the forces or mechanics of its evolution.

It should be noted that the Council of ICAO has amended in 1967 the traditional definition of "aircraft" ("any machine that can derive support in the atmosphere from the reactions of the air") by adding the words "other than the reactions of the air against the earth's surface." The new definition purports VERTOL aircraft come into existence.

(ii) Draft Definitions

10. a) The German Branch proposed the following definition:

"*Spacecraft*" means any object designed to move in outer space, not needing support from the reactions of air."

It subsequently suggested the deletion of all the words after "outer space".

b) The Hungarian Branch suggests the following draft:

"All artificial bodies (manufactured by man) shall be space objects which are launched from the earth, with or without crew, with the purpose of orbiting around the earth, moon or the sun by making use of the laws of Keppler (celestial mechanics) or of reaching from the earth another celestial body whether or not with the objective to stay at the place of destination."

Dr. Herczeg, author of the Hungarian reply, points out (i) that this definition "has the advantage of covering spacecraft in the strict sense of the term and space stations even though produced in space or on a celestial body, and of applying to manned and unmanned "objects" irrespective of whether they are controlled from the earth": in this respect, *see* also the comments of Professor de La Pradelle in d) hereunder; (ii) that under that definition "space objects would be defined not only by the distance from Earth, but by their characteristics laid down in the science of physics... but such definition would not cover space sounds" which "on account of their different functions (require) a distinct legal regulation."

c) The proposal of the Soviet Union Branch reads as follows:

"The definition of space object should (also) cover any object or its component part launched with the view of performing flight in outer space for exploration and use of space including the moon and other celestial bodies, till the moment of its scientific dismanteling or demolition.

N.B. It is recalled that, according to the Soviet Union Branch, the "chief criterion of a space object should be its purpose."

d) Professor de La Pradelle suggests the following definition:

"On entend par engin spatial tout appareil susceptible de se déplacer dans l'espace extra-atmosphérique (et destiné soit à s'y désintégrer, soit à s'y maintenir conformément aux lois de la physique astronomique)."

His comments read in part as follows:

"La définition s'appliquerait ainsi normalement et principalement aux capsules satellisables et à titre exceptionnel aux fusées-sondes et aux fusées de lancement dont les étages supérieurs peuvent être appelés à opérer une propulsion de la capsule en dehors de l'atmosphère ... (elle) n'est pas applicable aux établissements lunaires ...

e) Professor Cocca refers to the following conclusions reached by the First

Colloquium on the Progress in Cosmic Exploration and its Consequences (Buenos Aires, December 1966):

1st "A cosmic vehicle is necessarily a construction by men, the object of which is to travel in outer space.

3rd "All the component parts, in the moment of the launching, form part of the cosmic vehicle, no matter whatever the cause of any becoming separate later or eventually.

4th All that is launched to outer space by man is a cosmic vehicle and not a space object."

The definition adopted at that colloquium reads as follows:

"Cosmic vehicles in the regime of the Treaty are all artifacts launched by man for the exploration or use of outer space including the moon and other celestial bodies, with peaceful purposes".

f) Your Rapporteur offers the following definition:

"Space device means any object launched toward (in the direction of) space". ("Appareil spatial signifie tout objet lancé en direction de (vers) l'espace"). – *Alternative:* Space device means any object intended for launching into space." ("Appareil spatial signifie tout objet destiné à être lancé vers l'espace.")

Note: (1) The wording suggested in the above definition appears to be preferable to the wording "launched into spaces" which is used in the Agreement on Rescue and Return (see para. 5 above), because the latter expression may be construed as referring only to those objects which have reached outer space.

(2) As regards the alternative definition above, which, it is noted, would apply before the launching takes place, attention is drawn to the possibility that the use of the expression "capable" of being launched into space may give rise to difficulties in the event of abortive launchings, namely when the "object" proves to be incapable of being launched into, or reaching, space.

Classification of Spacecraft

11. a) There is general agreement that a classification of space craft according to both technical and legal criteria will be appropriate in due time.

b) The Soviet Union Branch comments as follows: "We should think that in the elaboration of a general definition of space object, there is no need to distinguish between or to enumerate individual kinds or types of space objects.... In the future development of norms of space law there invariably will rise a necessity for the elaboration of a definite system of the classification of space objects. Important from the point of view of principles in this field is a strict distinguishing of space objects used only for peaceful purposes and space objects used for military purposes (for legal regulation of celestial bodies concerning the elaboration of the Convention on the rescuing of cosmonauts and a Convention on the liability for damage done by space objects). In connection with partial demilitarization of celestial bodies, certain importance is attached to the distinguishing of objects depending on their position in outer space or on a celestial body. In connection with the elaboration of a Convention on the rescuing of cosmonauts, it is important to distinguish between a space object with personnel aboard (spacecraft) and those without personnel"... "Even greater importance is acquired by the classification of space objects depending on their purpose and use (communication satellites, meteorological satellites, navigational satellites)."

c) Professor de La Pradelle suggests to adopt a technical classification and a legal classification as follows:

Classification technique: "Une distinction fondamentale pourrait être faite entre les fusées et les satellites, soit entre les engins ou véhicules de lancement et les engins ou véhicules d'exploration et d'exploitation spatiales satellisables."

Classification juridique: "Elle pourrait prendre appui sur le rapport Cooper et les commentaires qui l'ont accompagnés, et ferait apparaître des catégories d'appartenance et de contrôle ayant une incidence sur le status des activités spatiales."

Examples:

Engins spatiaux publiques (Public spacecraft)

Engins spatiaux privés (Private spacecraft)

Engins spatiaux ou de groupement d'Etats, engins spatiaux d'organisations internationales, satellites d'information, etc.

Engins d'entreprises privées (télécommunications) engins d'organisations non-gouvernementales.

d) Professor Cocca suggests that a distinction be made between manned and unmanned spacecraft, and also between rockets, satellites and space probes.

e) Additional criteria and classifications have been suggested in the Questionnaire; see I-General, A, 1 (a).

Identification (Registration and Nationality)

12. The answers to the Questionnaire agree that "space objects" need to be identified and that such identification requires registration. In connection with such registration, the following questions appear to require examination:

1) Should there be an international agreement with the view to determine which State or organization shall be the "registration authority"?

2) Should there be an international rule specifying which State, international organization, or private entity shall be obliged to apply for registration?

3) Should there be international rules regarding the content of the registration and specifying the identification marks or methods?

13. As noted previously, Article VIII of the Treaty on Exploration, in line with the United Nations Resolution No. 1962, assumes that objects launched into space are registered within a State, but does not designate the State of registration nor prescribe any rules relating to registration.

The Space Law Committee has taken no position with respect to the questions 1 and 2 above, but resolved that spacecraft be registered by a State or inter-governmental organization in accordance with its own regulations; see paragraph 3 above.

14. National Registration The Committee's draft resolution provides that spacecraft be registered in a State in accordance with that State's regulations, but it does not designate the State where the registration shall take place. In this connection it must be noted that Article VII of the Treaty on Exploration declares "internationally liable": (i) the State that launches the object; (ii) the State which procures its launching; (iii) the State from whose territory the object is launched; (iv) the State from whose facility it is launched.

The Committee may want to examine whether it wishes to designate the State in which the object must be registered, and, subsidiarily, the State or international organization which shall apply for registration. In this connection it may wish to examine the question whether the object must be registered in each of the States mentioned in Article VII of the Treaty on Exploration or whether it would suffice to designate one particular State with, however, the proviso that the register of that State must mention the "other" States.

For reasons of simplicity and certainty, your Rapporteur has always preferred that the "object" be registered in the State from whose territory it has been launched or, in the case of launching on the high seas, in the State from whose facility it is launched.[1] That State, however, could be made responsible for mentioning on its registry all other States which might be liable internationally – or otherwise – for damages caused by the "object".[2]

15. Few comments deal with the problem of multiple (national) registration. Professor Lissitzyn admits multiple registration, but the German and Soviet Union Branches and Professor Cocca are opposed thereto.

16. International registration. The draft resolution adopted by the Space Law Committee in Paris provides for such registration. It appears to leave open the question whether such registration is to be effected with the launching organization or whether it can be effected with a general organization, e.g. the United Nations or a specialized agency provided their regulations permit such action; in a latter case, it would depend on these rules and regulations whether that organization would register objects launched by a State or a group of States. If so, the question of multiple registration would

[1] If that solution were adopted, there would be no need for international registration, except in the unlikely case of an object being launched from a ship, on the high seas, belonging to an international organization. For the time being, however, ships cannot be registered "internationally".

[2] It is recalled that the Questionnaire in Section II, Preliminary Remarks, para. 4, contains the following provisional list of those States which, theoretically, might be involved in the flight and activities of a spacecraft: (i) State of registration; (ii) State of manufacture of the booster (launch-vehicle); (iii) State of manufacture of the space capsule; (iv) State or States of the manufacturers of the embarked equipment; (iv) State from whose territory the spacecraft is launched; (vi) State whose nationals control and initiate the launching (vii) State whose nationals programme and/or control the flight and activities of the spacecraft (space navigation); (viii) States that provide ground stations necessary for space navigation; (ix) State or States whose nationals man the stations mentioned under (viii); (x) States through the air space of which the spacecraft passes; (xi) State of landing (whether planned landing or emergency landing); (xii) State of nationality of the astronauts.

arise. For comments on these questions *see* paragraphs 15 and 18 of this report.

The German Branch, Professor Lissitzyn and Mr. Hewitson also would permit registration with international organizations. The Soviet Union Branch "believes that the problem of international registration of space objects indisputably deserves attention and demands the most detailed study". They point out that "the solution of this question will largely depend on the general definition of the legal status of such organization in international affairs".

17. As regards the special case of "joint space activities of a number of States in launching objects into outer space," the Soviet Union Branch feels that "the parties to the agreement or members of the organization should themselves decide upon the question as to which State should carry the space object on its registry". This approach is in line with the resolution adopted on 14 December 1967 by the Council of the International Civil Aviation Organization with respect to the registration of aircraft operated by joint operating agencies.

18. Distinct from the question in the foregoing paragraph, namely registration of objects with the launching organization, a member of that organization or a party to an *ad hoc* agreement concerning a specific, individualized space activity, is the general question whether provision should be made for registration of space objects with an international agency having jurisdiction in space matters, e.g. the United Nations, or a new specialized agency, such registration being a complete substitute for national registration or registration with an international launching organization.[1]

a) The German Branch is in favor of "a special international register to be created preferably within the farmework of the United Nations."

b) The Soviet Union Branch refers in this connection to the proposals made by various Representatives during the sixth Session of the Legal Sub-Committee of the United Nations Committee on Peaceful Uses of Outer Space. They mention in particular the proposal by the Representative of Canada, who "felt that it was necessary to establish a special international agency for the registration of space objects."

c) Your Rapporteur has proposed previously, and remains an advocate of, the establishment of a specialized agency of the United Nations having jurisdiction with respect to space activities. The functions and responsibilities of such agency could be patterned according to, but would be different from, those of ICAO in the field of international civil aviation. This view is shared by Mr. Hewitson.

19. The draft resolution adopted at the Paris meeting does not specify the conditions and particulars of registration; instead it relies upon the State or organization concerned for the framing and enforcement of the required rules.

a) The Soviet Union Branch states: "The order of registration is indisputably a matter of internal competence of States. This, however, should not exclude the possibility that in the future a certain unification of such registering can be made on an international level."

b) The Hungarian Branch suggests that an international agreement specify that "States should be obliged, according to their respective mu-

[1] Such registration is different from the "notification" required under United Nations Resolution No. 1721 but could eventually replace it.

nicipal laws to take appropriate action; that domestic authorities should list all launchings licensed or effected from national territory with information susceptible of making identification, the requirement for salvage, eventual liability for damages and the establishment of property rights". In addition, it should contain "the minimum of particulars, e.g. place and date of launching, highest and lowest point of orbiting, bands of radio frequency used, outer recognizable signs, respectively markings, and the name of the State of registration".

c) Professor de La Pradelle proposes the following rules:

1) "Tout engin spatial destiné à se maintenir dans l'espace, avec ou sans retour prévu à la terre, doit être immatriculé sur un registre spécial tenu par l'Etat propriétaire du satellite (l'expression 'd'Etat' comprenant soit l'Etat individuel soit les groupements d'Etats et les organisations internationales) ou qui en assume le contrôle (pour les cas d'un satellite appartenant à une personne privée).

2) L'immatriculation des engins spatiaux munis d'un équipement radio-électrique doit être notifée aux organisations internationales spécialisées intéressées par l'Etat du lieu de lancement.

3) L'immatriculation des engins spatiaux d'exploration et d'exploitation doit faire l'objet d'une marque d'immatriculation, constituée par des lettres, des chiffres, ou par une combinaison de lettres et de chiffres, assignée par l'Etat d'immatriculation. Une marque de nationalité ou de supra-nationalité précédera la marque d'immatriculation et sera déterminée par l'indicatif d'appel radio attribué à l'Etat d'immatriculation par le Règlement international des Télécommunications.

4) Aucun lancement d'engin spatial ne peut être effectué sans l'autorisation et le contrôle d'un Etat.

20. A separate question is the choice of identification marks and methods.

a) The Soviet Union Branch report on the various details notified by the U.S.S.R. and the U.S.A. to the United Nations Secretary General in accordance with the United Nations Assembly Resolution No. 1721. They also point out that "identification markings make it possible to establish the State affiliation of a space object only after it has returned to Earth" and that "during the space flight such object can be identified with the help of special radio identification signals".

b) Other comments are to the effect that the designation of identification marks and means be left to the State of registry, but, as the Soviet Union Branch points out, this does not exclude "the possibility that in the future a certain unification of such registration can be made on an international level".

21. Nationality.

Professors Cocca, Lissitzyn and Mr. Hewitson agree with the Rapporteur that there is no need for nationality of space objects. This view is not shared by the German and Soviet Union Branches.

a) For the German Branch "the principle of nationality is indispensable for safe and orderly space navigation". In addition, it is believed to be "the basis for any responsibility for damage caused by, or to, spacecraft".

b) The Soviet Union Branch state that "one should not be in a hurry to dispose of the concept of nationality in determining the legal status of space objects". In their opinion "the fact that joint activities of States in the field of space activities (exploration and exploitation) will expand and the role of inter-governmental organizations will also increase, is not a sufficient argument in favor of rejecting the concept of 'nationality'".

CONCLUSIONS

In the light of the foregoing, your Rapporteur suggests that the Committee, at the forthcoming session, may wish to;

1. Express its appreciation to the National Branches and jurists who have submitted answers to, and comments on, the Questionnaire.
2. Decide to limit its study at this session to the questions of
   "definition of spacecraft" and
   "identification (registration) of spacecraft",
   which are dealt with in this Progress Report; *see* I-General of the Questionnaire reproduced in the Appendix hereto.
3. Examine the question of terminology and the various definitions suggested.
4. Formulate a definition.
5. Examine the question of classification and, if appropriate, establish criteria for such classification.
6. Endorse the draft resolution of the Committee with respect to registration; *see* paragraph 3 above.
7. Study the desirability or otherwise of adopting rules governing national and/or international registration, in particular
   a. designation of the State or organization with which space objects shall be registered.
   b. designation of the State(s), organization, or entity which shall apply for registration
   c. particulars to be registered
8. Study and recommend specific methods or means of identification of spacecraft.
9. Decide whether spacecraft shall have a "nationality".
   If the answer is affirmative, examine, and decide on, the international status of spacecraft owned or launched by an international organization or a group of States.
10. Give directions for further action with respect to the Questionnaire submitted to the fifty-second Conference, and, in general, the question of the Legal Status of spacecraft.

EXTRACTS FROM THE QUESTIONNAIRE

I.–GENERAL

A. *Definition of Spacecraft*

1. Should the definition of spacecraft be all-embracing (drafted in general terms) or proceed by distinguishing and enumerating classes or types of spacecraft?

(a) If a unique definition is adopted, should it be followed up by a classification of spacecraft (having regard to the possible need for providing exemptions or special rules for specific types of spacecraft), for instance:

manned and unmanned spacecraft
active and passive spacecraft
"stationary" spacecraft
classification by use such as
"space platforms"

(i) meteorological spacecraft
communications spacecraft
scientific research spacecraft
"navigational aids"

(ii) military and non-military spacecraft

(iii) spacecraft destined to return to earth, and spacecraft destined to disintegrate

(iv) experimental and "permanent" spacecraft.

2. Should the definition be formed so as

(a) to make the "instrumentality" a spacecraft from the beginning of its launching until its landing on earth or its disintegration, respectively, and

(b) to include

the launcher (booster)
débris
spent aircraft

3. How should the definition read?

Comment: (1) A definition using the word "space", *e.g.* object launched into, or being capable of moving through "space", seems to require a definition of at least the lower limit of space.

(2) It may appear that the reliance of spacecraft on the physical laws of astronautical flight could be used as criterion. However, experience shows that spacecraft can be manoeuvred, while in space, by men (on board or on the earth). Hence the criterion ought to be the "capability" of spacecraft to move under said physical laws, or any more appropriate definition of the forces of mechanics of its evolution.

Obiter: One may think of a definition modelled after, but contrary to, the definition of "aircraft" adopted by the Council of ICAO in Annex 6 to the Chicago Convention.

B. Identification of spacecraft

4. Should a spacecraft be registered and is registration sufficient?
   (a) Should aircraft be registered internationally or nationally?
   Note: UN resolutions provide in fact the possibility of both such registrations.
      (i) Are international and national registration compatible?
      (ii) If so, should there be a rule providing what spacecraft must be registered internationally and what spacecraft must be registered nationally?
   (b) In case of national registration, should multiple registration be permissible?
   Comment: While single registration [and nationality; see Comment under question (5) below] might be a convenience in the case of ships and aircraft (see, however, article 77 of the Chicago Convention), there appear to be no legal or technical difficulties for having more than one State accepting and fulfilling, individually, functions and responsibilities and enjoying rights, with respect to spacecraft.
   (c) In the case of international registration should there be only one single registering agency or organisation?
   if more than one international body are to be entitled to register spacecraft, should there be given a general definition of these bodies or a list of them?

Comment: (1) Registration in a State purports to channel international rights and responsibilities with respect to an object to that State and to subject such object to the latter's legal order and jurisdiction, in addition to providing for the identification of the aircraft. Therefore, in the case of international registration, the question of applying public and private law rules to spacecraft so registered needs special consideration inasmuch as international organisations have not yet made international public and private law rules of the kind necessary in this context *. This problem should be dealt with in the light of the question under II, III and IV.

(2) It will be apparent, it is believed, from questions asked under II that it may not be convenient nor practical to concentrate all international rights, responsibilities and functions with respect to spacecraft in one single State, *e.g.* State of launching, State of manufacture, etc.

(3) While there seems to arise no legal problem with respect to providing identification (registration) marks, there is, however, a technical problem, namely the marking of spacecraft in such a manner as to permit the

identification of parts of destroyed spacecraft and of objects or parts detached from spacecraft.

5. Should spacecraft have a nationality?

Comment: It is noted that "nationality" is not required for identification purposes. Like Professor Jennings (Tokyo Report 1964), this rapporteur is inclined to believe that while the "metaphor of nationality" was justified for ships remaining outside the jurisdiction of any State for a considerable time, when there was no comprehensive network either of international rules regulating the conduct of ships or of conflicts of law applicable to private relationships arising on board of the vessel, "nationality" is less relevant for aircraft. It has been shown by many writers, including this rapporteur, that it appears to be unnecessary for spacecraft. Nationality is but a technical device to link the craft to the national laws of given jurisdiction. However, other devices, *e.g.* registration, launching, etc., may provide such link efficiently. (The case of motorcars proves that registration is a sufficient device: when used for commercial purposes in a federal State, motorcars may have to be registered in all component States or Provinces where they are used.)

(a) If so, should multiple nationality be permitted?

See Comment under Question 4 (b) above.

* It will be noted that such international public law rules have been established with respect to aircraft and aerial navigation by the Chicago Convention and the Annexes thereto; *see also* Comments under questions 16 and 20 below, as well as "Aeronefs internationaux" in *Annuaire français de Droit international,* 1962, p. 685–717.

SELECTED BIBLIOGRAPHY

ALEXANDER, L. M., *The Law of the Sea. Offshore Boundaries and Zones.* Columbus, 1967.

ALLEN, E. W., "Freedom of the Sea," 60 *A.J.I.L.* 814–816 (1966).

Applicable Rules of International Law – Communications Satellite Legislation, 57 *A.J.I.L.* 427–428 (1963).

AVOKOV, M. M., "Vienna Conference on Consular Relations," *B.Y.I.L.* 271–287 (1963).

BARTON, G. P., "Foreign Armed Forces: Immunity from Supervisory Jurisdictional Immunity," 31 *B.Y.I.L.* 370 (1954).

BAXTER, R. R., "Constitutional Forms and Some Legal Problems of International Military Command," 29 *B.Y.I.L.* 265–283 (1952).

—, *The Law of International Waterways*, Cambridge, Mass. 1964.

BECKETT, W. E., "Criminal Jurisdiction Over Foreigners," 8 *B.Y.I.L.* 108–128 (1927).

—, "The Exercise of Criminal Jurisdiction over Foreigners," 6 *B.Y.I.L.* 44–60 (1925).

BERBER, F. J., *Rivers in International Law*, London, 1959.

BEST, R. S. B., "The Anglo-American Consular Convention of 1949," 25 *B.Y.I.L.* 293–295 (1948).

BISHOP, W. W., *International Law; Cases and Materials*, 2nd ed., Boston, 1962, pp. 439–626.

BLOOMFIELD, L. P., "Outer Space and International Co-operation," *International Organization* 603–621 (Summer 1965).

BOGGS, S. W., "Delimitation of Seaward Areas under National Jurisdiction," 45 *A.J.I.L.* 240–266 (1951).

—, "National Claims in Adjacent Seas," 41 *Geographical Review* (1951).

BRIERLY, J. L., *The Law of Nations*, 6th ed., edited by Waldock. Oxford, 1963, pp. 222–316.

—, "Matters of Domestic Jurisdiction," 6 *B.Y.I.L.* 8–19 (1925).

BRIGGS, H. W., (ed.), *The Law of Nations, cases, documents and notes*, New York, 1938.

—, "Removal of Enemy Persons from Neutral Vessels," 34 *A.J.I.L.* 249–259 (1940).

—, *International Law*, Oxford, 1965.

BRINGHAM, J. W., "The Continental Shelf and the Marginal Belt," 40 *A.J.I.L.* 173–178 (1946).

BROWN, E. D., "Deep-Sea Mining: The Legal Regime of 'Inner Space'," 22 *The Year Book of World Affairs 1968*, London, 1968, pp. 165–190.

BROWN, P. M., "Protective Jurisdiction," 34 *A.J.I.L.* 112–116 (1940).

BROWNLIE, I., "The Maintenance of International Peace and Security in Outer Space," 40 *B.Y.I.L.* 1–31 (1964).

CARLSTON, K. S., "The Grasp of Jurisdiction," *Proceedings of the American Society of International Law* 170–173 (1959).

CARROZ, J. E. & ROCHE, A. G., "The Proposed International Commission for the Conservation of Atlantic Tunas," 61 *A.J.I.L.* 673–702 (1967).

CHAUMONT, Ch., *Le Droit de L'Espace*, Paris, 1960.

CHENG, B., *General Principles of Law as Applied by International Courts and Tribunals*, London, 1953, pp. 51, 75–78, 124, 157–158, 306.
—, "International Law and High Altitude Flights: Balloons, Rockets and Man-made Satellites," 5 *I.C.L.Q.* 487–505 (1957).
—, "Inter Astra Silent Leges? A Prolegomenon to Jural Cartography," *GLIM* 1–6 (Michaelmas, 1961).
—, *The Law of International Air Transport*, The Library of World Affairs No. 47. London, 1962, pp. 65, 110, 120–127, 140–141, 143, 286.
—, "The Extra-Terrestrial Applications of International Law," *C.L.P.* 132–152 (1965).
—, "Nationality and Registration of Aircraft – Article 77 of the Chicago Convention," 32 *J.A.L.C.* 551 (1966).
—, "Le Traité de 1967 sur l'espace," 95 *Journal du Droit International* 532–645 (1968).
CHESHIRE, G. C., *Private International Law*, 7th ed., London, 1965, pp. 74–112.
CHRISTOL, C. Q., *The International Law of Outer Space*, Naval War College, International Law Studies, Vol. 55, Newport, 1966, pp. 416–430.
CHRISTY, Jr., F. T. & SCOTT, A., *The Common Wealth in Ocean Fisheries*, Baltimore, Maryland, 1965.
CLEMINSON, H. M., "Laws of Maritime Jurisdiction in Time of Peace, with Special Reference to Territorial Waters," 6 *B.Y.I.L.* 144–148 (1925).
COHEN, M., (ed.), *Law and Politics in Space*, First Conference on the Law of Outer Space, Montreal, 1964.
COHN, E. J., "Waiver of Immunity," 34 *B.Y.I.L.* 260–273 (1958).
COLOMBOS, C. J., *The International Law of the Sea*, 6th revised edition, London, 1967.
COOPER, J. C., "Nationality of Aircraft," 14 *J.A.L.C.* 292 (1950).
CSABAFI, I., "The U.N. General Assembly Resolutions on Outer Space as Sources of Space Law," 337–361 *Proceedings* of the VIIIth Colloquium of the International Institute of Space Law, Norman, Oklahoma, 1966, pp. 337–361.
CUKWURAH, A. O., *The Settlement of Boundary Disputes in International Law*, Manchester, 1967.
Current Problems in Space Law – A Symposium, *B.I.I.C.L.*, International Law Series 6, London, 1966.
DEMBLING, P. G. & ARONS, D. M., "Space Law and the United Nations: The Work of the Legal Sub-Committee of the United Nations Committee on the Peaceful Uses of Outer Space," 32 *J.A.L.C.* 329–386 (1966).
—, "The United Nations Celestial Bodies Convention," 32 *J.A.L.C.* 535–550 (1966).
FALK, R. A., "The Relevance of Contending Systems of Political Order to the Delimitation of Legal Competence," *Proceedings of the American Society of International Law* 173–181 (1959).
—, "On the Quasi-Legislative Competence of the General Assembly," 60 *A.J.I.L.* 782–79 (1966).
—, "New Approaches to the Study of International Law," 61 *A.J.I.L.* 477–495 (1967).
FALK, R. A. & MENDLOVITZ, S. H., (eds.), *The Strategy of World Order*, New York, 1966, Vol. I, pp. 314–353.
FALK, R. A. & NORDSTROM, R. J., (eds.), *Essays in International Jurisdiction*, Ohio, 1961.
FENSTON, J. & DE SAUSSURE, H., "Conflicts in Competence and Jurisdiction of Courts of Different States to Deal with Crimes Committed on Board Aircraft," 1 *McGill Law Journal* 66–89 (1952).
FENWICK, C. G., "The Sources of International Law," 16 *Mich. L. Rev.* 393–395 (1918).
FITZGERALD, G. F., "The Development of International Rules Concerning Offences and Certain Other Acts Committed on Board Aircraft," 1 *C.Y.I.L.* p. 11 (1963).
—, "Offences and Certain Acts Committed on Board Aircraft: The Tokyo Convention of 1963," 2 *C.Y.I.L.* 191–204 (1964).
FITZMAURICE, Sir G., "Some Results of the Geneva Conference on the Law of the Sea,

Part I – The Territorial Sea and Contiguous Zone and Related Topics," 3 *I.C.L.Q.* 73–121 (1959).

FRUTKIN, A. W., *International Cooperation in Space*, Englewood Cliffs, N.J., 1965.

GAL, GY., *Vilagürjog* (Space Law), Budapest, 1964, pp. 243–245.

GARNER, G. W., "Immunities of State-Owned Ships Employed in Commerce," 6 *B.Y.I.L.* 128–143 (1925).

GARRETSON, A. H., HAYTON, R. D. & OLMSTEAD, C. J., (eds.), *The Law International Drainage Basins*, Dobbs Ferry, N.Y., 1967.

GOEDHUIS, D., "Some Trends in the Political and Legal Thinking on the Conquest of Space," *Nederlands Tijdschrift voor Internationaal Recht* 113–136 (1962).

—, "Reflections on the Evolution of Space Law," *Nederlands Tijdschrift voor Internationaal Recht* 109–149 (1966).

—, "An Evaluation of the Leading Principles of the Treaty on Outer Space of 27th January 1967," 15 *Nederlands Tijdschrift voor Internationaal Recht* 17–41 (1968).

GOLDIE, L. F. E., "Recognition of Dual Nationality – A Problem of Flags of Convenience," 39 *B.Y.I.L.* 220–283 (1963).

GOODRICH & HAMBRO, *Charter of the U.N.*, 2nd ed., London, 1949.

GUTIERREZ, L., "Should the Tokyo Convention of 1963 be Ratified?" 31 *J.A.L.C.* 1–21 (1965).

GUTTERIDGE, H. C., "Conflicts of Jurisdiction in Matrimonial Suits," 19 *B.Y.I.L.* 28–30 (1938).

GUTZWILLER, *Le Développement Historique du Droit International Privé*. Rec. 29, (1929 IV).

HALL, W. E., *A Treatise on International Law*, 8th ed., Oxford, 1924.

Harvard Research 1935. II. Jurisdiction with Respect to Crimes (Dickinson), pp. 466–632. Territorial Waters, 23 *A.J.I.L.* Special Supplement (1929).

HAYTON, R. D., "Jurisdiction of the Littoral State in the 'Air Frontier'," 3 *Philippine International Law Journal* 369–398 (1964).

—, "The Antarctic Settlement of 1959," 54 *A.J.I.L.* 349–371 (1961).

HEAD, I. L., "ADIZ, International Law and Contiguous Airspace," 3 *Alberta Law Review* 182–196 (1964).

HERCZEGH, G., "A memzetköz9 folyovizek hasznositasanak néhany jogi kérdése," (Legal Questions Relative to the Utilization of International Rivers) 11 *Allam- és Jogtudomany* 12–30 (1968). [Published by the Institute of State and Law of the Hungarian Academy of Sciences.]

HIGGINS, R., *The Development of Customary International Law Through the Political Organs of the United Nations*, London, 1963.

HUBER, U., *De Conflictu Legum Diversarum in Diversis Imperiis*, 1648.

HURST, C., "The Continental Shelf," 2 *I.L.Q.* 640 (1948).

HYDE, C. C., *International Law, Chiefly as Interpreted and Applied by the United States*, Boston 1945, Vol. I.

JASENTULIYANA, N., "Regulatory Functions of I.T.U. in the Field of Space Telecommunications," 27 *J.A.L.C.* 62–78 (Winter 1968).

JENKS, W. C., *Space Law*, London, 1965, pp. 236–239, 240–241, 246, 273, 275.

—, *Common Law of Mankind*, New York, 1958.

—, "The Impact of International Organizations on International Law, 37 *Grotius Society Transactions* 23 (1951).

—, "Space Law Becomes a Reality," *Current Problems*, 22, 23, 24 (1966).

JESSUP, P. C., *Transnational Law*, New Haven, 1956.

—, *The Law of Territorial Waters and Maritime Jurisdiction*, New York, 1927.

—, *A Modern Law of Nations, and Introduction*, New York, 1952, pp. 41, 150, 168, 178, 180, 212.

JESSUP, P. C. & TAUBENFELD, H. J., *Controls for Outer Space*, New York, 1952, pp. 265–282.

JOHNSON, D. M., *The International Law of Fisheries*, New Haven, 1965.

KATZENBACH, N. DE, "Sharable and Strategic Resources: Outer Space, Polar Areas and the Ocean," *Proceedings of the American Society of International Law* 206–212 (1959).

KELSEN, H., *The Law of the United Nations; A Critical Analysis of its Fundamental Problems*, New York, 1951.

KEMP, J. M., *Evolution Toward a Space Treaty: An Historical Analysis*, NASA, HHN–64, 1966.

KISH, J. F., *A Nemzetközi Térségek Jogallasa* (The Legal Status of International Spaces), Budapest, 1964.

KOPAL, V., CSABAFI, I., BAKOTIC, B., "Space Law in the Socialist Countries of Eastern Europe: Czechoslovakia, Hungary and Yugoslavia," 1 *Canadian Slavic Studies* 60–78 (1967).

KOROVIN, E. A., ZHUKOV, G. P., KOVALEV, F. N., *Problemi kosmicheskovo prava* (Problems of Space Law), Moscow, 1966.

KOVALEV, F. N., CHEPROV, I. I., *Na puti kosmicheskomu pravu* (On the way toward space law), Moscow, 1962.

KUNZ, J. L., "The Nature of Customary International Law," 47 *A.J.I.L.* 662–669 (1953).

LACHS, M., "The International Law of Outer Space," 113 *Recueil des Cours* (1964, III.), Leyden, 1966, pp. 7–115.

LAUTERPACHT, H., "Sovereignty Over Submarine Areas," 27 *B.Y.I.L.* 376–433 (1950).

—, "The Problem of Jurisdictional Immunities of Foreign States," 28 *B.Y.I.L.* 220–272 (1951).

LAWRENCE, *The Principles of International Law*, 7th ed. Revised by P. H. Winfield, London, 1923.

League of Nations Conference for the Codification of International Law, "Territorial Waters," 1929.

LEE, L. T., "Jurisdiction Over Foreign Merchant Ships in the Territorial Sea," 55 *A.J.I.L.* 77 (1961).

LIPSON & KATZENBACH, *Report to the National Aeronautics and Space Administration on the Law of Outer Space*, American Bar Foundation, 1961, p. 847.

LYONS, A. B., "Immunities other than Jurisdictional of the Property of Diplomatic Envoys," 30 *B.Y.I.L.* 116–151 (1953).

—, "Personal Immunities of Diplomatic Agents," 31 *B.Y.I.L.* 299–340 (1954).

MANKIEWICZ, R. H., "Aéronefs internationaux," 8 *Annuaire Français de Droit International* 685–717 (1962).

MARTIN, L. W., "Ballistic Missile Defense and the Strategic Balance," 21 *The Year Book of World Affairs 1967* London, 1967, pp. 37–54.

MASTERSON, "The Hemisphere Zone of Security and the Law," 26 *A.B.A.J.* (1946).

MASTERSON, W. E., *Jurisdiction in Marginal Seas with Special Reference to Smuggling*, New York, 1929.

MATTE, N. M., *Utilisations Pacifiques de L'Espace et Droit Aérospatial*, Paris, 1968.

—, *Traité de Droit Aérien – Aéronautique* (*Evolution – Problèmes spatiaux*), Deuxième Edition, Paris, 1964.

McDOUGAL, A., "The Position of Foreigners on the Termination of Mixed Courts," 26 *B.Y.I.L.* 332–334 (1949).

McDOUGAL, BURKE & VLASIC, *Law and Public Order in Space*, New Haven, 1963, pp. 647–648, 691.

McDOUGAL, LASSWELL, VLASIC & SMITH, "The Enjoyment and Acquisition of Resources in Outer Space," 3 *U. Pen. L. Rev.* 521–529 (1963).

McNAIR, *The Law of the Air*, 3rd ed., London, 1964, pp. 259–345.

McWHINNEY, E., *Federal Constitution Making for a Multinational World*, Leyden, 1966, pp. 122, 126–127.

—, *"Peaceful Coexistence" and Soviet-Western International Law*, Leyden, 1964.

MEYERS, H., *The Nationality of Ships*, The Hague, 1967.

MOORE, J. B., *A Digest of International Law*, Washington, 1906, Vol. 2.

MOUTON, M. W., *The Continental Shelf*, The Hague, 1952.

O'CONNELL, O. P., *International Law*, New York, 1965, Vol. 2, pp. 655–957.

OPPENHEIM, L. F. L., *International Law, a Treatise*, 8th ed., edited by Lauterpacht, London, 1955, pp. 325–334, 594–606.

VAN PANHUYS, H. F. & VAN EMDE BOAS, M. J., "Legal Aspects of Pirate Broadcasting, A Dutch Approach," 60 *A.J.I.L.* 303–341 (1966).

PARRY, C., "Plural Nationality and Citizenship with Special Reference to the Commonwealth," 30 *B.Y.I.L.* 228–229, 259–261 (1953).

PHILLIMORE, Sir R. J., *Commentaries Upon International Law*, 3rd ed., London, (1879–1888) Vol. I.

POLLOCK, F., "The Sources of International Law," 2 *Colum. L. Rev.* 511–524 (1902).

RAYMOND, J. M., "A New Look at the Jurisdiction of ALCOA," 61 *A.J.I.L.* 558–570 (1967).

RIESENFELD, S. A., *Protection of Coastal Fisheries under International Law*, Washington, 1942.

SARKAR, L., "The Proper Law of Crime in International Law," 11 *I.C.L.Q.* 446–470 (1962).

SCHACHTER, O., "The Development of International Law Through the Legal Opinions of the U.N. Secretariat," 25 *B.Y.I.L.* 91–132 (1948).

—, "Law, Politics and Action in the U.N.," 109 *Recueil des Cours* (1963, II) Leyden, 1964, pp. 169–256.

SCHWARZENBERGER, G., *The Inductive Approach to International Law*, London, 1965.

—, *International Law as Applied by International Courts and Tribunals*, London, 1968, Vols. I–II.

SCHWEBEL, S. M., "The U.N. and the Challenge of a Changing International Law," *Proceedings of the American Society of International Law* 7 (1963).

SCHWELB, E., "The Nuclear Test Ban Treaty and International Law," 58 *A.J.I.L.* 643 (1964).

SHAWCROSS & BEAUMONT, *Air Law*, 3rd ed., London, 1966, pp. 28–29, 701–715.

SKUBISZEWSKI, K., "Forms of Participation of International Organizations in the Law Making Process," 4 *International Organization* 790–805 (1964).

SLOANE, F. B., "The Binding Force of the 'Recommendation' of the General Assembly of the United Nations," 25 *B.Y.I.L.* 1–33 (1948).

SØRENSEN, M., (ed.), *Manual of Public International Law*, London, 1968.

STARKE, J. G., *An Introduction to International Law*, 6th ed., London, 1967.

STROHL, M. P., *The International Law of Bays*, The Hague, 1963.

STUYT, *The General Principles of Law as Applied by International Tribunals to Disputes on Attribution and Exercise of State Jurisdiction*, The Hague, 1946, pp. 28–152.

The Status of Domestic Jurisdiction. Proceedings of the Fourth Summer Conference on International Law. Cornell Law School, Ithaca, New York, June 18–20, 1962.

TWISS, *The Law of Nations*, 2nd ed., 1884, Vol. I.

VERESCHETIN, "Legal Forms of the USSR's International Cooperation in the Peaceful Utilization of the Cosmos," (In Russian) No. 1 *S.G.I.P.* 69–73 (1967).

VERPLAETSE, J. G., *International Law in Vertical Space*, South Hackensack, N.J., 1960.

VLASIC, I. A., "The Growth of Space Law 1957–65: Achievements and Issues," *Yearbook of Air and Space Law*, Mankiewicz, ed., Montreal, 1965, pp. 365–405.

WALDOCK, C. H. M., "The Plea of Domestic Jurisdiction Before International Tribunals," 3 *B.Y.I.L.* 96–142 (1954).

WESTLAKE, J., *International Law*, 2nd ed., Cambridge, 1910–1913, Vol. I, pp. 246–281.

WHEATON, H., *Elements of International Law, with a Sketch of the History of the Science*, 8th ed., London, 1836.

WILBERFORCE, "Crime in Aircraft," 67 *Journal of the Royal Aeronautical Society* (1964).

YOUNG, E., "The Legal Status of Submarine Areas Beneath the High Seas," 45 *A.J.I.L.* 225–239 (1951).

—, "The Over-Extension of the Continental Shelf," 47 *A.J.I.L.* 454–456 (1953).
—, "The Geneva Convention on the Continental Shelf," 52 *A.J.I.L.* 733–738 (1958).
—, "The Development of the Law of Diplomatic Relations," 40 *B.Y.I.L.* 141–182 (1964).
ZHUKOV, G. P., *Kosmicheskoe Pravo* (Space Law), Moscow, 1966.

U.S. GOVERNMENT DOCUMENTS ON INTERNATIONAL SPACE ACTIVITIES

1. *Radio Frequency Control in Space Telecommunications.* By Edward Wenk, Jr. Committee print. 86th Congress, 2d session. March 19, 1960. 235 p.
2. *Policy Planning for Space Telecommunications.* Staff Report. Committee print. 86th Congress, 2d session. December 4, 1960. 207 p.
3. *Legal Problems of Space Exploration; A Symposium.* By Eilene Galloway. Senate Document No. 26. 87th Congress, 1st session. March 22, 1961. 1392 p.
4. *Communication Satellites: Technical, Economic and International Developments.* Staff Report. Committee print. 87th Congress, 2d session. February 25, 1962. 287 p.
5. *Soviet Space Programs: Organization, Plans, Goals, and International Implications.* Staff Report. Committee print. 87th Congress, 2d session. May 31, 1962. 399 p.
6. *Documents on International Aspects of the Exploration and Use of Outer Space, 1954–1962.* Staff Report. Senate Document No. 18. 88th Congress, 1st session. May 9, 1963. 407 p.
7. *United States International Space Programs: Texts of Executive Agreements, Memoranda of Understanding, and Other International Arrangements, 1959–1965.* Edited by Eilene Galloway. Senate Document No. 44. 89th Congress, 1st session. July 30, 1965. 575 p.
8. *International Cooperation and Organization for Outer Space.* By Eilene Galloway. Senate Document No. 56. 89th Congress, 1st session. August 12, 1965. 580 p.
9. *Space Treaty Proposals by the United States and U.S.S.R.* By Eilene Galloway. Committee print. 89th Congress, 2d session. July 1966. 52 p.
10. *Treaty on Principles Governing the Activities of States in the Exploration and Use of Outer Space, Including the Moon and Other Celestial Bodies. Analysis and Background Data.* Staff Report. Prepared for the Use of the Committee on Aeronautical and Space Sciences United States Senate, 90th Congress, 1st Session. March 1967. 84 p.
11. *Treaty on Outer Space.* Hearings before the Committee on Foreign Relations, United States Senate. 90th Congress, 1st Session on Executive D. March 7, 13 and April 12, 1967. 162 p.

SUBJECT INDEX

NAME INDEX